Beyond the Bend

The Journey of Normand Laub
from World War II to Peace of Mind

*Based on the writings and journals of Normand D. Laub
Compiled by Barbara R. Laub
Edited by Marci Andrews Wahlquist*

Copyright © Barbara R. Laub, 2017.

All rights reserved. No part of this book may be reproduced or transmitted in any form or by any means, electronic or mechanical, including photocopying, recording, or by an information storage and retrieval system, without permission in writing from the author.

The following photographs were originally published in *The 1st Cavalry Division in World War II,* compiled by Major B.C. Wright, 1947, printed in occupied Japan:
- Camp Strathpine on page 58
- Brisbane rodeo on page 59
- Leyte beachhead (top) on page 129
- Leyte swamp and machine gunners on page 130
- Filipinos packing supplies on page 131
- Flying column and Santo Tomas main building on page 160
- Caves and jungle patrols on Luzon on page 180
- High-point men on page 196

All other photographs came from Barbara Laub's personal collection.

Appendix A maps were copied or adapted from various Internet sources, including the following:
- baby.indstate.edu/gga/gga_cart/index.htm, Indiana State University's cartography pages; map of "Up the Ladder" strategy
- www.onwar.com, maps showing the battle for Leyte Gulf and the battle for Leyte Island (scans by Ralph Zuljan)
- www.yahoo.com, maps of Utah and the Arizona Strip

Maps of the Admiralty Islands came from Barbara Laub's personal papers, including a travel brochure of the Admiralties.

ISBN-13: 9780997890440
ISBN-10: 0997890444
Published by Idea Creations Press
www.ideacreationspress.com
Printed in the U.S.A.

Here now is a story of peace and war,
Of sorrow, of hate, and love evermore.

Table of Contents

Introduction ix
Author's Preface x

1 Clouds of War 1
   The World Grows Stormy
   Call to Arms
   Enlisting Together
   Training at Ft. Riley, Kansas
   Photographs

2 Growing Up Together 23
   Early Years in Enterprise
   The Journey
   Two Alone
   Photographs

3 Training in California and Australia 43
   The PRD
   Shipping Out for Places Unknown
   Camp Strathpine, Australia
   Photographs

4 Cowboy Days 60
   Movie Cowboys
   Great Horses
   Real Cowboy Jobs
   Photographs

5 Admiralty Islands 72
   Los Negros Beachhead
   Manus Mission
   Koroniat, Our Island Paradise
   Photographs

6 Leyte Campaign 109
   MacArthur's Return to the Philippines

The Night Before
Leyte Beachhead
The World Came to an End
Battle of Leyte Gulf
Campaign Continues
Mission Bagatoon
End of the Leyte Campaign
Photographs

7 Return to Leyte **133**
Into the Past
An Extraordinary Time
Everything I Had Hoped
Photographs

8 Liberation of Santo Tomas POW Camp... **149**
Flying Column to the Rescue
Reunion Fifty Years Later
Photographs

9 Retaking Manila..................................... **162**
A Building at a Time
Philippine General Hospital
Horrors of War
Photographs

10 Southern Luzon Campaign **170**
Moving South from Manila
I Will Fight No More
Photographs

11 End of the War.. **182**
Last Letter from the Front
Waiting to Go to Japan
Troop Celebration August 1945
My Courage Failed
Photographs

12 My Mission and My Marriage 197
So Much Guilt
Home Together
A Special Christmas Present
Home from My Mission
Courtship and Marriage
The Most Important Day
Photographs

13 Life Goes On 217
Starting a Farm
Junior's Death
Our Homestead 1954–1958
A Journal Entry
An Unexploded Bomb
Faith to Live
Photographs

14 Sentimental Journeys 226
A Date with Destiny
Visit to Hawaii
Journey to Japan
My Return to the Philippines
Photographs

15 Searching the Arizona Strip................. 250
The Past Comes Close
Toroweap Valley
Call of the Wild
Mystery of My Life
Photographs

16 Epilogue: Redemption in Leyte 264
Sending a Sacred Book
Miracle in Leyte
Photographs

Appendix: Maps **273**
   The Pacific Theatre Operations in World War II
   1st Cavalry Division Assignments
   The Admiralty Islands
   The Battle of Leyte
   Invading the Philippines
   Return to Leyte
   Southern Utah
   The Arizona Strip

Introduction

We often long to go back into the past to one experience or another and change the way we acted, or to change an outcome to one we wish we had been able to effect at the time. Few of us ever realize even a portion of such a longing, but Normand Laub did. After suffering a nearly soul-destroying loss in World War II, he spent the rest of his life endeavoring to find peace and replace his loss. But peace kept eluding him. He returned to the places where he suffered and where he recovered himself in the war to find the most significant sites nearly untouched since those long-ago days, making it seem he had been able to step back into the past, to see "beyond the bend" to a place in the river of time left behind long before. There he found a measure of redemption from his sorrows. And then he went to each of the places significant in the development of his early life and was able to realize the exquisite relief of facing the past with over 40 years of a changed life to help him heal. In each of his experiences, he reflected on and wrote his thoughts and feelings, and he never stopped trying to spread a message of faith that he himself believed with his whole heart and soul. This is the story of a truly extraordinary man with a truly extraordinary life.

—Marci Andrews Wahlquist
May 2006

Author's Preface

Ever since the end of World War II when I found myself back in the good old USA, I have been plagued and troubled with a buried sense of guilt behind my gratitude that I did make it back. I have wanted and tried to tell this story for many years, possibly ever since I and that flag-draped casket made that final trip home together in 1948. I remember how I tried to forget. I wanted to forget. I wanted to make the reality not so, but it wouldn't go away and I buried it deep inside.

Why was I, with little learning and no letters, continually obsessed with an unquenchable urge to write a story of peace and war? Why, though I made countless attempts over the years, turning out pages and pages of notes and camouflaged manuscripts, was I never able to complete the story, or tap that deep submerged river of buried feelings and troubled emotions that often threatened to surge into a raging torrent through my tormented soul? Why, fifteen years after the War, was there still an unexploded bomb inside me that came dangerously close to destroying me?

Why was I often plagued with a seemingly impossible dream to return to the land of the setting sun, down where the blue waters of the trackless Pacific idly splash on the quiet shores of a thousand forgotten islands, where the ruins of death and destruction even now peacefully sleep in the suns of perpetual summer? Why would I even think of returning to a place where, as a young soldier, I had experienced the deepest pain and sorrow I have ever been called to bear?

And why would I make a pilgrimage to a places of my early childhood, the badlands of Arizona where two little boys shared challenging experiences in the isolated canyon wilderness. Why did it seen to me that something there forever stamp the fabric of those two young lives and weld them inseparably, though the War seemed to forever shatter the links?

It wasn't until that long-needed, long-hoped-for, but never-expected trip back to the island war zones that I really found myself and the words to write the story. It seemed that trip unlocked the deep, secret, personal vaults of my soul, sealed with that strange sense of guilt, and sealed with a kind of sacred, untouchable reverence, deep hurt, and haunting respect that made talking about it so difficult.

Now I read the stories and books of others about the pivotal, monumental period of World War II, realizing that those who lived it that era that is nearly forgotten are nearly all gone, I feel a deep compulsion to try to express what is deep inside, that something that has been suppressed fo all these years.

And finally, as I stood alone on the rim of a deep canyon abyss, the amazing sequence began to unfold in a sad and touching review. That tiny computer that makes up the human brain clicked on and my ears began hearing sounds that had fallen silent decades ago, and my tear-dimmed eyes began seeing scenes that had long since faded. Was this the call of the wild, the wonderful world of memory, or the road that leads Beyond the Bend?

Although.my story spans more than half a century, fewer than five years, from 1941–1945, form the real bend in my road, in my world and my life. My story has a bit of hope, tragedy, and despair, a story of revenge and hate that has turned into an experience of love and gratitude.

Normand Laub

Chapter 1

Clouds of War

The World Grows Stormy

War was something one read about in history books, or maybe an occasional newspaper, if one were inclined to read, which I wasn't. But it certainly had little to do with me, my life, or even America when I was a teenager. Then after that December Sunday in 1941, the big, black, three-letter word, "War," burning across the top of every paper in the country seemed almost to pounce on you from its frightful headline position, as a stunned nation heard the shocking news of the Japanese attack on Hawaii. Pearl Harbor and December 7, 1941 would not only become a date that would live in infamy as Franklin Delano Roosevelt predicted, but in its smoldering aftermath, "Remember Pearl Harbor" would also become a rallying point and battle cry that would arouse and galvanize into united action a slumbering, divided nation.

We have since learned that this attack may not have come as a total surprise to some of our national leaders, but it was quite a shock to a generation of youth much like myself who had grown up quite unconcerned or troubled by the horrors and fears of war. Even then, in spite of the underlying effect or personal implications, its smoke and blood and din were still quite remote from most of us. Many did not sense the magnitude of its national or international consequences and didn't expect it to last long or amount to much, but as history painfully records, it took nearly four years. So it was that war suddenly burst around us and became the greatest subject of the day and was whispered on every lip.

Most of the Americans who would fight and die in World War II had not yet been born or at least were babies when the war to end all wars, World War I, was over. It should be noted that the 23-year span between the two world wars marked one of America's longest war-free periods. Of course, if we read the paper or listened to the radio back in the thirties, we could have been disturbed by the Japanese sacking of Nanking in China, Mussolini's invasion of Ethiopia, or the Spanish civil war. But these events concerned people and places that were a long way off and quite easily ignored or forgotten. What most of us didn't know as we innocently occupied our time with just plain living and growing up in the midst of the Great Depression, was the fact that the sinister seeds of global conflict and our own inevitable involvement were even then being secretly plotted and planted on two widely separate fronts.

In the west, a scheming German corporal with a gift for satanic intrigue rose from a Landsburg prison to rally, inspire, and deceive his people like few leaders ever have, talking peace while he secretly prepared for war to avenge and restore the fatherland. Telling his listeners it was better to be a street cleaner in the Third Reich than a king in a foreign land; shouting, "Those who want to live should fight, and those who do not want to fight, do not deserve to live!"—with this sort of rhetoric and persuasion, he illegally transformed the restricted Germans into one of the greatest military powers in the world. "Today we rule Germany—tomorrow the world," the Führer promised. The people responded, "We are the master race. Heil Hitler!"

On the other side of the globe, another group of equally sinister and ambitious leaders were also very carefully but aggressively plotting and planning their own brand of world domination. Cultivating the spirit of the ancient Samurai with their own view of divine rule through murder and assassination, the Black Dragon Society or Showa of Japan violently took control of that country's politics and destiny and eventually challenged and defied the free world with their sweeping military aggression and fanaticism, symbolized by their flag, the "Rising Sun."

By 1941, though most of us still didn't know it, the deadly clouds of war from both the east and the west were rapidly closing in. All of Europe seemed to be doomed. The only bright spot left in the west, after the fall of France and the hopeless British retreat, was the tragic miracle of Dunkirk. Even so, the spirit of American isolationism was pretty strong. Supported by two of the nation's biggest newspapers, along with the respected opinion of an American hero, Charles Lindbergh, the American people didn't believe we should get involved in a foreign conflict. We already had excellent defensive barriers, a broad ocean on either side of us.

In 1940, America had finally decided to engage in a bit of protective prudence. President Roosevelt asked for and received a fair-sized defense and rearmament budget, and in September Congress enacted the selective service system. Now all healthy, single American males between the ages of 20 and 44 were being called into military service for 12 months of training by a systematic lottery draft. For the first time, America began to build a peacetime army, which would mushroom from less than half a million men in 1940 to a combined military force of over 16 million men and a quarter million women before the war was over. In fact, the American casualty list from World War II would be nearly double its total peacetime army number and would nearly equal the battle losses of all its previous wars combined.

It would mark the beginning of a change in the world like few things ever have before or since. Man and the world in which he lived would never return to the former casual, carefree ways. People, nations and things would never be the same again. This was a major bend in the road, a road that had seemingly gone on and on, up and down, round and round, with gradual, but little change for countless generations.

Call to Arms

Despite my lack of formal learning, I had read enough to identify and appreciate the great patriots of the American Revolution and had even tried to understand the tragic feelings of a nation torn by the scourge of the civil war. Nor had the dashing, but imprudent courage of Custer or the matchless glory of the Alamo totally escaped my early years of learning. All of these must have sometime and in some way been etched and filed in the hidden recesses of my subconscious mind, so not unlike millions of fellow Americans, I was similarly struck and affected by this sudden cry of battle and challenge to freedom. It seemed to awaken and strike a responsive chord, for never in the history of men or nations has a total populace met the challenge and like a single body risen to answer the call.

The first young man from our peaceful little community to be caught up in this new military machine was a close personal friend, William T. Hunt. Bill, a former high school basketball star and top rodeo hand, was already kind of a local hero. So this first lottery call to arms from our area became quite a significant moment for us all. Although Bill was a bit older than my brother and I were, we had grown up together and he was a special cowboy friend. So before he left for that great unknown, we took some final rides together, did some rodeoing, and took some cowboy pictures. But for most of us the fear of war was still a long way off, even though the military draft had now become an inevitable reality. Yet, before very many of these first draftees had served their initial term, the deadly vial of war was dumped from the Pacific sky and spread like a plague 'til it held the entire globe locked in the cold grip of death.

With the military draft gobbling up all the eligible young men in the nation at an increasing rate, it was only a matter of time until my brother Merril would be called up. That would end our inseparable buddy brotherhood. We talked about it. We worried about it and we discussed our concern with our folks and finally decided there was a solution. If he went, so would I. We would both enlist so we could go together. But when, where, and into which branch of service?

By a stroke of luck, or coincidence, it was about this time that *Life Magazine* ran an impressive article on the 1st Cavalry Division down at Ft. Bliss, Texas, complete with horses, soldiers, and some mock battle scenes. Although not all that historically well-read, we were acquainted with the deeds and actions of some of the great horse soldiers of the past, but we hadn't realized a modern army still rode horses into battle, so we were quite impressed.

It was no secret that next to each other, our first love, second love, and our only love was horses. We had practically lived on and with them all of our lives. They were our joy, our security, and our transportation. If we had to join the army or go to war, what better way than on horseback? Of course, the pressing necessity of this decision was still a few months off as Merril was only 19 years old and I barely 17. It did give us something to think and dream about however, but that dream became a shocking reality much sooner than we thought on December 7th, 1941.

There were those in our country, of course, who still didn't think the war with Japan would ever amount to very much. I remember one armchair general, a very prominent man in our community, making the statement soon after Pearl Harbor, that if the Japanese kept coming and tried to land in America, he'd take a buggy whip and personally go drive them all off into the ocean. It took the almost simultaneous attacks on and fall of Singapore, Hong Kong, Shanghai, Manila, Wake Island, and Guam, after Pearl Harbor, to alert and alarm the world to the magnitude, desire, and unbelievable power of the Japanese war machine.

Although some historians may question and lament America's seeming ignorance and reluctance to accept the hard reality before Pearl Harbor, they can never forget and must ever applaud the singleness of her commitment after that shocking event, the impossible success of her military achievements and patriotism. Neither my family nor I nor anyone else that I knew would escape the onrushing tide of change, disruption, and destiny. So the Laubs, the ranchers and the cowboys, accepted and prepared for war.

After Pearl Harbor, the slumbering nation was transformed into a beehive of action. The most productive, efficient military force in all the world was beginning to take shape. A few months later, my brother turned 20 years old and as I had reached the mature age of 18, we began to make plans for the inevitable. We dug out that old *Life Magazine* and fired a letter off to Major General Innis P. Swift, commanding general of the 1st Cavalry Division in Ft. Bliss, Texas. We told him we knew how to ride horses, wanted to continue to do so and would like to join his galloping military brigade. But he would have to promise us one thing—that we got to stay together. In due time we got a reply back from the gracious General. I don't remember now exactly what all he said and can only guess what he must have thought, but to our sad disappointment he didn't instruct us to bring our saddles and catch the next bus south.

In looking back now, I'm amused at how innocent and naive we must have been. But as we were soon to learn, there would be a quite a few disappointments, adjustments, and hard learning experiences before we would be able to mount up and ride for Uncle Sam. General Swift did suggest we go to our nearest recruiting station, enlist, and make our wishes known.

Like most parents, our folks were not really anxious to see us go, but they also realized our only chance to be able to stay together would be to go together. If we didn't, Merril would be drafted, then if and when I was called (they weren't drafting 18-year-old boys yet) he would already be gone.

By now, it was the middle of summer 1942, so we decided to help the folks get a few needed things done before we left. Because of Mother's poor health, Pa tried to stay quite close to home, so my brother Merril and I had to run the ranch, care for the stock, and try to do our share. With a team and wagon we hauled the folks some winter wood, helped harvest the crops, and gathered the cattle from the hills.

By then it was October and time for Utah's very popular big-game deer hunt to begin. We had always hunted before, even as kids with Pa, but this time it became a totally new and different experience. I tried to imagine what war would be like as I now carried my loaded gun through the hills. Would we hunt and stalk the enemy like we hunted the wily buck? Would they sneak around and try to outsmart us as our four-legged quarry often did? And when the crack of a rifle or boom of a gun echoed from a nearby hill, I tried to imagine that it was the enemy shooting back. Often as we galloped our sure-footed horses through the dark, I tried to get a feel for what it might be like to charge an enemy position in the dead of night. Would our faithful ponies, who seemed able to see in the dark better than we, sense the danger and carry us over rough ground and through tight spots like they had in the reckless midnight rides of our youth? I was sure they would and often felt a surge of comfort and optimism for what might yet lay ahead. At the end of the deer hunt, we stood our 30-30 guns in the corner of the old ranch house.

Once we had finally decided to join the army, we began to follow with growing interest and attention the various battles and campaigns being waged around the world. We were quite aware that after nearly nine months of tragic defeat and retreat in the Pacific, the American forces had at long last turned on the Japanese at bay. And we followed with keen interest the gripping and bloody action of the U.S. Marines on a small, unknown ditch called Guadalcanal. We were also touched by the hardships and unbelievable sacrifices made by a handful of rugged Australian bush fighters, supported by a few American soldiers, on another unknown island in the southwest Pacific, as the impassable, slippery mountain path called the Kokoda Trail, over the steep jungle-covered Owen Stanley Mountains of New Guinea, became a very familiar and much-talked-about thoroughfare.

We were also impressed, about this same time, by a daring and fearless commando attack on Hitler's fortress, Europe, when a group of Canadian, British, and American commandos hit the French city of Dieppe in a costly one-day raid. But I think the battle that really caught our attention at that moment was being waged in a land of ancient intrigue, the North African campaign. I don't believe the Desert Fox (Rommel, the respected German field commander), and his Afrika

Korps who had swept across the Libyan desert into Egypt like an oncoming storm, was our real interest here. It was rather the country itself, the wide open desert spaces of Africa that really caught our attention. We lived in a semi-desert area and were quite at home in barren terrain. This African landscape looked more like a battlefield where one might have room and space to use a horse, while the pictures we had seen of the jungle-covered beaches of Guadalcanal or New Guinea didn't strike us as being very desirable Cavalry country, nor did those bleak cliffs along the French coasts. So picking up the theme of a popular western ballad, "Don't Fence Me In," we dreamed of riding off to war in a thrilling Cavalry charge. Rather affectionately we rode our favorite horses for the last time, patting them on the necks and saying, "I wish I could take you with me old pal." And we wondered what army horses and life would be like.

Enlisting Together

> *You've heard of Doug MacArthur*
> *Who set the Japs at bay,*
> *But there's others in this nation*
> *And they're starting on their way.*
> *So you slant eyed little fellows*
> *Who's on a one way track,*
> *You had better get to driftin',*
> *'Cause you're not a comin' back.*

These words are part of a song Pa wrote for my brother and me to sing at the farewell of another friend who took pretty hard his call to the war. It was sung to the tune of a snappy railroad song, "The Wabash Cannonball." Merril played the guitar and I the mandolin, and we did a bit of singing and entertaining as we grew up. Now that we were going into the army ourselves, the words of this song seemed quite appropriate for us as well, although we didn't then know it would be the Japanese we would be fighting.

It was kind of a sad farewell, that November morning in 1942 when my brother and I bid a last goodbye to our folks and family. It was almost ten years to the day since we had rode out of this little town of Enterprise for an Arizona adventure. Only this time it was just the two of us going. I think Mother took it the hardest, yet who more than a mother could worry about the hazards and unknowns of the future. We had arranged to catch a ride to Salt Lake City, Utah with an uncle in his truck. Salt Lake was three hundred miles away and our closest military induction center.

It was night when we reached the city, so we put up in a small hotel. I remember trying to use a pay phone the next morning to find out where the induction center was. A kind lady finally helped me operate this strange, 5-cent contraption. The induction center wasn't at the nearby Fort Douglas, but on the ground floor of a downtown office building, so we had a taxi take us over there.

We were both pretty nervous and country shy, but we were glad to be there together. The center was a very busy place that morning and probably served parts of several other nearby states. We got our first experience at standing in those traditional army lines right off the bat as we waited our turn to say yes. We tried to stay together, but somehow we got separated and I must have gotten ahead. At least when we ended up with our official military brand (serial number) mine was 19171808, several digits ahead of my brother's, 19171820. If they signed us up in numerical order, I don't know how 12 people ever got between us, but they did. We did tell them we were enlisting together so we could be together and that we wanted to join the Horse Cavalry, which was also something different. Most of the volunteers were requesting the Navy, the Air Force, or the Marines. At that time a volunteer could supposedly choose his branch of service, while most of the draftees were being sent to the plain old infantry, but that was not for us. Ha ha.

This was a whole new experience for us, and I suspect we fit to a tee the words of another amusing war song that was made up down in the islands during the war, called "That Crazy War." Some of its lines went something like this:

> *Now I was just a country boy who lived down on the farm,*
> *I never ever hurt a flea or done no one no harm,*
> *'Til that war, that crazy war.*
> *The sheriff he walked up to me, said Come along my son,*
> *Your Uncle Sammy needs you to help him tote a gun,*
> *In this war, that crazy war.*
> *They took me to the courthouse, my head was in a whirl,*
> *And when the doctors jumped on me, I wished I'd been a girl.*
> *In that war, that crazy war.*

This song pretty well described us during that first hour. We were given a brief physical exam, asked some questions, filled out some papers, took a test, made a pledge, signed our names and "presto," we were in, just like that. The way I remember it, the whole thing probably took less than an hour, and then with a whole group of mass-inducted soldiers, we were loaded into a bus and driven up to old Fort Douglas, which now had rows and rows of brand-new, pre-fab army barracks and buildings.

A lot of things began to happen, new to us then, but soon very routine. We were assigned to a barracks and a bunk, met our new platoon leader, and were forthwith mass-marched down to the quartermaster building to receive a complete new wardrobe, which, though not always made to order or fit, was very durable and would be our standard dress for the next three years, with some slight seasonal variations. I suppose I had always felt a bit of patriotism, clear back to the time when as a fifth grader in school I helped lead an Armistice Day parade by carrying the American flag on my horse. I remember quite well the keen, but humble sense of pride I felt as I slipped on that heavy O.D. dress jacket and donned the uniform of the greatest nation in the world.

Of course, the whole country was now caught up in a growing sense of patriotism and national commitment. For young men, this was the only thing to do. This patriotism was reflected in nearly every home, business, and public meeting. There were slogans, songs, and blazing posters everywhere. "A slip of the lip may sink a ship," read one catchy slogan. "Scrap your fat," went an amusing little song that was made to encourage saving and sacrifice. "Rosy, the Riveter" was a popular ballad that praised and encouraged the female defense worker. And a stern-looking bewhiskered Uncle Sam, with a star-spangled top hat, pointed a long finger at you from posters all over the country, which read, "I Need You."

So, in spite of this demanding new life style, we began to feel pretty good about joining the army. But, had I known where this uniform would take me during the next three years and some of the things it would ask me to do, I wonder, would I have stopped or turned back? I doubt it, nor do I think my brother would have either. But it's good some of those things were still hidden beyond the bend, and I was not permitted to foresee the heartbroken soldier that would one day return to this same fort to be mustered out of the service alone.

But for now, a new, exciting, and entirely different life lay before us. We were young, healthy, and eager to pursue it. And as long as we had each other, what else mattered? Together we could face anything, come what may. Even the high-sounding but lowly rated kitchen police duty, KP, seemed all right then. I think my very first army assignment was KP over at the sprawling little kitchen, which some of the local men affectionately called the Greasy Spoon. But it wasn't all that bad. Peeling potatoes and washing dishes was something I had done before.

"Fall out!" "Fall in!" "Hit the deck!" "On the double!" These were all new commands and moves to us, as they were for hundreds of other new recruits, GIs as well. The letters *GI* stand for government issue, and that's what we were about to become. Government property. Government owned and controlled robots. We would become part of a massive human machine that would operate and function quite like a massive, well-organized orchestra, learning to respond and take orders from whomever swung the military baton.

At first I used to question why the army had to use and enforce such strict, hard regulations. Why they needed to drill us day after day and why the leaders and drill masters needed to be so hard, cold, and seemingly cruel, especially during those first few weeks of basic training. But when we got overseas and went into combat, I began to understand its real purpose and value. Our human psyches were being trained to operate almost automatically, to obey orders on command. Later on, when the captain said, "Sergeant, take your squad and go take that hill," you went. You didn't say, "No sir, they're shooting real bullets up there and I could get shot!" You took your squad and went into the face of the cannon without question or hesitation because that's what you had been trained to do.

Another thing that seemed quite strange and difficult at first was the military division of rank and social barriers that seemed to prevail. It was hard for me to see, and respect, any real difference between a captain and a corporal, or any officer for that matter, especially if the captain was the younger, which quite often they were. To me, they were all equal people. But I wasn't rebellious and soon learned to recognize, respect, and salute the brass when the occasion required.

We did a lot of close-order drill, with pretty awkward feet at first, during our three-week stay at Ft. Douglas. We were also given a number of orientation and training lectures. And we were continually, it seemed, cleaning the barracks and policing the area, picking up all the cans, papers, and cigarette butts. And the pressure of predawn reveille every morning, getting up, dressed, out of the barracks, and onto the company street in acceptable dress and formation, in the limited time allowed, was quite a worry at first, especially in view of the sharp tongue lashings and other punishments often meted out to those who didn't do everything right or may have committed some other small infraction. And though we didn't know why we were being kept there so long, we were at least learning army discipline by the numbers.

I think the military formation I liked the best was the one held at the end of the day, Retreat. Now that we were soldiers preparing to go to war, it always gave me a sense of pride and a case of goose pimples to hear the military band strike up the national anthem as the various troop formations came to rigid attention and gave that snappy salute as the stars and stripes descended their gleaming pole.

We spent our first army Thanksgiving at Fort Douglas. The folks had sent us some special goodies from home, including some of my mother's homemade cheese, which we shared with some of our newly made buddies. I think it was at about this point that the army newness began to wear off and we began to experience those deep, empty breast pangs known as homesickness. Even though we had each other, we still missed our home, our family, and our horses.

We still had hopes of getting some horses, and this may have been the reason for our lengthy detention at the induction center. We were also waiting for the arrival of some other horse soldiers. Most of the guys we came in with that first day, and a lot since, had long gone to some other base or port. Not only did we eagerly anticipate those daily roll call musters when a list of names would be read off with the instructions, "Pack your bags, you're shipping out," but we began to sweat them out too. For there seemed to be no apparent order or system, alphabetical, age or otherwise, dictating who may be taken and who may be left. Knowing now how screwed up the army red tape and paperwork can sometimes be, I count it a miracle or sign of divine intervention that we were not separated or shipped out in different directions, then or on any number of other occasions during those first few months. But we weren't; in fact, we were able to serve in the same troop, platoon, and even the same squad most of the time.

Then one wintry afternoon, nearly a month after enlisting, a whistle blew, followed by the order to "Fall out and form up." Grabbing our caps and jackets, we hit the street at the double quick. Striding up to the formation with a paper in hand, an officer clerk from down the street whom we had seen before, wearing the tree chevrons and rocker of a staff sergeant, took command. "The following," he ordered, examining his paper, "will pack their bags and get ready to ship out at 0500." Then he read a list of 25 names, with spelling variations, that ran the full range of the alphabet from Abbott to Zimmerman. Both our names were on the list. We didn't know where we were going, but at this point it didn't really matter, so long as we were doing it together. Most of us were packed and ready long before 5 p.m. when we and our bulky drawstring barrack bags were loaded on the back of a canvas-covered army 6x6 truck and taken to the downtown Union Pacific railroad depot.

We were not the only people on the move. As we marched into the huge railroad waiting room, it looked like half of America was on the move and most of them were in the service. There were soldiers, sailors, and marines, girlfriends, old friends, and families. While some were exchanging cheerful greetings of welcome, others were trying to bid a tearful, last goodbye.

We didn't even have to buy our tickets. That was one of the fringe benefits of our new position. In fact, most of our transportation from now on was prepaid by Uncle Sam. We did have to wait and often stand in lines, but not to buy a ticket. And since we were shipping out under special secret orders, the officer in charge kept us well chaperoned and herded together. There were no close friends or personal goodbyes for us. It wouldn't do for an enemy saboteur to know who we were or where we were going. He might try to derail the train or blow up the track. And it was comforting to know, in our war-alert country watching for any sabateurs, that our 68-year-old Grandfather Bowler was even now one of the many special guards employed by the government to guard railroad bridges and tunnels. He had been guarding a tunnel in southern Nevada since right after Pearl Harbor.

It was quite late that night when our special train finally got under way. The porter came and made our beds, and on that first army trip we really traveled in style. It wouldn't always be so. Midnight found us being rocked to sleep as this army special rattled across the Continental Divide in Wyoming, headed for a new world and a new life.

Training at Ft. Riley, Kansas
December 1942

The Continental Divide, at the top of the Rocky Mountains, was the farthest east we had ever been, so our journey from there on would be all new country for us. A brief stop in Denver, Colorado was something of a highlight for us. The name was pretty familiar to us, because back in the Depression days the big Montgomery Ward catalog out of Denver was a pretty popular shopping mall for lots of country families. I had bought my first new saddle, my mandolin, and lots of other things from it. After a two-hour layover in Denver, we headed east across the flat country of the Great Plains. Again, some new sights to us hill country people.

We first took our training at the Cavalry Replacement Training Center near Junction City, Kansas. Those of us who got off the train there were picked up by a GI 6x6 truck and hauled out to a fairly new military base with rows and rows of new two-story barracks, very similar to those we had been housed in back at Ft. Douglas.

We had picked up a cowboy from Montana, one from Wyoming, some rodeo cowboys from Oklahoma and Texas, and some race horse jockeys from Kentucky, but surprisingly, many of our new army cavalry buddies were so-called "horsemen" from the eastern United States, some of whom had never been around horses. Quite interestingly, this was very acceptable to the army, as we were soon to find out, because as with everything else, there was the right way, the wrong way, and the Army Way, especially when it came to riding horses. No matter how good or how much you knew about riding horses, the army had its own way and style that it wanted to train in you, but even that was quite a way on down the road.

The two months there of basic training were pretty disappointing and frustrating. The strict, tough, uncompromising discipline and regimentation of military life was a real challenge for most of the recruits, especially those of us who had led a life of carefree country boys. The adjustments were many and difficult and we hardly ever got to see a horse. It was close-order drills, calisthenics, obstacle courses, lectures, short hikes with full packs, weapons training, and target practice. It was a whole new routine for us, but we accepted it and did get along pretty well. We had a lot of learning to do and there were many things that were now different, but I didn't think we were dumb. We knew how to take orders and be obedient and had never been guilty of trying to cheat, deceive, not do our share, or avoid doing what we had been asked to do, but we learned that there were such people in the world and that strict discipline and obedience were very necessary.

Just before Christmas, when we were starting to feel homesick, Bill Hunt got a chance to stop by and see us. He was on his way home to Enterprise on a furlough and had gotten off the train to look us up even though it delayed him a few days. He said that he was anxious to see us and how we were getting along with army life, and boy, we were happy to see him. We had a great visit together, recalling all of our happy cowboy days together. We knew it would be some time before we would see each other again, as no one could see what was beyond the bend.

The troopers of the horse cavalry were influenced and motivated by a sense of elitism which drew its honor, pride, and confidence from a long and colorful history of mounted warriors who were a stirring and inspiring tribute to honor and courage. The cavalry troops always considered themselves a little apart and above their common cousins of the infantry. Even though we became dismounted, that pride and ego we learned to have as the Cavalry remained with the 1st Cavalry Division up though the islands.

Amid all of the new, fast-moving, ongoing training, the thing that was the greatest shock, and hardest for me to take, was the time they had this crusty old World War I veteran, I think he was a major, come and tell us what it was like to kill someone. We were seated in a training room and he told us about being in the trenches in France and of killing a German in the trench with his trench shovel. The gory details of spattering brains on his shoes and legs triggered a somber reaction in me, especially later as I stood guard in a lonely little guard house, on the bleak plains of Kansas, as a winter blizzard howled about me. When anyone thinks of war, it's almost always a picture of fighting, of death and destruction, dying and wounded. At its best, war is terrible, at its worst it's unthinkable. If I was going to have to kill somebody, I wanted to do it on horseback—it seemed easier and a lot cleaner, especially after what the major had just told us.

When we finished basic training, some of us with a little better than average horsemanship skills had been assigned to Ft. Riley, Kansas, as cadre for the Cavalry's O.C.S. (Officer Candidate School). We were then assigned to the newly formed 29th Cavalry Regiment and were mounted on reassigned GI horses and equipment from the ranks of the 1st Cavalry Division of Ft. Bliss, Texas.

Not only was Ft. Riley quite centrally and safely located, it boasted one of the nation's older and better-organized military training schools and army posts, even though it was still very equestran oriented. It was one of the more desirable, picturesque, historical American forts, with its stone buildings, brick streets, stables and corrals. It had oak-shaded streets and river bottom, and it had equestrian obstacle and English steeple courses which were standard military also. So for nearly six months we rode, drilled, and performed with the short-lived 29th Cavalry, commissioned in 1943 and decommissioned in 1944, as though this war would be fought and won by the fast-riding U.S. horse soldiers. It really was a great experience, however, and had it not been for the press of war and the urge for action, it could indeed have been for us that proverbial "Life of Riley."

As I said before, we had to learn to ride all over again, the Army Way. But we did very well and seemed to get along very well. My brother and I were even able to help show the army brass how to swim horses across the river without drowning some of them in a mock forced river crossing.

We enjoyed the thrilling opportunity to ride in some of the last big Cavalry charges across the Kansas plains as part of our military training. While still stationed at Ft. Riley we reenacted some of the thundering battle scenes of the Old West, and as part of that final phase out, we provided a mounted parade and review for our Commander-in-Chief, President Franklin D. Roosevelt, while he rode in Cadillac One, his black convertible. We really were experiencing the Life of Riley!

In July 1943 we were given a furlough and took the train home to see our family. It was a special time, but the last time we would ever be together again. We were special guests with one of our friends, Clawson Hunt, at the annual 4th of July Independence Day celebration. After the program we had our pictures taken with three other friends. By the end of the war, of the six of us, two had been killed in action, one was a POW in Germany, and one had missed the draft because of health reasons. Quite a sacrifice from six young friends.

With all of our army involvement, we never lost our sense of values, our need to ensure our togetherness, nor our concern for each other; Merril especially, being more mature and responsible, kept watching out for me, his carefree younger brother. At times it was a struggle and we felt the fear of separation as divisions were made among us at times in Ft. Riley.

We were assigned to a newly formed Cavalry heavy machine gun squad, and the training was very intensive. One day after we had been assigned to a line outfit, there came the rumor of a really big move, the one at which all the previous training and preliminaries had been aimed. Amid the excitement and bustle of this scene, my brother was called into the office of the troop commander.

"We are to leave a few capable men at the fort as cadre," the Captain told him. "You are one of those few, if you would like to stay."

"Thanks for the honor, Captain," Merril said, "I'd rather not. My brother will be shipping. We enlisted so we could be together, and I joined this man's army to fight. Thanks, but I'd really rather go."

Our excitement was high and our enthusiasm hard to contain in mid-summer 1943 when we boarded that troop train for parts unknown, as well as for some very dramatic and challenging experiences. Early in 1943, someone in the War Department decided horses were obsolete in this modern war, so we hung up our army spurs and saddles, put our horses out to pasture, and prepared to ship out. I suppose we thought at that time that our horses would follow, but they didn't. Where we were going, horses would only be a handicap.

Pfc. Normand D. Laub

Merril and Normand were together in uniform as in all else.

The Laub Family in July 1943:
Back: Milton (Dad), Normand, Merril;
Center: Ruby, LaRee, Luella (Mom); Front: Stephen, Derril, Farren.

Below: Farren, Derril, and Stephen Laub
wearing their big brothers' hats.

Six friends together for the last time, July 4, 1943:
Merril Laub, Stan Staheli, Clawson Hunt,
Normand Laub, Alma Hunt, Ken Staheli.

Below: Normand revisits their old barracks at Ft. Riley.

Chapter 2

Growing Up Together

Early Years in Enterprise

March 1926 in the little pioneer town of Enterprise, Utah, which was barely 30 years old, found my parents, Milton Fay Laub and Luella Celestia Bowler Laub, along with my grandparents, Walter Wallace Bowler and Mary Ann Hunt Bowler, and possibly several others, standing in the bare yard of the Bowler home in Enterprise on 2nd South and 1st East. Their home was located across the street south of the new yellow brick, two-story Enterprise High School, which had only recently been completed in December 1921. The occasion was stamped indelibly on my little memory—I was barely two years old, having been born January 6, 1924—because my mother was softly weeping, my father trying to comfort her as was her mother, Grandma Bowler, while my four-year-old brother, Merril, born March 29, 1922, and some other little ones were just sort of milling or playing around. Although the sun was probably shining, my best recollection was sort of a sad, melancholy scene. This day, I have been told, would have been the day of the funeral for my older brother, Milton Fay, four years older than I, who had died following a short but serious illness. The somber scene and setting still linger in my mind, but the proud old school building, along with my grandparents' large two-story cinder-block house, are gone now to make room for the expanded Enterprise Elementary School, which now blocks the street and occupies the very place we must have stood all those years ago.

Nearly a year later I remember Merril and I fighting to hold or tend our baby sister, LaRee, who had been born June 8, 1926. We had a little pot-bellied wood stove in the front room of our two-room house that my father had built on a lot given him by his father, John Franklin Laub. He had built it with lumber he had hauled from Cedar Mountain by team and wagon. I had won this time, and as I sat there, enjoying this special privilege, the chair either rocked forward or I slipped off the edge, causing LaRee to fall against the stove, burning her face and hands (I think mostly her hands, as I remember her wearing some white bandages on her hands for some time after). Again there was a wail of woe and sadness in our little family circle, especially from me, which probably helped stamp this incident in my earliest memory bank also.

Another little sister, Ruby, came to our family for us to play with on March 27, 1928.

To move on down the road apiece, when I was about five and a half I was pretty aware of the big wide world around me. We had horses, and being young, my brother Merril and I rode double most of the time on one horse, Merril being the driver. Not only were the horses fun to ride, they were our only means of transportation and source of employment too, as my father helped drive and gather cattle for others. A drive had been scheduled, and my brother and I were to get to help. But the morning of the drive I woke up with the red measles. Although I wasn't really all that sick, it was determined that it wouldn't be good for me to go. So with tears of real sadness I remember watching my father and brother saddle up and ride away.

Sometime during my first five years was our move to Sacramento, California. My father and his older brother Raymond decided to try and make their fortunes in the famous gold fields of California, so we loaded our belongings in an old motor vehicle, I think they called it a Star. It had a canvas top and sides, a front and back seat and long running board on each side with a rail to also carry and store things on. I'm not sure whom it belonged to. I don't know what else they may have done, but they did find some gold by panning in the sands of the American River. I remember seeing some little flakes or grains of gold in a small glass vial my father had.

My most vivid recollection of California was getting run over by a car. Merril was probably in school and LaRee and I were playing at a neighbor's house across the street. As we started to cross the street, a car was coming and I told LaRee to wait for it to pass while I tried to beat it. But she didn't wait and tried to follow me. In trying to miss her, the car swerved and hit me, running over me with at least one wheel. It probably wasn't going very fast and wasn't a very heavy car. I don't remember being hurt all that bad, just bruised and bumped, but it did shake up the couple driving it, as well as my mother.

Another big journey, maybe in that same old Star car, was our move to Ogden, Utah to find work. It may have even been from Ogden that we made the journey to Sacramento for the winter months. The only part of that journey I remember is getting to Beaver the first night and camping by a little pond and unpacking some camp things from those running board side trays.

Pa worked down on Washington Blvd. somewhere, and Merril and I would sometimes take his lunch down to him. I remember crossing a bridge over a pretty good-sized creek or stream with cement-type rail and trying to be smart and walk on the rail. I fell off on some rocks on the streambed, but it didn't have much water at that time. Merril came running down the bank to see if I was hurt, but fortunately I was only bruised.

We must have been back in Enterprise when I turned six, because I started school at that fairly new Enterprise School which still had no landscaping around it. About this time in 1930 during the Great Depression, my father lost our little two-room house and lot. I think he had mortgaged it to buy a truck to haul posts with his brother Raymond, which didn't work out for them, and they lost the truck too.

During the Depression I knew the government was buying and killing stock as a subsidy. We had a little spotted bull calf, and this government agent came to our corral one day. He took out a large pocketknife, and grabbing the little calf by one ear, twisted its head and cut its throat. Merril and I had to drag the little calf's carcass away. I thought how cruel and ruthless this government agent was in his striped bib overalls. I think he gave my dad $2.50 for the calf, which was used to buy us clothes to start school. This was a government welfare program to help get rid of the farm surplus, and they bought and disposed of quite a few animals this way, including some full grown ones.

After losing our little home, my father rented and fixed up a two-room rock house with an attic where Merril and I slept. The house had been vacant for years and was up on the outskirts of town across the Spring Creek Wash. We lived there for a couple of years until my father decided to stake his future and fortune on a new start out on the Arizona Strip.

The Journey

October 1932

Turning back the flap of my little denim coat, I proudly tapped the butt of the full-sized revolver that hung from a special belt my dad had made. That's my courage and my protection, I silently assured my wide-eyed little classmates as I stopped my pony to bid them a last farewell. Of course, this was only a bit of showing off by a small eight-year-old boy, not a threat to anyone's life or safety since it took both my hands and all of my strength just to hold that weapon up, let alone take aim or pull the trigger.

As a dashing young cowboy of 17, my father had ridden and loved the wide-open range of the Arizona Strip, an isolated little slice of land north of the Grand Canyon and south of the Utah border. So the badlands of Arizona would be our new home. It was pretty difficult for an eight-year-old boy of that time to comprehend or explain to his little friends where it was we were going or how far away it would be, but it was definitely beyond the bend.

And so on a crisp fall day of 1932, we left the little southern Utah town of Enterprise where I was born. With my father driving the wagon loaded with most of our possessions, Merril, who was 10 years old, and I followed on horseback, driving the extra stock. My mother and two younger sisters stayed behind to be picked up later.

We hadn't gone too far when it was discovered some small item had been forgotten, and I was sent back to fetch it. It was on this little errand, as I galloped across the school ground, I met my little friends going home from school and did my little show. My dad had a pair of nickel-plated .45 Colts and he let each of us wear one. I'm not sure why, except that we wanted to. At least we were armed, although I'm sure without bullets! But it did make us feel important and grown up. Of course, my friends knew we were leaving for a wild, unsettled country, and I suspect the wisdom and hazards of our family move had already been much of the talk of the town.

The 120-mile journey to the lower Toweep [now named Toroweap] Valley down near the north rim of the Grand Canyon took over ten days, and we camped out every night. Although it involved some long days of hard riding for two little boys, we loved it. In looking back now, however, I marvel at the courage, the patience, and the ability of my father, barely 32 years old himself, and I wonder how he ever made it. Every morning there was wood to rustle, fires to build, breakfast to cook, horses to wrangle and saddle or harness, cattle to gather, and camp to break. We didn't have feed or water for our stock, so they had to forage as well as get their rest at night. And if grass was short or scarce, they might be pretty scattered by dawn. To make finding and catching them easier, some of the horses were hobbled as well as belled.

When we left St. George, Utah, the closest settlement to where we were going 80 miles away, Pa said he needed to do some shopping. He helped us cross the shallow Virgin River with the stock, pointed the direction we should go, and said he would catch us later. I don't know how far or long we traveled, but to two little boys in a strange, silent, uninhabited world of endless chaparral, it seemed mighty far, and there was still no sign of a wagon following or catching up. We must have watched the back trail like a couple of outlaws on the dodge with a stolen herd. Even though we were armed, our childish courage and independence finally failed. We held a brotherly council and decided we'd better go back and see what had happened to Pa.

What about the stock? We'd have to leave them, especially the cows; we couldn't let anything that slow restrict our pressing retreat. Abandoning the herd, we headed back for St. George, slowly at first, but the further we went the faster we went, until rounding a bend at a full gallop, we ran head on into a very welcome sight, Pa's team and wagon.

Pa had a good laugh, shared with us some goodies he had bought and a pair of new gauntlet gloves to wear. The mornings were getting pretty chilly now, especially before sun-up, as little fingers tried to fasten cinches, tug harnesses, and do other needful chores.

This little experience was only one of many Merril and I were to share and was a valuable lesson for our little minds, showing that in spite of life's many uncertainties and anxieties, hope and assurance often lies just beyond the bend.

Despite the fact that the mighty Colorado slices across the northwest corner of Arizona with its unsurpassed canyon, the entire territory is notoriously famous for its lack of water, with no other rivers or streams and very few springs in all of its canyon wilderness. And in most of the area, even wells drilled to great depths had been disappointingly dry. Ponds, dams, and natural water pockets that collect limited rain comprise the water supply for most of the strip's inhabitants, man and beast. At our first camp south of the Utah border, we had to park the wagon and drive the stock quite a ways up a deep, narrow canyon to a small spring called Moquack (an Indian name) to get a drink. It was long after dark that night before we had our supper and got to bed.

The dry, rough road took its toll on the stock, as well as on the wagon. One day one of the wagon tires, or steel bands that hold the wheel together came loose. One of the best solutions to this problem would be to drive the wagon into water or otherwise to soak the wheel overnight, so the wooden fellies would swell, making the rim tight again. We didn't have that kind of water, so the next best thing to do was to take the wheel off, heat the steel band, hammer and try to shrink it so it could be driven tightly back onto the wheel. Although a very common practice in the team and wagon days, it was still a pretty difficult precision chore, even for a blacksmith with all his tools—a bellows, forge, anvil, and tongs. But with a brush fire and a rock for a bench, it was a very challenging task.

Pa tackled the job that had to be done, pointing us on alone again with instructions to keep going until he could catch up to us. We got quite a ways ahead this time, but we did keep going. Going up a little draw about noon, we met a couple of horsemen leading a pack horse on the way down. They were surprised to see two little boys with their cattle, so far from civilization and seemingly all alone.

"Where are you boys going?" one of them asked.

"To Arizona," was our prompt reply.

"You're already in Arizona," he laughed and to our puzzlement tried to explain the territory without success. Arizona, firmly fixed in our young minds, was a place, not a state. I don't know who they were or what they thought, but after a short visit we headed on and so did they.

Wolf Hole and Little Tank were a couple of permanent camping places along the way, spaced about a day's journey apart. The water in their deep ponds was low and muddy and filled with wigglers, which we had to strain through a thick cloth for drinking, but we used it and so did the stock.

Although it wasn't easy, this journey was a growing and learning experience for my brother and me, and we had an excellent teacher and outdoor guide in our father. We learned to handle and drive both the horses and cattle, which weren't always cooperative or compatible. But after a few days on the trail together, they settled down pretty good and our main job was to see that everyone kept moving and didn't stray. So we often had time to scan the naked hills, explore the roadside nooks, savor our freedom from school and enjoy the wild wilderness.

To reach the lower Toweep Valley where we were going, down along a lesser-known and little-visited but spectacular strip of the awesome Colorado River, we had to cross one of Arizona's many high mesa plateaus from west to east. It was up on this high timbered mesa of Mt. Trumbull near the famous Nixon Springs that we would spend the next summer and some special times together. The primitive road to the top was steep and narrow and winding and far—too far for a team pulling a heavy wagon to go without many a stop to rest. Leaving the stock to follow at will, my brother and I helped with the wagon. Pa told me to take the lead with my pony, because she was the strongest. Hooking a rope on the end of the wagon tongue and around my saddle horn, I was to help the team start the load and pull the wagon up the steepest parts of the hill. Following behind on foot, my brother was to grab a rock each time the wagon stopped and place it behind a rear wheel, so the wagon wouldn't roll back and the team could rest without strain.

This was a very tense and challenging experience for a small boy and his pony. We tried to keep pace with a suddenly starting and stopping team. I tried to keep the saddle from turning so as to keep the straining pony calm and in line. I remember being pretty nervous at times, especially where the road was narrow. As we neared the top, looking down into the deep canyon below, I worried what it would be like if the wagon started backwards, pulling me and the team in a tangled mess over the edge and down the mountainside. But we made it, although it took a good while. Then we had to go back and gather the stock. Some had followed, but not all of them.

We camped at the top with plenty of grass but no water, and a good view of the part of the world we had just left behind. In the distance about 30 miles away was Gun Sight Butte, standing all by itself on the plain, a narrow wedge-shaped peak we had passed a few days ago, so named because it looked like the front site of Pa's 30-30 Winchester. In the dim blue far away were the towering Pine Valley Mountains, nearly 80 miles off, near St. George, Utah, which we had recently passed through. This was a mighty big world for a little 8-year-old boy who now felt he had nearly seen it all. And in the words of Bert Price, the old-time cowboy country sage and the local area's own Will Rogers, "As long as I could see the Pine Valley Mountain, I would never be lost," he quipped.

The next day we made it over to Nixon Springs, a very interesting, even amazing geological miracle. About halfway up the side of Mt. Trumbull, a large volcanic lava dome with towering pines, a cool clear fountain of delicious water gurgles out of a black ledge. It is a strange paradox in nature's underground plumbing, as it finds its release from the highest point in the entire area. It ignores gravity and the low lands on all sides, especially the 5,000-foot drop to the Colorado River not many miles away. It's one of the few springs and the only good one in this whole area, the only source for miles around for man or beast of this life-giving fluid. Wells have been drilled on both sides of this great mountain, but no water was ever found, so ranchers from both sides of Mt. Trumbull made their regular trips here to fill their barrels and replenish their jugs.

Sunup the next morning found our little three-man caravan dropping off the east side of Mt. Trumbull into the isolated Toweep Valley. It took our little pioneer caravan most of the day to traverse the narrow, winding road down to the big Kent Ranch at the head of Toweep Valley, where we were quite warmly welcomed by the Kents. Bud and his wife had already moved down to the big sprawling ranch house for the winter from up at Nixon Springs. Bud's parents, the older Kents, had built and lived there for some time and their daughter and granddaughter, the Bob Sullivans, were spending the winter there also. Their granddaughter, Ruth, who was about the age of my brother and me, would be given some home schooling by her mother and grandmother, as the closest formal school was nearly a hundred miles away at Fredonia.

After our stock had been watered and cared for, we were invited into the big house, with its fancy center table and high-backed chairs, for supper with the Kents. This was a different experience after traveling and eating our meals in the saddle and from a tin plate by a campfire for the last two weeks. We gained permission from them to move into a small, one-roomed cabin with a lean-to on the back at the lower end of the valley and to turn our stock into the big, lower Kent pasture.

This established a basis for friendship, and we would visit many times during the next six months, because this was also the only post office and place to mail and receive letters for miles around. One of the chores given to Merril and me would be to ride our ponies from the lower place about eleven miles down the valley every week to pick up the mail.

It was an interesting experience for a couple of wide-eyed little boys to wander around the Kent's home ranch, with its big stockade corrals with cattle and horses being caught and worked by the ranch hands. We had an extra hour that morning to do this while Pa took advantage of their well-equipped blacksmith shop to do some work on the wagon, which was showing the wear and tear after our long wilderness journey. But we had our horses caught, saddled, and ready to roll before Pa. In fact, the stock being slower than the wagon as usual, Pa instructed us to head down the road with them and he would catch us.

Like the many other experiences we had been having, this last day of our journey also proved to be new and exciting as we worked our way down the deepening Toweep Valley to the lower place near the awesome chasm of the mighty Colorado River. We went down past the John Schmutz place and then to Bill Cunningham's, where young

Rass [short for Erastus] Cunningham was breaking and working some fiery young broncs in a small round corral, where they could buck or run and never get in a corner. Young Rass was a good cowboy and a top bronc rider and we had to linger and watch him top out a big, ornery, roan colt that didn't think it wanted to be ridden. Of course we had heard of Rass before, since his mother originally came from Enterprise.

It was near sundown when we pulled into the lower Kent ranch, which really wasn't all that much of a spread. We found the little cabin, with a couple of young tamarack trees out in front, a large earthen pond on one side, and a huge stockade corral, divided in the middle with kind of a fenced lane leading to the corral on the other side. A bunkhouse and an outhouse made up this isolated wilderness homestead that was fitted into a small swell in the lowest part of the wide Toweep Valley, so you couldn't see it until you got pretty close.

This journey to our new home had been an exciting and growing experience for two little boys 8 and 10 years old, and we tried as best we could to make the most of it and take it all in. This is where we would spend the wild and lonesome winter.

Leaving our wagon and stock, we caught a ride back to Utah in the back of an old truck with Rass Cunningham. He was one of the great cowboys of that time whom we came to admire and even tried to imitate on our horses. I learned later that Pa had hired him to take us back and get the rest of our family and belongings.

It took us a couple of days to make it back to Enterprise where we spent Thanksgiving. Then we loaded the rest of our few belongings in a 1929 Chevy, with my mother and two little sisters who were 4 and 6 years old. We headed back to the Arizona badlands where we would spend a pretty isolated winter. There were no schools for miles around so we didn't attend, which pleased me. But in 1932, nearly one third of a million kids in America were out of school because of lack of money to run them. With the Great Depression in its third year, millions of people were out of jobs, out of homes, out of food, and out of nearly everything else. But while these terrible troubles and trials were testing the nation, we were getting along pretty well. We were poor, but so was everybody else. We had a house and food to eat, and my brother and I were really enjoying our life and the world.

Shortly after we moved out to the Toweep Valley, Merril and I had ridden our ponies bareback to a good grazing spot to hobble for the night. Pulling the bridles off, we headed back for the house on foot, two little boys out in the middle of nowhere. These little guys were a strange sight in this part of the country, and soon a half dozen big long-horned steers came headed our way to see what was what. They weren't really angry or after us, just plain curious, but our young minds didn't know that. There weren't any trees to climb or hide behind, just a few scattered clumps of Spanish dagger. But if a body wasn't careful, the sharp flinty points of the bushes could be about as dangerous as the menacing horns of the curious steers.

We were smart enough to know it wouldn't do any good to run, so when one would seem to be getting too close, we'd stoop down, pick up a rock or handful of dirt and throw it at the animal, who would stop or jump and run for a minute. While the cattle were stopped, we'd scurry to the next clump of bushes and drop down behind it, grab a handful of dirt—the dust worked best to frighten the cattle—and throw it at them. While they were distracted, we'd hurry on. And thus the big-horned steers played an amusing game of cat and mouse with two very sober and frightened little boys until the procession topped a ridge above the house and corrals. At the sight of the man-made structures, the big steers had gone as far as they wanted, and throwing their tails in the air, they snorted and headed back for the hills. It was a pretty harrowing experience for us.

Before long the winter snows began. It was a long, cold winter and the snow was deep, and it made it hard for Merril and me to ride our horses down to the Kent homestead to get the mail. We made a trip to town before Christmas and ran into a full blown winter storm on the way back. At one point to get enough traction, Pa had to back the old car up a hill to make it up through the snow in order to get home.

While the Arizona Strip wasn't the most desirable place for a family to live, we did have a good family life. I remember Pa leaning out the window and singing for Mother, "Look down, look down, that lonesome road." But Mother's health was not real good, she was so lonesome, it was hard on her, and at times she found it almost more than she could bear. For this reason, Father spent more and more time with and attending to her. This meant that the horses and livestock became more and more the responsibility of Merril and me.

Of course we didn't mind most of the time, and it probably helped us mature beyond our years. It also tended to bind us closer together, making us exceptionally dependent on and trusting of one another. Of course Father was there to guide, encourage, and back us up. Sometimes he had to go with and show us how to do the impossible when our little minds became stumped, overwhelmed, or discouraged, like the time we couldn't find the horses and "knew" they had been stolen by the outlaws.

There in the lower Toweep Valley were no springs or wells, and we had to depend on water from a pond which was close to the house, as did all of the stock in the area, ours and others too. Because of this, all the good feed close by the pond was grazed off, and because of a very limited supply of hay and grain, all the livestock, including the milk cows, saddle horses, and the team had to be grazed on the open range. Fences and pastures were few and far between in that part of the country in those days. Some of the horses were usually hobbled to make it easier for a footman to catch them and to keep them from wandering too far away. On this particular morning we needed the team, so Merril and I struck out over the hill with bridles in hand to fetch them.

Hunting loose horses on the open range requires a combination of intuition, luck, skill, a little common horse sense, and the ability to read animal signs and follow tracks. We found where the horses had been during the night and began to follow their tracks.

"It looks like they went this way," called Merril, as he headed down a draw, looking and pointing. Then turning west they had grazed up over a rocky ridge, with only an occasional print showing now and then when a horse happened to strike a soft spot, and tracking became slow and difficult. Separating, we each made a circle to look for tracks, hoping to pick up the trail farther on where the earth was softer and not so rocky.

"I found them," I yelled, as I came onto an old trail bearing fresh horse tracks, some of them with shoes. Our team was shod and the trail clearly showed a three-quarter circle, the distinct print of a steel shoe.

"It looks like someone's been driving these horses," observed Merril after we had followed the tracks for some time.

"They sure ain't been grazing," I added, "and I don't think we're ever going to catch up to them." By then we had walked quite a few miles and were beginning to get tired. "No need to follow these tracks anymore," I said as I stopped, dropping one knee to the ground.

"What are we gonna do then?" Merril asked, coming back.

"I don't know" I said, intently studying the tracks before me, "but I bet somebody has stole our horses."

"We best get back and tell Pa someone's made off with the team," Merril said as he gathered up his bridle and headed out in a jog. No wonder we couldn't find them, we consoled ourselves, as we headed back for the ranch house.

"You're sure it was outlaws?" Father asked, though not really all that excited. "I haven't heard of any being around these parts for quite a spell now, but I better go look. You say you lost the trail for a time when the horses went over Blue Ridge?" After questioning us quite thoroughly about what we had found and not found, where the tracks and signs were, Pa struck out in a different direction and pretty soon was back with the lost horses.

It was often that way with the milk cows too. Sometimes we'd search and search for them until it was dark and have to come home without them. Then the next morning Pa could go out before breakfast and bring them in. He'd keep telling us, you have to look for tracks and read the signs all right, but then you gotta apply a little instinct and reasoning, a tracking short cut, he called it. "If you took the time to follow these geezers everywhere they went, you never would catch up to them. You gotta figure where they've been, where they're going, and where they'll be, and then go there." The milk cows were harder to track and wandered more, and we didn't hobble them, but we did put a bell on one of them, which helped to locate them in the thick brush or trees. We'd go a little ways and then stop and listen for the bell, go a little further and then cock an ear, hold our breath, and listen for the tinkle, tinkle of the bell.

There were days and hours that we spent tracking animals that had grazed off during the night and hid up in a clump of trees. We became skilled trackers, almost with the sense of a bloodhound, as we followed a trail through the sage and trees, reading signs that became like a printed page. Our skills were honed in the late afternoons by hunting cows that had strayed farther away in search of green feed, pressed on by the setting sun and the urgency to locate the critters before darkness blotted out all signs and evidence, pausing every few minutes to listen for the tinkle of a bell that would disclose what hillside, thicket, or valley the cows might be in. They usually fed and stayed together, but it was quite disappointing sometimes, after an anxious and pressing search, to catch the distant sound of a bell on the night wind and find part of the herd, but with one still missing, and then to have to try to determine where the stray might be. Sometimes we'd track on foot and sometimes on horseback, galloping down a canyon or over a rocky hill, through the trees and little hollows, watching deer or gray coyotes slink away, and sometimes catching the heavy odor of skunk that hung in the air for days.

Two Alone

When we moved up on Trumbull Mountain for the summer, the folks decided they needed to make a trip back to Enterprise for some reason. But we still had our stock to drive to water at Nixon Springs and chores to do, so it was decided that Merril and I would stay there and do the chores while Pa took my mother and two sisters in the old Chevy back to Utah for a week. Even at this early age, we had been well taught and instilled with a positive spirit of confidence and reliability and this became a test of our courage and wilderness survival skills. Leaving us alone so far away was a concern to our parents because we were far from everything. The nearest ranch was about four miles away and the nearest little town, Bundyville, was about ten miles down on the west side of the mountain.

Again, this was a growing and learning experience for us, but we really never thought much about it. At first we busied ourselves with the daily routine of home life and ranch chores. We had to prepare our own meals from limited supplies without the aid of electricity or running water, and without fast food stores to run to, but we did have cows to get our milk from. We had to drive some of our stock and horses to Nixon Springs for water, then nearly ten miles to pasture to a place my dad was trying to homestead. We kept the cows closer to the little cabin he had built by locking the calves in the corral.

One day we went to take the horses to water and like normal boys, we did some playing and exploring along the way. We went a little too far and were late heading home. To make up for lost time we were hurrying, running our ponies farther than prudent. Mine, a pinto we had traded for back in Utah, wasn't used to roughing it like our other horses were. Being hobbled so we could catch him, he was probably undernourished. Anyway, the extra press caught up with him and he began to falter, stagger, and finally fell to his knees in the dark.

A panicky cry from me brought my brother back. A quick check in the dark showed a jaded, giving-out horse, trembling and sweating.

We held an anxious and urgent council as to what to do. It was already dark and late and we still had miles to go, cows to gather from the hills, and chores to do when we did get home. After a short rest, we decided to try to go on and take the pinto too. So we two climbed on the other horse, riding double and leading the pinto. It was kinda like the song of long ago:

Two Little boys

Had two little toys,

Each a wooden horse;

Gaily they playe

Each summer's day –

Warriors both of course,

One little chap

Then had a mishap,

Broke off his horse's head;

Cried for his toy,

Then cried for joy

As his young playmate said:

"Did you think I would leave you crying

When there's room on my horse for two?

Climb up here, Jack. We'll soon be flying;

I can go just as fast with two."

It was much slower going and well past midnight when we finally got to the shadow of the lonesome pines. And we were so tired, we turned the hungry horses into the little grain field, which was kind of a no-no. The cows had finally got lonesome and come home on their own and were standing by the corral gate lowing for their calves. We put them in the corral and went to bed more tired than hungry.

Then there was the time after our folks returned when it rained. It was kind of like Noah's flood, at least that's what we thought when it caught us halfway between Nixon Springs and the big pasture. I suppose there have been rains like that before, but not in our young lives. We tried to brave it out and ride in it, but the water came down in drenching sheets with hail beating on us. Within minutes, water was standing and running everywhere. We got off our ponies and tried to take shelter under a good-sized tree, but the rain and hail seemed to beat right through the branches. Our minds conjured visions of a second Noah's flood as we watched the rising water fill the dry gullies and washes we would have to cross to get back to the cabin. I remember thinking the end of the world must be upon us, and having been somewhat familiar with the story of Noah, thinking this is a repeat performance. So amid shattering thunder and streaks of lightning and a dark sky at midday, not wanting to be caught in the end of the world without mom and dad, we climbed on our ponies and, keeping to the high ground, raced for home and the security of our family.

Despite the many challenges of caring for ourselves and the stock, of tracking and finding lost strays, it was a fun and growing time for us. Our experiences made us men long before our time. I'm sure the folks did worry about us, but for us it only served to weld and bond us even closer, especially me, depending on my older brother Merril. So you can see, with the draft and the war coming, joining the army together was both needed and important.

The Laub children on "Old Lola"—Merril, LaRee, Ruby, Normand, about 1930, at the old stone house in Enterprise, Utah.

The cattle country of the Arizona Strip where two little boys forged an unbreakable bond.

The pond in the lower Toroweap Valley where young Merril and Normand could water their stock.

Normand recalls how he and Merril hid behind clumps of Spanish dagger from the curious long-horned cattle.

Chapter 3
Training in California and Australia

The PRD

Our detachment of Cavalry troops arrived in the San Francisco Bay Area on a slow troop train from Ft. Riley, Kansas. This train ride was quite different from our first one out of Salt Lake City about nine months before. There were a lot more of us for one thing, and for another, our quarters and chow were pretty typical army, nothing fancy like we had before. We enjoyed our ride back through the mountains and deserts of the west after our training on the rolling hills and great plains of Kansas. We, "the Brothers" as we had become to be known, joked and talked and watched the Nevada wilderness with its familiar scenery, as we proudly explained western cowboy and ranch life to our eastern buddies and friends.

It was hot dry summer when the troop train dropped us off at the PRD, or Pittsburgh Replacement Depot, just outside of Oakland, California behind the coastal hills of the San Francisco Bay Area. While life and business appeared to be going on quite normally, there was a very noticeable difference. There were a lot of military personnel, vehicles, and equipment to be seen everywhere in America, but particularly in the Bay Area since it was one of the main points of embarkation for soldiers and equipment for overseas destinations. Our quarters at PRD were pretty cheap and flimsy compared to the tree-shaded, beautiful old stone quarters of Ft. Riley, Kansas. Most of our quarters in California were long, single story, tar-paper-and-lumber buildings, with rows and rows of bunks for sleeping. There wasn't a lot to do either. We spent quite a lot of time executing various military training maneuvers, making long marches, mostly in the daytime, but sometimes at night. We hiked and climbed the steep hills that were covered in grass that was yellow and dry. It was quite hot. I think we must have spent about three weeks at PRD, drilling on long marches with full pack, in the hot, dry California sun, learning, I guess, to be foot soldiers. If we had been sent to North Africa, we were getting in shape, but where we were going was quite a different place from these hot, dry, California hills. But we didn't know that yet. And we still had hopes of getting horses.

I don't suppose there was anywhere where rumors were more plentiful than in the army among a group of soldiers awaiting shipping orders. It was always the latest thing and the straight dope. One of the rumors was that we were going to New Caledonia, wherever that was. Another was Australia.

Our camp life, however, wasn't all that pressing or busy. We had plenty of time for bull sessions, card games, and dice rolling, although Merril and I didn't gamble or drink. Somehow I had managed to bring a short piece of rope and sometimes I amused myself and others by roping someone's feet as they walked by. But this little pastime nearly got me into trouble several times. Merril kept telling me I needed to be careful and that if I tripped someone up and he came after me, he wouldn't help me or even claim any relation. But it was kind of fun.

Weekend passes were available for most of our group while we were there, and most of the soldiers got at least one. Some got several and some crawled through a hole in the fence and went without a pass. My brother and I finally got a weekend pass which we intended to use to visit Oakland, where we had an aunt living. So we got all spruced up in our best khaki uniforms and got out on the highway with the swarms of GIs trying to hitch a ride into Oakland or Frisco. But there were a lot more soldiers lined up on the road than there were cars, and by time they got to us, they were already loaded. After walking and trying for about an hour to catch a ride, we gave up and crossed the road to the other side to thumb a ride back to camp, and it wasn't long until we got a ride going the other way. So we went back to camp and spent the weekend writing letters, reading, and visiting.

We did manage to get another pass later. This time, a group of us pooled our money and hired a taxi to take us to town. While the rest of the soldiers went out on the town, my brother and I went and visited our Aunt Mel in Oakland. After dinner with her and her husband, he drove us back to camp. But gas was rationed, so civilians didn't do a lot of driving during the war.

Being horse soldiers with quite a few cowboys in our ranks, someone decided we ought to put on a rodeo for fun and to pass time. So somebody arranged for some rodeo stock, roping calves, horses to ride, and some bucking stock. Some of us went to some local ranches to help load and get the stock and then we spent a little time helping fix up a ball park into a rodeo arena with chutes and pens and the likes. In the bucking events I drew a Hereford steer that didn't buck very hard, but Merril drew a brindle Brahma cow that really gave him a ride, raking the back of his legs and spurs with her hind feet nearly every jump. This rodeo wasn't anything big or special, but it was fun and something to do.

There were a number of things happening there that were new to us country boys, even though we had been in the army nearly ten months now and out in the big wide world. A couple or three of the slick-looking dudes would spruce up and take off somewhere nearly every night with or without a pass. It was rumored they were pimps and had something going. We had never heard of homosexuals and back in those days if there were any around, they were never talked about openly, but I kind of think now they might have been.

Then there was ex-Sgt. Stewart, a good-looking soldier. He was about 26 and had been in the service during peace time. He was married, but his wife was back in his home state of Louisiana. Yet he had a girlfriend in Frisco, and he spent nearly every night with her. She had a good job or must have been quite well-to-do because she had her own car and would come and pick "Dick" up at night and bring him back the next morning in time for regular duty. And he was one who often took a hole-in-the-fence pass. He was a good soldier and having been in before and being older than most of us, had been kind of an example up to now. But after this double-standard cheating example, I lost my respect for him and felt sorry for his wife whom we had seen a few times back at Ft. Riley.

But as we quickly learned, there was a lot of this cheating and sub-moral conduct going on in the army, especially on the west coast where the pressure for a final fling created desperation in soldiers headed for combat overseas. The war seemed to give them a license or excuse for dropping the bars and compromising their moral standards.

The day of departure finally arrived. I don't remember how far in advance we knew, but it must have been a day or two because the night before we shipped out, a couple of the guys crawled through the hole in the fence and didn't come back. I never did know what happened to them, but evidently they didn't want to go to war with us.

February 13, 1985

So here we are, Barbara and I, crossing the cactus-strewn desert of the Mormon Mesas, Nevada, headed for the land of the setting sun, where the blue waters of the trackless Pacific idly splash on the quiet shores of green tropical islands, that mystical land beyond the distant horizon where part of me died and was buried a long time ago, and where a new, uncertain, but struggling soul was born and began an endless quest for personal identity, that elusive but important search for the real purpose and meaning of life. It will be interesting and rewarding to go back and open those locked doors and, as it were, re-enter those sad and haunting silent halls of long ago. Hence, this "Sentimental Journey" into the past and beyond the bend.

As we left home this morning, after some last-minute counsel and instructions and a touching farewell to Craig and RueThella, and Larry and Lynda, I asked Barbara why we were going on this trip. She said, "I guess because you wanted to," which is probably quite right. I really have kind of wanted to but never thought we really would. But here we are, just the two of us, on our way. It should be quite an experience.

And now, as we cross down across the sunlit desert of southern Nevada, my mind reverts to a train ride across northern Nevada, a troop train headed for the west coast of America and the uncertainty and unknown beyond. It was wartime then and the nation and all of the people were caught up in a strange, different world. We were so young then, so carefree but kind of sober too, as we tried to anticipate what lay ahead.

Today as we came over the summit from the north and looked down onto Las Vegas, we were greeted by a wing of jet fighters, sweeping low over Nellis A.F.B and then climbing sharply into the sky. The world has seen a lot of changes in the last 40 years, but perhaps few greater than in the military means of waging war.

Shipping Out for Places Unknown

It was another of those new and interesting experiences to board an ocean liner and sail under the Golden Gate Bridge into the wild blue Pacific Ocean. The biggest boat we had ever been in was a small rowboat and the biggest pond we had ever sailed on was the Enterprise Reservoir, so this became quite interesting for some of us country boys. I remember spending a lot of time on the main deck standing at the rail, watching the ocean. I continually marveled at the deep blue of the water. And at night it was fascinating to stand on the bow and watch the nose of the ship slice through the ink-black water and see the streaks of white as they fell away on either side.

Of course, at night we traveled under strict blackout conditions, and we did a lot of zigzagging to outsmart any enemy subs that might try to get a fix on us or a shot at us. I think we only saw one other ship during the two-week voyage, and we gave it a pretty wide berth, so I don't know whether it was friendly or enemy.

Although it was war time and we were traveling under strict orders in very risky conditions, there was a big celebration onboard the ship as we crossed that deep, invisible dateline, and when we sailed over the rim of the equator and started down the bottom side of the earth. Each of us was issued a special little card with our name and a picture of some deep sea monster, something about Davey Jones' Locker and the mystic spell of the deep and some other notes I had never heard of before. Some of the sailors shaved their heads when we crossed over. There were a lot of new and strange things this dumb little country boy had never known or heard of before that we were seeing or being exposed to.

There wasn't a lot new or different to do during this long voyage. Our life aboard ship felt like kind of a paradox. You got up every morning in the very same place you were before, but you weren't really in the same place anymore. You rolled out of your sack when the lights or signal flashed in the morning, showered in the same sticky salt-water shower, shaved, and ate your breakfast in the gallery. You had already been all over the ship from top to bottom and from stem to stern, so there wasn't anything new to see. The people were always the same, no new faces and no pretty girls, unfortunately, no girls at all. Aside from the routine fire drill, boat drill, and emergency abandon ship dry-run practices, there wasn't much else to do. The vast, placid blue Pacific didn't change all that much. Sometimes we would pass through a little rain squall or a bit of fog, or under clouds, but for the most part it was the blue sky, blue ocean, and sunshine for which the broad Pacific is famous.

The ship did have a pretty good library and I read a couple books. The only one I remember now was by that famous Western author Zane Grey. He had lived and written quite a few of his stories about our own neck of the woods, Utah, Arizona, and Nevada, and about our people, the Mormons, cowboys, outlaws, and Indians. Not all true of course, but very interesting reading. Zane had a terrific imagination and a unique feel and flare for words, descriptions and feelings. I liked his books and had read a quite a few before this voyage I was on. In fact the very first book I read was a Zane Grey novel, *Wild Fire,* about a great red mustang stallion, a heroic wild horse hunter, a pretty girl, and an outlaw gang in the wild, impassible country of the Grand Canyon. This was my country, my love, and my life. I had an old bachelor rancher uncle who had nearly all of the Zane Grey books, but one I found in the ship's library, *30,000 on the Hoof,* was one I hadn't read. It was about an ambitious cowboy who built his own cattle empire in the West near the turn of the century, whose three sons were caught up in the tragedy of World War I and two of them were killed in France. So this book and the pressure and significance of the moment in our own lives left quite an impression on me. In his story, Zane Grey added a fourth dimension to his world of life and living. Both Merril and I read it. But little did we know how closely we would relate to its war aspect as well as to its cowboy, horse, and country connections.

There were constant card and crap games going on. Somehow these two vices seemed to both attract and pacify the minds and needs of soldiers, at least it was probably the greatest single pastime during leisure moments. Even during 10-minute breaks someone would break out a deck of cards or set of dice. But these tools of the devil, as my pious old puritan grandmother would call them, often became more than an idle pastime. To some they became a passion, an obsession. Many times a game was going or the betting was on before the ink was hardly dry on some of the soldiers' paychecks. Of course we never got paid by check; it was always cash, often in the currency of the country we were in.

But Merril and I never got involved in cards, gambling, or betting. I might have done if it hadn't been for him, but I'm glad I didn't. I have seen soldiers lose their entire paycheck in not much more time than it took them to stand in line to collect it. Of course, it wasn't a total disaster since Uncle Sam still paid most of their bills, including food, clothes, and lodging. But there were some sad cases, some disappointed soldiers, and occasionally some violence, especially when there were card sharks or a big winner, one soldier with sole possession of several others' pay. Quite often my brother and I were loaning money to some poor GI whose luck was bad but was bound to get better. But we didn't have a lot of money to lend, because we had most of our $50 a month overseas pay sent directly home to help pay for the ranch.

There was a lot of time to think, to meditate, and to anticipate. I remember standing on the bow at night searching the sky for the Southern Cross. We were down where the constellations were different from those in the Northern hemisphere. And I remember wondering about the meaning and purpose of life and our existence and feeling overwhelmed at the size and vastness of the world and universe. What strange new land were we going to? What would it and the people be like? We had never been this far from home before.

We were headed for war and combat, but where? What would it be like? It was both a time of eager expectation and anxious anticipation. I don't recall that I ever felt any undue fear or concern. Most soldiers didn't think about it too hard. We had kind of gotten conditioned to take what came and not to sweat it. Besides, what could you do if you did? In looking back now, one can't help wonder how we were able to take some of the conditions, the adverse and sometimes miserable and deadly consequences as calmly and matter-of-factly as we did. It was simply a way of life for the moment, the only world there was, and the world we lived in. Besides, we were stuck. What else could we do? In the words of a very common and accepted saying back then, "We were in for the duration plus six" (the duration of the war, plus six months).

I recall that one morning we suddenly hit some rough water, no storm, just some giant swells. Some of us were thrown clear out of bed, if you could call that piece of white camp canvas laced to a metal frame we used for a bunk, a bed. On these converted troop ships these bunks were hung about five high, 30 inches wide and 80 inches long.

The ship was pitching and rolling. You could be walking down the deck and all of a sudden the floor would drop out from under you and leave you walking on air for just a moment. The water in the shower and bathrooms was sloshing back and forth across the floor about four inches deep. And when we went down to the mess hall for chow, I just got my tray of scrambled eggs and toast when we hit a giant wave, and trays, food, and utensils all slid down and off the end of the long table in a clattering, messy heap. This literally was a soldiers' mess. But there weren't too many diners, as a lot of the soldiers and some of the sailors were suddenly struck with that dreaded plague of the ocean, seasickness, when there is more coming up than is going down. And you don't dare eat even if you were hungry and felt like it for fear it would come right back up. We did a lot of sailing in the Pacific in the next year, but this was the roughest water we ever hit and the closest I ever came to being seasick. My brother did get sick and didn't feel like eating anything.

Of course, our ocean voyage did provide some other interesting and exciting experiences too. There were the schools of sharks and porpoises and an occasional whale that crossed our path or followed or paralleled our course. Sometimes for only a fleeting glimpse, but sometimes for hours they would escort and entertain us, or check us out, darting and jumping out of the water. But the little ocean creature that fascinated me most and which I had thought was only a fancy line in Rudyard Kipling's moving poem, "On the Road to Mandalay," was the little flying fish. I didn't know fish really had wings or could fly, so it was a real fascination to me to watch these little schools break from the water and skim across the surface with their little sets of transparent wings shining in the bright sunlight.

Then for the first time in many days, we were joined by a flock of sea gulls. Like weary and desperate ocean voyagers of the past, we were heartened by the occasional sight of bits of floating sea grass or other land-connected particles, indicating land of some type was not too far distant. So the big question and exciting expectation was, where were we? At what strange and foreign land were we about to arrive? What would our reception or landing be like? And would it be friendly or hostile? I think somewhere along here we received the official word that we would be landing in Australia, the Land Down Under, and we were given a brief lecture about the people, conditions, and customs, and some do's and don'ts of etiquette and language, particularly around the ladies.

The end of this voyage also brought a bit of relief. We had traversed 7,000 miles of enemy-infested waters without incident on our slow boat. As I look back now, I'm reminded of some lines from a tribute to Abraham Lincoln after his assassination: "Oh, captain, my captain, the fearful trip is done,/ The ship has weathered every storm, the prize we sought is won."

Camp Strathpine, Australia

It was mid-morning under cloudy skies as the ship made its way to Brisbane. We steamed up a good-sized river inland a short distance to the dock. The heavily wooded green hills and landscape were covered with broad leaf eucalyptus and other jungle type trees. One of the things that really caught my attention as we marched off the boat onto the docks were the teams of big draft horses they were using down on the waterfront for power and mobility to move the loads of things around. We found the country quite behind America in many respects besides that.

Here we were, not only thousands of miles from home, but two hemispheres away too. We were in the Eastern hemisphere as well as the Southern hemisphere. This was an upside-down world to the soldier of 1943. We were eager to see and learn about these new people in this far-off land. They spoke with a sharp, crisp brogue, kind of accenting A for I and I for E, but they were a very jolly, chipper, country group of people. We were young country boys, involved in one of history's epic moments which scattered young men like us all over the world, many of them to places and among people they knew very little about or had never heard of before.

As part of a special detachment from the 29th Cavalry, Ft. Riley, Kansas, my brother Merril and I were sent here as part of a re-enforcement detail to beef up the troops of the 1st Cavalry Division already quartered at Camp Strathpine, a base camp of about 15,000 American soldiers, carved out of the gum tree forest of northeastern Australia. Upon our arrival we were assigned to the newly formed D (Dog) troop of the 5th Regiment, under the astute command of Col. Hugh Hoffman. D troop was a heavy weapons troop with two platoons. Lt. Bill Swan was one of the military strategists and trainers and quite involved in helping set up part of the camp, particularly in some of our military training and maneuvers here. He chose Merril and me to go with him into the jungle for some special training, and he became a special friend to us.

I started looking for horses so we didn't have to walk. We had heard that we were to get them here, but the only horse I ever saw in Australia was one ridden by General Swift. One time as we were being marched along he rode by, and my eyes followed, turning my head around, and the drill sergeant got on me for turning my head. Strict military discipline requires that a soldier keep his eyes riveted on the back of the head of the soldier in front of him and not look to the right or left, no matter what. Our stop in the tropics of Australia, between the dry deserts of America and the dense jungles of New Guinea and of the Pacific islands where we were soon to be plunged into battle, without the horses on which we had been trained, was a very necessary and desirable stop. The training and conditioning we received here proved invaluable for what awaited us as we joined the Allied forces in that long, jungle island hopping march up through the southwest Pacific towards our destination, Japan.

While here we met and talked to some of the battle-weary soldiers of the American 32nd Infantry Division who were being rotated back from the New Guinea battles. This was one of the first

American army units to be committed to action in the Pacific, and in those early months of learning warfare in the jungles, they were not too well trained or prepared for either the Japanese or the jungle, and so they suffered immense hardships and casualties. So our first contact with veterans of actual combat were these weary battered troops, and they gave us a not very appealing report of malaria, mud, and rain. In fact, in those early days of the jungle war, malaria took a heavier toll on our troops than did the enemy bullets. A brave and energetic soldier, when struck with malaria in a damp, dark tropical jungle, can literally lose the will and desire to fight or even to live. Even though he had been fighting with all the skill and ability he had to live, the effects of this plague on his physical being can waste him away until he no longer cares about anything; in fact, he can reach such a low point that death would be welcome. Try to imagine the depth of this silent, hidden enemy and its devastating effects on the soldier. How many died from malaria? What was its total casualties? It must be conceded that the 32nd was very ill prepared or trained for the conditions that they were to face. Our leaders had learned much from their costly experiences.

I have a few fond memories of our time in Australia. Merril and I were able to find our church [The Church of Jesus Christ of Latter-day Saints] and mingle with some of the special saints in that area. Also we were able to participate in some of their rodeos, which provided us with some excitement and good times when we had some time off from our training.

We now knew that we were not going to be mounted and ride into battle on our beloved four-footed chargers. We became known as "Dismounted Cavalry," a term we were to accept with a bit of disappointment but still a bit of the pride and spirit of the famous horse soldiers of the U.S. Army. We thus identified ourselves through much of the rest of the war, as we realized that we would be ordinary foot soldiers fighting on some of these south sea jungle islands.

In fact, we spent no small amount of time in the division briefing rooms, studying and poring over some huge wall maps of the southwest Pacific area, New Guinea, Java, Borneo, and countless other smaller islands, learning about their people, conditions, features, and wondering which ones we could be going to. They were strange-sounding names, unknown islands of very minor consequence that very few had heard of half a century ago.

We also followed with keen intent the different battle lines and progress and the slow, bloody ground that was being taken by the Marines on Guadalcanal or on the coasts of New Guinea by the Aussies and Americans. We felt good in helping the struggling Aussies build their limited defense, since most of their troops were already away fighting. I remember counting those many islands and thinking, what a long war this was going to be by the time we drove the Japanese from all of them.

Soon after the first of the year 1944, a shipload of soldiers, in fact all 15,000 of us had left Brisbane. It was a moment of wonder and anticipation as we marched down to the river dock and loaded back on a troop ship again and sailed back down the river to the open sea and north into the mysterious never-never land of the southwest Pacific. We were heading into the enemy-infested wilderness. We were about to meet him now. He was on part of many of the islands we were headed towards. Can anyone capture the feeling, the anticipation, the wonder that occupied the minds and thoughts of us soldiers as our boat sailed among these tropical isles as they rose like studded green jade jewels from the great blue mass of the ocean? I celebrated my 20th birthday somewhere in this area, but I don't remember a thing about it.

From Australia, we were sent to New Guinea to help back up the hard-pressed Aussie and American forces trying to check a sweeping Japanese advance down through the southwest Pacific toward Australia. The cruise from Brisbane to Port Moresby, New Guinea was an interesting one for the soldier headed for the battlefield. Once again we were closing in on the enemy and getting closer to our date with destiny. Most of us had never heard of New Guinea before World War II, and even now it was not a familiar landmark. But it was becoming more of a well-known place to us because it was an active battlefield.

This was the Allies' last and about only remaining outpost and line of defense against the advancing Japanese war machine, so it held a special as well as strategic significance. The Owen Stanley mountain range, over 13,000 feet high and covered with dense jungle, formed a natural barrier running the entire length of eastern New Guinea. The Kokoda Trail (winding foot trails) was the only means of crossing it. It was this formidable barrier, not the Aussies or Americans, that finally stopped that sweeping Japanese advance toward Australia. The mountains not only stopped the Japanese, but they stopped the Aussies as they tried to climb the gold stairs, 2,000 steps that were dug into the sticky, impossible mud and jungle of this mighty Owen Stanley jungle fortress. It was here the native New Guinea tribesmen became our greatest allies as they faithfully and tirelessly carried supplies into and packed the wounded out of the jungle for us. These admirable natives were known as the Fuzzy Wuzzy Angels of New Guinea.

Our visit to Port Moresby was very brief. Most of the troops never got off the ship. The natives swam or paddled out to our ship in there little boats. Some of the soldiers would toss coins overboard into the blue-green water just to watch those expert swimmers and divers who would follow a silver coin clear out of sight down in the water. The villagers built their huts on stilts out into the harbor with their canoes and boats anchored to or tied up underneath, with a ladder rope or steps down into the water.

The tens of thousands of servicemen, soldiers, sailors, and Marines, most of them young, green Americans like my brother and me, didn't have time to explore or even to wonder about the unique country we suddenly found ourselves in. The southwest Pacific campaign was waged among primitive people and often in difficult and primitive conditions. Those beautiful islands with their white beaches looking like the opening of paradise became bloody, deadly jungles and costly beachheads where young men in the beginning of life were to live only for a brief moment more and then die unaware of the beautiful land of mystery into which they had sailed.

As soldiers, we looked at the sunken ships and other signs of war. This was our first contact with the real effects of the war, so it was a moment of high excitement and interest. We then sailed south around the southern tip of New Guinea and made another brief stop at Milne Bay.

May 8, 1988

As I sat there in the predawn light of Port Moresby, New Guinea, from somewhere out of that fading past, I could feel, almost see and hear some of the scenes and events of long ago. But my pen had not the ability or time to record the thoughts, the feelings, and the fleeting scenes that were intermittently flashing through my mind. And I guess it was because there were the two of us, my brother Merril and me, who were on this part of the journey, who knew, experienced, and lived these scenes of the past. I was drawn with a strong cord to this area like few may ever have reason to be. Perhaps that's why the rusty skeleton of the sunken ship sticking up out of the water in the nearby bay was a key that suddenly unlocked the door to a vast bank of memories and feelings, like the dead and abandoned remains of the once-mighty ocean vessel that sailed into this port with her cargo of men and supplies during World War II, among which were my brother Merril and me.

Camp Strathpine, Australia

LDS Servicemen in Brisbane, Australia, early 1944;
Normand is 2nd from back right and Merril is kneeling far right.

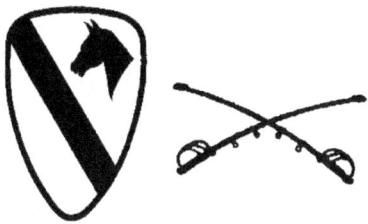

Cavalry Emblems

The 1st Cavalry Division held a rodeo in Brisbane.

Chapter 4

Cowboy Days

Movie Cowboys

Because my mother's health was not good, and because living on the Arizona Strip was not a desirable place for her and my two little sisters, we moved back to Utah. The Democratic administration under President Roosevelt had initiated some new welfare work projects. My dad was able to get a little work on one of these projects, and we found and started to buy another little run-down ranch in the Enterprise area. Growing up together, Merril and I began staying part time on the ranch and fixing it up. We finally had the little place doing pretty well and were buying a few more cattle to build up our herd. We were really enjoying our cattle, our horses, and our western cowboy life and world. The blight and aftermath of the Great Depression still hung pretty heavy on much of the area, but we felt rich and prosperous, even if we weren't those things in reality. Our father had always instilled within us a positive, self-sufficient attitude. We didn't have to hang our heads or take a back seat to anybody, even if we didn't always have fancy clothes, other nice things, or even some of the things we may have liked or wanted. We were happy, and we had talents and opportunities.

Hollywood people came into our part of the country in the fall of 1938. They were filming part of the movie *Union Pacific* out at Desert Mound along a branch line of the railroad that ran up to Iron Mountain. I first learned of the filming from an advertisement that said they needed pinto horses for the Indians to ride and were paying good dollars to rent them. It also mentioned that if you were six feet tall and dark complected you might be hired on as an extra. Unfortunately, I wasn't dark complected, nor was I six feet tall, and even worse I was only 14 years old, too young to be hired even if I had met the other requirements, so there went my chance to become a teenage movie star. However, Merril did qualify, and we had some pinto horses that we were excited to rent to the movie people. Merril was going to deliver our horses to the Desert Mound stock yards, and so I went with him like I had all my life. The few local guys that I knew besides my brother were Terry Tait, who was also from Enterprise, Uriah Jones from New Castle furnished a team of mules, and Jess Guyman from Parowan with a team and wagon.

Most of the filming was done on the branch rail line that ran southwest from the corrals and stock yards. This was quite an impressive sight for a country boy, with all their big tents, trucks, trailers, lights, cameras, and filming equipment. They even had some big tents where they kept their fancy Hollywood horses indoors with special grooms to care for and polish them up.

They brought up a band of Navajos from Arizona whom they housed in some tents and "wicky ups" down across the creek by themselves. The Navajos had some sweat lodges where they made steam with hot rocks and did some of their Indian ceremonies. They were very colorful with their blankets and long black braids. It was in the fall, and we had some cold weather and a little snow one night. On one cold, cloudy day between shots, Uriah Jones and someone else persuaded the Indians to do a ceremonial dance in one of the tents for us.

Merril and I had a small tent up on the side of the hill where we slept and fixed our own meals. There was a bus or taxi service into Cedar City night and morning, so most of the stars, directors, staff, and extras stayed in town. The movie was directed by Cecil B. DeMille and starred Joel McCrea, Robert Preston, Barbara Stanwyck, Brian Donlevy, and other notables. They did have a cook shack out at the camp which provided snacks and a noon meal for everyone, so we did mingle and eat with the movie stars during lunch. Also, there was time between shots and scenes when we were able to walk around the set and mingle freely with everyone.

One of the main scenes was when the Indians pulled down a wooden water tank to block the train and then attacked the train, killing the passengers and robbing the supplies, clothing, and goods that were on the train. Merril was an extra "Indian" in this scene. Our job (and I did get to help even though I didn't get paid) was to wrangle the loose horses when the Indians would swoop down on the stalled train, jump off their horses, and attack the train and people. With all of the shooting, noise, and excitement, the yards of cloth on the horses, and kettles tied to their necks and tails, they would scatter. Several times they stampeded, and we would round them up and bring them back. Quite often they would have to stop the filming while we got them back in place for the "lights, camera, action." Of course there was always plenty of action, both on and off the set.

We must have been there for a couple of weeks or more, and I think they paid us every week. I remember Merril had to take a bus into town to get his check. I can't remember now how much it paid, but I think it was two or three dollars a day for him, and the rent for the horses was one or two dollars per head per day. Back during the Depression this was pretty big money for our family. Participating in this movie was a very interesting and impressive experience for us.

Great Horses

I was just a kid when I first learned about a notorious little mustang stallion. It was during the early thirties and the hard times of the Great Depression plus a prolonged drought hung heavy over the ranges of the dry southwest. The bands of wild, free roaming horses (mustangs) were seriously competing with the ranchers' cattle for the limited grass on their dry ranges. Because they belonged to no one in particular and had no value back then, they were systematically removed by trapping, catching, or outright killing. In our area the 30-30 Winchester helped remove most of them. An avid horse lover even as a kid, I found this a sad situation, and it was that way also for my dad who liked to chase the wild bunch and occasionally caught and brought one home for us to love and admire. He often talked against these ruthless horse-killing raids, until the mustangs were finally all gone from our southwestern Utah range. There were still a few left in the headwaters country of eastern Nevada, but a state line fence kept them out of our area.

Then, one spring, the stallion showed up on the Utah side. No one seemed to know where he came from or how he got there. He joined the ranchers' horses and made them hard to catch or corral, because he was too fast and fleet for anyone to rope or run down, though many often tried over the next two or three years. He wasn't very large, but he was a picture to behold with his long black flowing mane and tail, a blood-red bay with a wide bald face and four white stockings that were nearly belly high. Talk about speed and action, nobody had seen his like in many years as he swept over the hills and rocks with the ease and grace of an antelope. Because of his speed and cunning herd control, there was a band of mares the ranchers hadn't been able to corral for over a year and the talk began to build that something had to be done.

It was a beautiful time in the spring of 1937 and the cattle roundup was in full swing. Merril and I, old enough to join in the roundup, were joyfully helping with the cattle drive. Early one morning, as the different cowboys and ranchers assembled for the day's assignment at one of the bigger ranch headquarters, the word was spread that the certain band of mares and their unbranded colts needed to be brought in that day, "with or without ol' White Rock Bally." Adding a somber bit of finality to this declaration was the 30-30 rifle that one of the prominent ranchers had strapped to his saddle.

By late afternoon, most of the riders were finally assembled at the big rock hole stockade corral with their numerous bunches of cattle, including me and my brother. And then some sharp-eyed cowboy yelled, "There they come."

Looking up we saw a band of speeding horses headed our way, with three wild riding cowboys in hot pursuit, with arms and hats waving. Hurriedly grabbing our horses, some of us mounted up and fanned out to help haze them in. Although this was his band, White Rock Bally wasn't with them.

"What happened to him?" someone finally asked, and one of the riders and old timers said he wouldn't come so he had to be shot. And then someone else asked about the shooting and the proud rifle-carrying rider announced that the little stud had been hit just a little to the left of square between the eyes.

But then as the work of branding and talk went one, we heard old Pat tell some of the other ranchers about the chase. They had found the horses all right and got them headed in the right direction, but the shepherding little stallion kept interfering, so the rifle carrier finally used his gun, hitting him in the shoulder and breaking a front leg. But this majestic little monarch and proud mustang stud still refused to leave his band of mares, though old Pat said that if the little stallion had left the band and run away for his own safety, he doubted there was a horse in their group fast enough to have caught up to him, even running on only three legs. The rancher with the rifle finally roped him, catching him only because he wouldn't leave his mares and colts. Then with our little White Rock Bally fighting and choking down at the end of a 35-foot rope, he shot him, "This one just a little to the left of square between the eyes." Of course to me and my brother, this only made the little mustang stallion all the more a hero and our respect for the braggado rifle-carrying rancher even less.

With a touch of sadness and a growing personal interest and concern, we asked where the end had come and were directed to a low bare ridge by a little valley a few miles away. Taking our leave of this more mature cowboy group, Merril and I mounted up and headed for that ridge. Sitting on our own precious ponies, staring down at this tragic heap of wild death, my feelings were deep and mixed. Here lay the silent remains of all that was once so wild and free. Gone forever.

Though but a youth, I found myself feeling much like Frederic Remington must have felt a half century earlier when he tried to capture on canvas the fading Western scene. "I knew the wild riders and the vacant land were about to vanish forever," he said, "And the more I considered the subject, the bigger that forever loomed."

And for me, that forever had just come to pass. No more would his piercing whistle peal across the valley as he stood on the ridge, his head held high, his tail outstretched and his red nostrils flared. Almost with a sense of hushed reverence, we dismounted to have a closer look. The pool of red blood had turned dark and hardened, but it was that glazed, empty stare in his unseeing eyes I would never forget. Gone was the life, the light, and the fire that was once his noble spirit. I surely thought there must be more to his life than mere breath. Surely one little lead bullet could not destroy what was once so magnificent. Surely horses too have spirits, I reasoned.

My favorite horse during those years was Ol' Paints. He was born in 1930 when I was only six years old, so we grew up together. He was a sorrel pinto from a common sorrel bally mare, but his sire was a famous black and white stud owned by Mayor Harmon Perry of Ogden, Utah. For years, the mayor rode him to lead the Ogden City 24th of July Pioneer Parade, many times having the stallion dancing on his hind legs along the route.

When Ol' Paints was only two he was chased by a dog and got his right front foot caught in "the curse of the Western ranges," a barbed wire fence. The sharp barbs nearly sawed his foot off just below the ankle before he finally got it out. He had nearly bled to death when we found him, but my father was able to doctor him up, sew his foot back together, and with a lot of tender care and attention, we were able to save him. But it left him with a club foot which bothered him a bit when running.

Staying on the old Laub Ranch above Enterprise in the fall of 1939, now 15 years old, I was running a small trap line for coyotes to help make some money during the Depression. In one of my traps up by Eagle Rock I caught a big dog coyote, but I had tied the chain to a clump of rabbit brush for an anchor and he had chewed the brush off and got away with my trap. Merril was working on a neighbor's ranch at the time, and he really kidded me about being a great trapper, letting a coyote get away with one of my traps.

A couple of days later while riding Ol' Paints, I was going around my trap line again. About a mile farther on up the canyon I saw a big coyote break out of the willows and dart up a trail on the side of the canyon. I could see by the way he was running that he was dangling a steel trap on one front foot. There's my trap, the coyote, and a chance to redeem my reputation, I thought. So I unbuckled my lasso rope and took off after him.

When I had about caught up to him he swung off the trail and started back down the hill. At about that point the canyon turned into a row of low ledges, and the coyote, looking for a way off, ran out onto the rim. I couldn't get Ol' Paints to follow him out on the ledge, so I jumped off with the rope in my hand and ran out to see where the coyote had disappeared to. He had found a little bush-laced crevice down the side of the ledge. The ledge sloped quite steep before it dropped off, and in my enthusiasm to recapture my bounty and reputation, I didn't notice until it was too late.

My leather-soled cowboy boots slipped out from under me and I went over the edge feet first. About 20 feet down there was a little shelf about 3 feet wide. I remember thinking. "Good, I'll catch myself on it." I landed on the little shelf on my feet all right, but the speed and momentum of my fall to my horror like in my worst nightmare merely served as a springboard to catapult me head first over the edge down about another 20 feet to another little shelf, where I landed on my head and shoulders, only to roll off it down about another 30 feet to the creek bed below.

I lay there stunned, thinking, "Am I still alive?" And then I heard the rattle of steel and chain on the rocks and realized that I had beaten the coyote to the bottom. But as I tried to pick myself up to continue the chase, among my many other pains I discovered I had a broken leg (or ankle), and I had lost both my rope and hat on the way down. Then looking up, I saw Ol' Paints standing out on the edge of the cliff looking down, I guess to see what had happened to me.

The sound of the chain and the trap soon faded, for I had a much bigger problem now than a lost trap and coyote. I needed to get back up that ledge to where my horse was. Crawling on my hands and knees I discovered those two little shelves formed part of a zigzag pattern of shelves connected on the face of the cliff all the way back to the top. As I crawled along the lower shelf, I found my hat where I had landed on my head and shoulders. As I zigzagged back along the next one where I landed on my feet and probably where my ankle broke, I found my rope. And then when I got to the top there was my faithful Ol' Paints standing a few feet back, waiting for me.

The fact he hadn't wandered off or left me was a blessing—most of our other horses probably would have. Also that he would let me crawl up to him on my hands and knees and get the bridle reins and let me lead him close by a big rock so I could crawl up on it and over into the saddle was also amazing. I don't think there are many horses, even gentle ones, that won't shy away from someone trying to approach them on hands and knees. But with my right leg broken, I couldn't stand on it to get my foot in the stirrup. That he was willing to follow a crawling cowboy and stand close to the rock I led him to so I could get on was miraculous, but more than all that it was a miracle I survived the fall itself.

Still another amazing part of this experience was when I got back to the ranch house and found my brother was there to help me. Somehow he had the feeling he needed to ride the several miles over to the home place and check on me. And about the same time, my father drove up from Enterprise about 10 miles away, having had the same impression. My foot and leg were so swollen they had to cut my boot to get it off. My father then took me back to town where I got my leg fixed, while my brother filled in for me at the ranch.

The next day my father and brother found and caught that coyote in a side canyon not far from where I fell and brought it back alive for me to see before it was killed and skinned. The pelt brought about $3.00 and the bounty was about $2.00, making about $5.00 in all, pretty good money back then. But it didn't quite pay for my broken leg.

Real Cowboy Jobs

We prided ourselves once we were teenagers in being good horsemen and good cowboys and being able to go anywhere in our tri-state area—Utah, Arizona, or Nevada—and get a job making it as competent cowboys and helpful ranch hands, and we often did. This satisfying experience with my best and closest friend, my older brother Merril, made it seem as though we had everything in life as we took turns working abroad and tending our own little spread. Whatever one could do, the other could do equally well. We loved our area and our lifestyle and wouldn't have swapped it for anything we knew about. Of course, my family and most of the people I then knew were poor and still struggling from the Great Depression. This by no means excluded, however, the idea that the future still held all the sheer joy of living and fulfillment that most ordinary folks, even though poor, could both wish and hope for.

At age 17 my biggest concern was getting and holding a job as a cowboy. An invitation to work for one of the last big cattle ranches of the old west, the Ryan Cattle Company of Nevada, was the ultimate achievement of a life-long dream. My job, as the newest and youngest buckaroo, was to ride with the elite cattle company crew. This was the absolute pinnacle of joy and success for me. Forty dollars per month was more money than I'd earned in my whole life and I wasn't lazy either. I'd done my share of pitching hay, building fences, clearing land, and rustling wood, plus countless other ranch and country chores. But if the truth had been known, I'd have taken the job for board alone, even furnishing my own horse! So $40 a month, a whole ramada to ride, and the unsettled wilds of the nation's most sparsely populated state to ride them in—what more could anyone want?

But though I'd never admit it, I did get homesick at times for my home and family in Utah. I was not used to the new menu of lots of beef, beans, and coffee, and one night out near Caliente when most of the cowboys had gone into town to celebrate, I lay in my bed pretty sick, thinking I might die. I prayed and promised the Lord if he'd let me live I'd never drink coffee again, and I never did. Finally, secretly nursing some broken ribs I acquired in a spill from a falling horse in a reckless and unapproved dash after a wild stallion, I was glad to swap places with my brother Merril and go home for a rest.

Normand and Merrli
as young cowboys

Normand, Ken Staheli, Merril.
September 5, 1940

The old Laub ranch, summer and winter.

The cliff from which Normand fell while chasing a coyote.

Chapter 5

Admiralty Islands

Los Negros Beachhead – March 2, 1944

As the Allies began to turn the tide of the war, General MacArthur sent the 1st Cavalry Division on a daring reconnaissance mission deep into enemy territory to seize a little group of islands called the Admiralty Islands. If our mission succeeded, we could bypass New Britain and the big Japanese base at Rabaul, thereby effectively neutralizing a large number of enemy soldiers and leaving them, as Gen. MacArthur put it, "to die on the vine." Our little beachhead was unexpected, an extra surprise since it wasn't on Manus in the big Seeadler Harbor, where the enemy had prepared their defense. The UPI called our offensive one of the most brilliant maneuvers of the war. The 2nd Squadron, 5th Cavalry landed February 29th, and we followed March 2nd at Hyane Harbor, on a rough coral reef shoreline. The AP described it as a masterful strategy. But it wasn't a pushover and the enemy had us outnumbered two to one to start with. For the first few days they gave us a pretty rough time. I had often tried to imagine what war would be like, but despite my most concentrated efforts and the Army's most intense training, even with live bullets under barbed wire, we were still not prepared for war's grim, harsh reality.

> *Have you ever spent the night in a jungle foxhole*
> *While the enemy prowls like a demonic fiend,*
> *'Mid the heavy deluge of a tropical storm,*
> *And you wait as death rides the wind?*
> *If you have, then you know what I mean.*
> *If you haven't, thank the Powers that Be.*
> *If you would like to know what war is really like,*
> *Spend the next few minutes with me.*

This was our first beachhead and we were pretty inexperienced, while our enemies were big Imperial Marines who had fought in China and other places. They were amazingly effective at infiltration and night fighting. Snipers were all over us that first night, even trying to get in our fox holes by singing "Deep in the Heart of Texas," and asking, "Got a cigarette, Joe?" An Air Force liaison observer who landed with us claimed he had made beachheads before, and he wasn't going to sleep in any fox hole, so he stretched his hammock between two trees. The next morning we found him dead, his throat cut from ear to ear.

We stood on that war-torn shore with the restless water lapping at our feet, suddenly struck with war's cold, terrible reality. As we scanned the beach littered with ruin and destruction, an anxious, empty feeling crept over me. The mocking waves haunted me as they rose and fell around a half-sunk barge—thundering the fate of those who landed in the gray of dawn, so recently alive but now gone. The sharp chatter of machine-gun fire, backed up by the hollow boom of heavier weapons, suddenly added a grim note to the scene, already heavy with gloom. Then from out of the west, a wave of American bombers (twin engine B25s) swooped down over a tiny island not far from where we stood, in a tree-top-level bombing, their last supporting strafing run for the night.

Moving cautiously inland through the shredded and tangled jungle to the front, we crouched among the enemy dead lying scattered like so many dead animals. We passed weary, bedraggled soldiers, busy consolidating their slim beachhead. Grim, dirty-faced soldiers were busy digging in, while others stood by in silence, watching, waiting, while others gathered up our dead and carefully placed them in rows on the beach they so recently had charged across. I got a sudden feeling that life is futile and useless. So this was war, the real thing, but the worst was yet to come.

My number one job was to kill—kill people—something I had never done or even thought of doing, something so horribly foreign to all my early Christian upbringing. To violently kill another human being was sickeningly repulsive, especially to me, for whom giving a bloody nose in a youthful scuffle was the most violent act I had ever committed. But psychologically, the war had rearranged my thinking so I no longer considered the enemy human. Part of this restructured view of human worth was probably influenced by that "blazing day of infamy" at Pearl Harbor that shocked our slumbering nation into action. Along with the reports of the prisoners of the Bataan Death March and other brutal atrocities, this branded my enemy as anything but human.

During the temporary battle lull created by the recent bombing run, we decided to try to eat, realizing we hadn't had a chance since landing. Digging now into our cumbersome backpacks, we broke out small boxes of army K-rations. I should have been hungry, but I wasn't. I didn't seem to have any appetite for food although I knew I needed to eat. But somehow the dry crackers and small square of processed cheese just wouldn't go down. Crouching among the enemy dead among the shattered jungle vegetation, I began to wish this was just a bad dream from which I hoped to awaken, but I knew I couldn't.

On the south and west end of Los Negros was the small Momote air strip built in the middle of a coconut grove. It was less than a mile long and only a couple of hundred yards wide, right along the beach. The Japanese had pushed up some eight-foot-high, three-sided bunkers, or revetments, along side the little air strip to park their airplanes in, and these made good elevated bunkers and banks to dig fox holes in. We were pretty well able to take the little Momote air strip where we landed that first day without too much opposition.

The main Japanese force seemed to be on Manus, the big island, barely separated by a narrow little ocean channel. Manus, 50 miles long and about 20 miles wide, was the main Admiralty Island and the main base of shelter for the big harbor. It appeared to be mostly undeveloped except for a couple of native villages and a small coconut grove on the southeast side. Most of the Army development was on the little Los Negros horseshoe-shaped island, where we were. And having taken that little air strip, we consolidated our tiny beachhead and waited for the rest of the division to come ashore.

General MacArthur had already come ashore for a personal inspection and had awarded a Distinguished Service Cross to Lieutenant Marvin Henshaw for bravery in action and for being the first man on the beach. Unfortunately, Lt. Henshaw lost his life a few days later when a little boat he was in swamped and sank in a follow-up mini-beachhead. He was a good swimmer, but some of the men weren't, and he drowned trying to help them to shore.

There had been a few skirmishes after the initial beachhead, but the main enemy counterattack didn't come until the third night sometime after midnight, and we nearly got pushed off into the ocean. The darkness settled, thick and black. We couldn't see a hand before our face. We crawled into our holes to wait. We kind of sensed something was building and it did. All the jungle around was filled with weird noises. We'd strain our ears for the sound of movement that might be the enemy, but there was nothing to see. The minutes grew long and tense as we tried to distinguish the many sounds. From somewhere out front came an unmistakable crash, someone stumbling on a limb. We stiffened and ceased to breathe. A prickly feeling ran up my spine, and breaking out in a cold sweat, I nervously fingered my gun. Hearts pounding and breath restrained, we waited for that next step. It was hell to sit there and wait. We knew the enemy was out there, but what was he doing or what was he going to do? For that matter, what were we going to do? What could we do? Wait, but for how long?

Then like the rumble of a thousand drums, great drops of rain begin falling. We were soon drenched to the skin and sitting in water, discomfort multiplied by danger, and still we waited.

But we didn't have to wait very long then. All at once, all hell broke loose as here they came. Drunk on saké, singing, shouting, and banging on tin pans, the crazed fanatical enemy began their charge. Out of the night they came, wave on wave, breaking into a run. Our nerves, strained to the breaking point, snapped as every man on the line opened fire. Searing tracers lit up the jungle as we gave them everything we had, but still they came. Only then, while firmly gripping the handle of the heavy 30-caliber machine gun swinging freely in my hand, my qualms about killing were replaced with the comforting assurance provided by the rapid, deadly wall of fire spouting out of the mouth of my weapon. The rule in war is kill or be killed, and that's what I learned to do.

But we could thank God that we were hit only by a small force. The main banzai charge was concentrated in one area to our right by 100 yards. Wave on wave, out of the night they came, advancing over their own dead, advancing with total disregard and sheer weight of numbers. It was soon evident that some of our troops would have to pull back or be overrun by a sea of enemy men. With their ammunition running out, our leaders made a hasty decision to pull back and blanket the area with mortar and artillery.

It was the 2nd Squadron, 5th Cavalry that had taken it on the chin, and what happened to them isn't easy to forget. Sgt. Troy A. McGill, a G troop squad leader, held one of the forward revetments. His squad gave the Japanese everything they had, but still the enemy came. With all of his squad killed or wounded but one, Sgt. McGill told him to fall back to the next line and he would try to hold out a little longer as they called for mortar and artillery support. With enemy soldiers crawling up his revetment like ants, McGill ran out of ammo. Instead of surrendering, he took his gun in his hand as a club and went down over the bank to meet the Japanese, and there he was found the next morning, a hero among the dead. I shall never forget walking down in front of Sgt. McGill's bunker that next morning, with the dead piled two and three deep in places. The dead in front of his bunker numbered 105. Such a slaughter of men. It was a sickening sight and one from which I had to turn away. Sgt. McGill, from Ada, Oklahoma, was awarded the Congressional Medal of Honor posthumously for his action that night, the first of the 1st Cavalry to receive it in World War II.

> *But this was only the beginning.*
> *There were other battles and other nights,*
> *a hundred islands and a thousand fights.*
> *This was only one night of hell,*
> *many others came, many others fell.*

This then was war, ruthless, real, deadly in its style and cost. And it took us nearly 80 days of this to clear the Admiralty Islands.

Our next big action, a few days later, was at a small ridge called Hill 260, a steep, heavy jungle area of razor-back peaks, where some of troop B had been pretty badly shot up and had had to fall back the day before. We tried again, and Lt. Ralph E. Hill was killed and others wounded, including Red Carolton and Merril's and my buddy Merle Kincaid from Williams, Arizona. Our heavy machine gun squad, led by Lt. Bill Swan, then moved in. Lt. Swan was hit and our little Indian friend, Aaron Attaberry, saved his life. But then Lt. Swan, bandaging his own arm, urged us on. The trail was narrow and muddy, and we had to crawl over the bodies of our own dead troops who had been left the day before. The corpses had begun to swell and smell. It was unlike anything we'd ever experienced before. Afterwards, Lt. Swan was awarded a Silver Star for helping silence the enemy position, and we were able to retrieve our dead buddy and move on. Unable to mount any large-scale attack again, the Japanese continued to carry out small obstructions and defensive measures.

That first month there, I found out about some of the tragedies of war: the accidents, mistakes, and "trigger-happy" soldiers who often fired on our own troops.

One early morning we were dug in, in two-man holes; a kid and I were in a hole together. Tanner and my brother were in the hole next to us. This Spanish kid I was with had the last shift on guard and it was just coming daylight. Tanner raised up to peek over the coconut log on the side of the hole, and I heard the kid yell, "There's a Jap!" then swing his rifle around and fire. The bullet went in the rim of Tanner's helmet, circled the inside of the helmet from the left ear over the top of the head to the right side, leaving a half-inch furrowed crease, then finally ripped a slash through the right side, emerging about the level of the right ear. Tanner survived this, but it broke his eardrum and gave him a ringing headache.

Once one of our buddies left his rifle lying in his foxhole in the rain while he went back to visit the rear. When he came back to take up his position on the line for the night, he picked up his gun and fired a shot in the air and said, "Yep it still works," then climbed in his foxhole for the night.

Los Negros was a horseshoe-shaped island. The southern section of the island where the little Momote air strip was located and where we had landed was generally flat and well drained. Its beaches were narrow and rocky, and the entrance to Hyane Harbor was only a narrow channel 50 feet wide through the protecting coral reef. This is why the Japanese didn't expect us to land there but prepared their defenses on the other side of the island at the big Seeadler Harbor with its sandy beaches. The northern prong of the horseshoe, however, was pretty rugged, with narrow razor-backed hills covered with dense rainforest jungle. This is where we did most of our fighting. In fact, the Japanese kept bringing reinforcements over from Manus, and with their skilled jungle fighting tactics, they kept us engaged for days on end. While winning the beachhead may have been fairly easy, the continuing battle was not. With no major roads on Los Negros, it wasn't possible to mount a large-scale attack. So it was small troop or squad action day after day. But as General MacArthur told us, "You have your teeth in him. Don't let him go."

The rain, the mud, the disease, and the jungle were a second enemy, and being blond and fair-skinned, I got caught by that enemy. From continually sleeping in wet clothes, in mud and rain, I developed a case of jungle rot and fungus that wouldn't quit. I had a mass of sores and scabs from my waist down. I was finally pulled off the line to our little field hospital where they told me I needed to be shipped back to Australia or to a drier area or I would lose my legs. Not wanting to leave my brother, I persuaded them to let me stay. By being able to leave my pants and jungle boots off for a few days and letting my legs and feet stay dry while being painted and doctored, my jungle rot cleared up, and amazingly I was never bothered by it again.

During the night of March 8th, two enemy planes made four runs over Los Negros and knocked out a 50-caliber machine gun. We had not been bothered much by enemy planes, but there was one lone plane that did fly over at night, which we christened Washing Machine Charlie. He was more a harassment than anything else. The bad weather had kept the Japanese and our own support planes away.

I remember particularly at night sitting in my foxhole and hearing the big naval guns firing from the ocean and hearing the winging swish of the incoming shells. As long as you could hear them swishing overhead you felt safe, but if the sound should fade before it reached you, you'd better duck, because it was going to drop somewhere close.

Also on the 8th of March, the 7th Cavalry landed unopposed at Lombrum Plantation on the north side of Los Negros. That same day, two mine sweepers and two destroyers entered Seeadler Harbor, preparing the way for six L.S.T.s and one aircraft carrier to arrive. About this time, 69 Sikhs made their way into our lines. They said they were from Singapore and had been brought here as forced labor. We also captured our first Japanese prisoner. He said the Japanese soldiers had been instructed repeatedly that to be a prisoner was not only a great disgrace but an embarrassment to their family and relatives. They were told that it was better to commit suicide than fall into enemy hands. We observed the results of this cruel indoctrination in later battles too.

ADMIRALTY ISLANDS

By the 11th of March, our attention began to focus on Manus, the big island where the main enemy base had been. By now they had lost about half of their total number. Their final death count was 3,317. Our losses were 290 killed, 977 wounded, and 4 missing. For the Cavalry's first dismounted combat engagement, this was a pretty favorable ratio.

But probably the most rewarding benefit of this little mission was that while the fighting was still going on, we had provided General Hanford MacNider, commander of the U.S. Army Service and Supply Task Force, a place for his very able crew and equipment to move in. By the April 7th deadline, we had expanded the little Momote air strip to a smooth 7000-foot strip, and by April 22nd we had completed an even longer 8000-foot bomber strip out on the northeast end of Los Negros. This became a very busy and very helpful base for the American and Australian planes doing bombing runs. We even got to see the famous British Spitfires which were flown in by the Aussies. The Aussies also flew some reconnaissance night missions in the brand-new American Black Widow night fighter.

Manus Mission

As part of the mopping-up operation after the main campaign was over, Merril and I, with 26 other troopers, were sent on a scouting mission to the large island of Manus. As we churned across the blue-green waters of Seeadler Harbor in a flat-bottomed L.C.I., someone spotted this old relic nestled back in a cove. It was just a plain white house, not unlike any other two-story house of colonial design, except this one was deserted and a bit out of place. Since we hadn't seen anything half so civilized since leaving Australia months before, we decided to put in and have a look.

It was definitely the work of Anglos and had been there for a number of years. Aside from this limited information, our careful and cautious search revealed nothing but questions. Who and why? Why in heaven's name, someone wondered, would anyone want to build a house like this way out in this forsaken wilderness? Even in our short Pacific sojourn, we had discovered the sad truth that not all South Sea islands are the romantic, wonderful places many people think or dream about. I was still wondering about this silent old building and its builders when we took off for the island's interior, a dark mysterious world of jungle.

Had I been fully aware of what our fate could have been had it not been for the benevolent work of the builders of that house, I should have had even more cause for concern, because 28 unsuspecting soldiers pushing down a narrow jungle path were suddenly swallowed by the dense foliage of the Manus jungle. It was barely four decades ago that the natives right here on Manus were still among the world's most savage cannibals. This little section of the globe, known as the Bismarck Archipelago, held the dubious distinction of having contained more man eaters than any other area in the world.

But since it was the Japanese invaders, not the terrible citizens of Manus we were after, we gave little thought to their importance until we suddenly met them. Blending with the dark shadows of their natural habitat, they saw us long before we saw them, and had they so desired, it would probably have been a very one-sided meeting. After shadowing us for awhile however, they had decided to make their presence known. Suddenly there they were, standing in the trail only a few feet away. Clad only in crude hemp breechcloths with their stained teeth and bushy auburn hair, they were a fearsome sight, but they didn't appear to be hostile. While they didn't speak our language, they did seem to partially understand us and in a friendly gesture bid us follow them. So we did.

Following our native guides, we were led through realms of tropical splendor seldom seen by Anglo eyes. Down long velvety corridors, one after another they led us. Indeed, there seemed to be no limit to the green halls of their spacious habitation, and the floors had soft oozing carpets (of mud) in every room. Even the walls of their stately mansions were all bedecked with rare palms, ferns, and climbing vines. Indeed, all manner of fancy curtains and tapestries hung from above, through which we had to weave and pick our way. The lighting in this dense tropical rainforest was simply exquisite, very soft and blending with just an occasional bright splash of light. The whole place spoke of extravagance beyond compare. In fact, our entire trip was a marvelous display of architecture and interior decorating expertly done, a natural creation complete with birds and snakes.

But there was one little flaw in our friends' superb jungle home—the roof leaked. Before we had completed our inspection, we realized this unpleasant drawback. It was a dreary experience. The lights went out and the water filtered through the ceiling in sheets until we were thoroughly drenched and the floor was fairly sloshing. After hours of marching down dark, seemingly endless hallways, we arrived on the banks of a wide river. Clustered on the opposite shore stood a group of native huts. Uttering a deep guttural noise, our guide summoned his fellow townsmen to our welcome. Immediately, a half dozen sleek canoes manned by youthful skippers bore down upon us. Since they seemed anxious to transport us and our gear across the river, we were very glad to accept. All 28 of us were ferried safely across, except for one mishap. A heavy 30-caliber machine gun we had brought with us fell overboard, but it was quickly recovered with the aid of their expert swimmers and divers.

We were introduced to the chief, who spoke a type of pidgin English, as did a few of his "number one" boys (special councilmen and guides). He received us graciously and bid us stay all night if we liked. He even offered us the village council hall as quarters and told us that on the morrow he would send some "number one" boys to help us pursue the enemy, saying, "Me no like the Jap-an-esse sol-dier. He no good."

As we gathered around the huge fire that had been kindled among the towering palms, the villagers proceeded to entertain us with a traditional tribal dance. Keyed to the rhythm of crude wooden drums and bamboo instruments played by a half-dozen musicians, a group of deep-voiced vocalists began a weird chant. The dancers were strictly male. The young ladies retiring in the background may not have been dressed for the occasion; in fact, they were scarcely dressed at all. The dance itself was unlike anything I had ever seen. There were times when the music's rising tempo would propel the writhing forms into a frenzy of movements and maneuvers.

It was at moments like this, when I had become familiar with the gruesome fate suffered by a Reverend Williams and other early visitors to this area, I could have easily pictured the festival being held in their "honor." I can see them now, lashed to a ceremonial pole, the center of attraction as they somberly await their part on the program as well as on the menu. So ours was quite a different reception from the one Reverend Williams or the other missionary explorers, "bless them," had received when they first came to this area. The feast this time was for us and not of us.

The star of our show was a pint-sized chap whose only costume was his own brightly painted skin. I don't think he had been booked for a part on this program, but he managed to slip in toward the close anyway. With some fancy steps and very difficult maneuvers of his own, he fairly stole the show. And then to our amazement, our hosts brought the entertaining program to a close with what appeared to be their own version of the patriotic British anthem, "God Save the King."

We stayed in their large ceremonial hall and spread out ponchos on the clean white sand of the floor. We slept in dry peace with a native guard at the door and listened to the heavy beat of a tropical downpour outside. It was a night to remember and our hearts had been touched. But our gratitude would have increased tenfold as we spread our ponchos on the soft sands of the village hall to enjoy the peaceful comfort of a dry night's sleep had we realized then the price this native courtesy to us had cost the Anglos before us.

During the next few days, the three "number one" boys the chief sent to help us really proved their worth and skills. Going down a blind jungle path, the leader whispered back, "Jap-an-esse very soon," and sure enough, in fewer than 50 yards we made contact. "How did you know?" we questioned.

"Me smell," was his simple reply. (And why not? Hadn't he descended from a long line of ancestors who once possessed a very keen taste for this kind of chow?!) Motioning us to wait, our three boys with one rifle and two long bolo knives disappeared like silent shadows into the jungle. A few tense minutes later we heard a sudden commotion, one shot, and some wild yells and shouts. Pressing forward, we found our three grinning, red-toothed guides standing by a small native shack with three dead Japanese soldiers inside and one lying in the yard.

When we got back to the old white house the next day, we were a couple of hours early for our pre-arranged rendezvous with the barge to pick us up, so we had time for some thoughtful meditation as we leaned on the rail along its large upper veranda and scanned the harbor for any sign of our scheduled transportation. While we waited, one of our number one boys told us, "One day the Jap-an-esse took all the people who lived in this house away and we never saw them again." In the trials of war criminals at Yokohama after the war was over, we learned the tragic story of how the Japanese executed the Manus missionaries, along with 60 other missionaries from all over the area. They were gathered up and taken aboard a Japanese ship, where they were shot and their corpses thrown into the sea.

Koroniat, Our Island Paradise

The major part of the battle campaign had ended by May 10th. The 5th Cavalry set up a base camp on Koroniat Island, the first little island off the northeast coast of Los Negros, in the coral reef chain that makes the outer barrier for the Seeadler Harbor. It was a beautiful little island, less than two miles long and not a half mile wide, a reward for making the initial landing. It had some Japanese defense trenches and pill boxes. It was a clean, neat little island, and my brother and I really enjoyed this part of our southwest Pacific stay.

The fearful battle and dark haunting nights of the Los Negros battle were over. This was our south sea island paradise. We had won the battle and survived the terrors of war, that nightmare experience, our first real battle and test of our courage, but even though it was over it was not without its aftereffects. In the middle of the night some poor soldier would awake from a nightmare with wild screams of fear and terror. One or two finally had to be taken away for medical treatment. They called it battle fatigue—the nightmares that wouldn't go away.

One day we received word that the army needed some volunteers who had had some experience with horses and mules and packing to go to China and help with the battle of the Burma Road. My brother and I turned in our names, being willing to go, but our C.O. Capt. Brown wouldn't let us. A few of the Cavalry troops went, but I don't know how many. Instead, we got to do close-order drills, haul sand in the back of the weapons carrier to spread on the floor of the mess tent, take the metal pots and pans from the kitchen down to the beach and polish and scour the black grease stains off them, and any other little chores to keep us partly busy.

Our regiment was laid out and lined up with H.Q. troop first on the very southern end with a double row of tents running across the island from west to east. Col. Hoffman, C.O., was on the tip overlooking the south end of the harbor and the little water inlet that separated Los Negros to the south. The A, B, C, and D troops, then E, F, G, and H were all lined up in neat rows. We had a parade ground, a little chapel, and a meeting place made from palm and bamboo branches (I think by the natives). Each little square tent had four men, with folding cots and mosquito nets fastened above our beds. Each of us had a box or crate for a desk and table on which we set a canteen lantern. We made these lanterns from army canteens filled with fuel oil and an old rag rolled up and stuffed in the neck for a wick. At night we would read or write or draw pictures, or just visit by the light of these crude lanterns. The regiment had a portable generator for the office and mess hall, but our individual quarters had no electricity. Our morning shower came with the rain. It could rain any time without warning or time for preparation. The atmosphere was always so damp, so saturated with moisture that it was almost like living in a giant Turkish steam bath all of the time.

We spent five months there on that island paradise, waiting, resting and to a degree preparing for the next landing and battle. My brother Merril and I and the troops of the 5th Cavalry leisurely sailed, swam, and relaxed in this peaceful blue water of the southwest Pacific islands. It was here, after the test of war, nearly two years and many thousands of miles from home, that Merril and I had time to pause and remember and to get homesick, to dream about our beloved home and life that we loved and left. We did a lot of drawing—horses, old ranches and other Western scenes, and pretty American girls—things we didn't have that we missed and probably dreamed about, and we sent the drawings home to our family. We wrote letters, visited with our friends and buddies, and took some pictures of us with our machine gun and battle flags. Sometimes we just relaxed on the beach in the shade of a little cluster of trees.

Letters from Merril and Normand

Australia
November 16, 1943

Dear Stan,

I will answer your letter I received a few days ago. I was glad to hear from you, but sorry to hear you had to go to the army so soon. You may be in by now, but if you are, your folks can send this letter on to you. I hope you get into something you will like, which will be pretty hard to find. I guess things will be pretty rough for a while, but after a while you will get used to it. Keep us posted as to where you are and if you ever get over in this neighborhood, we may get to see you. Things are going pretty good here for us. We have found a branch of the church near here and we go most every Sunday. We are getting along fine and learning a lot of new things and are quite pleased with the new things we are learning. Well I will close for now. Write soon.

Love, Normand

New Guinea
Feb 6, 1944

Dear Folks,

We are still okey and things are still as ever here. Well perhaps you would be interested in some of the lines Norm and I are spreading here in our tents to some of the boys. Starting off with, we were talking about money, horses, cows and places and one thing led to another. Normand said, I guess he'd work up an outfit like the Lyle boys have, a good little outfit in Nevada, and one in Arizona. If we get Uncle John's place, with ours, we'd make our home ranch there, and then be partners. He'd do the riding, with a few hired hands to cook and brand, etc. and of course there was a little disagreement as to which one would see to the hay at home, and drive the chuck wagon.

Now we came to a better idea, we will have Uncle John sorta be the Duffen, all he'll do is ride the chuck lines and keep us in grain, and then Dad could be like the hired boss, and then there would have to be farm work done. Norm says to have me and dad do that or have it done, but I'm writing this big future history story, so I'll say Norm is the biggest and is supposed to do the most work. So him, and some help, with dad to oversee, can put up the hay and me, Stephen, Farren, and Derril [Merril's and Normand's three little brothers] could spend two months in Nevada, two in Arizona, and then two in Utah, and then start over, for we got the most good horses, Diamond, Blue Rocket, and if he's not too big, Silver Tail, then the Adams filly and Skunky, then of course I could trade for another one or two from someone. I could make come real old cow punchers out of the little boys and a little Joe the Wrangler, or Billy the Kid out of Derril.

When we would get in from a big days round up to camp in Water canyon or somewhere on Clover Mountain, or out on the strip to Big Springs, I could recline back on a bed roll and tell of some of the big tales of being in New Guinea or somewhere else, while Stephen and Farren cooks super. Derril could see to the horses and give them a little extra oats to kinda make me happy. Then we'd eat and I could continue while the boys washed the dishes. Then we could all rest around the little curling fire, with the little jagged flames leaping in the air, refueling with a few pieces of sage brush and maybe more a little later.

And while the darkness of the world creeps over our section, as the coyotes start to howl, and the hoot owl and the night hawks begin to fly around, we could then talk of what cows we found, how they looked, or how many calves we branded too, or how many steers to hold and ship, then make plans for the next days ride and so on.

By that time the fire would be about died down to glowing coals and the coyote had ceased to howl, 'till day light, and went to prowling. We could go and water the horses again, and throw them a little more hay. Then me and Derril could roll out our bed and kick off our boots and spurs and get between the blankets, while Steve and Kid [Farren Laub's nickname] did the same. At any rate, stretch out flat on our backs and go to sleep. Watch the man in the moon, who is a cowhand, ride across the Milky Way, and rest in beautiful dreams, to rise early and greet a new day, with the nicker of a horse, that crackle of a growling fire, and the melancholy voice of a cowboy singing some roundup songs.

Well, I better close before I get some of these steers stampeding down this troop street and get a soldier run over. We'll be seeing you someday at the Laub Cowboy Outfit. I better sign off for the Sand Man's riding old Champ across the sky, to bring sweet dreams to us all. Every night, after we go to sleep, we've been wearing boots, spurs and levis, and big black hats, somewhere in the Rocky Mountains, about like Utah. This is spread pretty thick, but I believe it would work out pretty good, except with a few exceptions, where Norm might change things.

"Be back tomorrow, same time, same station, with a bit of Ranch plans."

Love,
Merril

Mar. 29, 1944

Dear Stan,

Well I have thought for a long time we would be getting a letter from you any day, for you had our address, but we never had yours until the other day your mother sent it to us, so I will write you. We have left New Guinea and are now in the South West Pacific fighting. We have saw some great sights and some bad ones, and had quite some thrilling experiences. Your foxhole and gun are your best friends. Good old mother earth has saved my life more than once. I am now in the hospital, but hope to be out soon. Merril is still doing fine they tell me. I hope you don't ever have to get into this or Alma either. Well how do you like the army? Ken says you got homesick. I guess things are pretty rough at first. It sure will be a happy day when we can all return home again with those we love.

Love,
Normand

[Alma Hunt was killed in action later and Stan Steheli was taken prisoner of war in Germany.]

May 17, 1944
Admiralty Islands

Dear Folks,

Well, at last we made a haul, we got a whole mess of mail. We got 6 air mail letters dated from April 17th, to April 27th, and two V mail, May 1st, and 2nd. So we really had some reading and was sure glad when it came piling in like that. Well, I see LaRee is getting along fine with herself. That Wes, riding on Merril's horse now, we sure kidded Merril about it. Kincaid asked if Merril wouldn't put in a good word for him, he'd help take over Wes's place and he'd furnish his own horses and let Merril ride some good horses. As for Ruby, there is a big husky fellow, like Bill Hunt, got his eyes on her. You should hear the arguments and plans made last night for doing away with Wes, when we got these pictures, they sure were good. The girls have got to be fine looking girls now. It seems they have changed some I think. They certainly look fine.

We sure was glad to get that one of dad and mother together. It is the only one of that kind we got and we sure like it. Dad looks like he used to and those horses like the ones he took a long time ago and as for the picture of the little boys and the girls, we sure got a kick out of it. Steve with those levis and his hat pushed back on his head and his hands shoved in his hind pickets. We got quite a laugh out of it. Kinda reminds us of that picture dad has of little Jerry Card Gilbert, kind of a rough hombre. He's getting to be a pretty good sized fellow now. I told Merril I guessed he'd show him where to head in at and Kincaid said the three of them would throw the two of us off the place when we got back home. Kiddie with that mischievous little smile of his and Derril with his bashful little looks. We sure like the pictures and they sure mean a lot to us.

Well, I guess you just as well build a lean to on the side of the house for Merril and Kincaid, for they're just like Merril and Ken was. They have the ring already. They built it out of Australian money, 32 cents. Ha Ha.

I'm wondering what you meant by that letter telling of something you said we mentioned in our letters, the ones John took out to dad. I don't just remember what I said in the letter, but the way you talked and if I remember that was the one where we told of our plans to get into the quarter horses and registered Herefords, and of our plans at the layout in Dixie and Nevada. If that was it, we sure are glad of the interest John is taking in helping to get us a start and go in together. We are waiting dads answer.

We were surprised to hear of young Amos Terry. It was news to us of his being missing at all and then being dead and for almost a year, it was a surprise. How come you never told us of it before. Explain to us what happened and if he was missing last June, how come they just found the body now? What happened and was their anything to that about him turning kind of wild and taking up with bad habits? We sure would like to know.

I am sending two more pictures and I am selling one, like the fellow running that steer for $3.50. Well I guess I will close for now. Hoping to hear from you soon again and a lot of letters.

As ever, All my love,
Normand

Admiralty Islands
May 17, 1944

Dear Stan,

I guess you will sure be somewhat surprised to hear from me, perhaps you think I have forgotten you, but I haven't, not for one minute. I never knew what your address was, until a while back, while we were giving those little Japs a merry chase for their money, and I did not get to write then, and then we couldn't find your address, we thought we'd destroyed it with some old letters, but low and behold Normand found it the other day somewhere, so here I am trying to write you a few lines to let you know all is well with us.

I see by the last letter we got from home, that you were home on a furlough, about the first of May as I remember. Good for you, and I'll sure bet you enjoyed it, while you were there, but I guess by now you are back in the same old line, the army way or you could be on your way somewhere east or west, leaving the USA.

I hope you are still there and don't have to leave the good old USA. However, there's not a question or doubt in my mind that you won't make out swell where ever you are, for you're just the kind of person that will make the best of anything that's put before you. You'll never know how much I think of you and I'm certainly happy to know that I'm one of your best friends, for I've certainly admired you in many ways, and I'll never forget the days we spent together, and I'm sure hoping it won't be long until we can all be together again and enjoy some of those good old times we used to have.

And you and Ken and all your folks have sure been the best of people to us and your home will be next to my own as long as I live. Your mother really treated us well and we've got some of the best letters from her I've ever received since we've been over here and they surely helped carry us on, and will forever.

They tell me you found, or met some pretty nice girls back there, and that they are going to Idaho. I guess you better see if you can't get me one of them, that's pretty good, and we'll go to Idaho or somewhere after we get home and see if we can catch them again. Ha Ha

You probably found out at home, all the news, up till now, about us. There's not much to say only we are at a rest camp here on a beautiful little coconut island, here in the southwest Pacific. It's quite a different land over here than at home. It rains most anytime it gets ready and it don't take long to get ready. Also we can't tell summer from winter, but I'll still take the Rockies.

Write soon and let us know how you're getting along and how you found things at home. Good luck and God bless you at all times.

As Ever and always your friend,
Merril

Admiralty Islands
June 13, 1944

Dear Uncle Vasco [their father's youngest brother],

We received your letter last night and the pictures and we certainly was glad to hear from you again and the pictures were good. It sure would be nice to see some snow again, even as bad as I used to hate it. You sure look good with that silver leaf on. I sure would like to see you again. We have learned to appreciate what rank of that kind stands for and we are mighty proud of you and hope you can continue to progress.

Well, things are going along pretty much the same as usual here. We just got back off of a short mission yesterday, had a short boat ride and saw some new country. We got along okey, only it rained most of the time and you know what that is like in the jungle. But we had a lot of fun. We went through several native villages in our travels and learned a lot from them. They sure like the Yankees and they sure hate the Japs. So we're lucky for that.

We had a bunch of the kids doing their native dances and the grown ones singing. Then we had a bunch of about 30, all the way from the size of a small kid to a grown person, dancing and some others singing and playing their drums, that they made out of a log. It sure was interesting and funny to watch. They sure can dance and they sing some songs also and they really can harmonize and it sounds good. I sure would have liked to had a camera and got some pictures of them.

We had several creeks to cross and one small river we were going to wade it, but the natives wouldn't let us. There was a village near by and they hauled us across on their canoes and our equipment. They sure can handle these little boats. We saw one crocodile that the natives had just caught and were going to kill. We had a very interesting trip and learned a quite a bit about the natives and jungle and how to get along in and with both.

Thanks for sending the camera I hope we will be able to get some pictures of this country and things over here and then we can compare them with those you have of places you have been and things you saw over in the other side of the world. We sure were glad to hear the news of the second front. I guess things are really a popping over there now. Well, there is very little news from here to write about, but we sure will be glad to hear from you again and are looking forward to the day we can all get together again and have a good hunting trip or camping trip in the mountains again. Well, I will close for now and may you have the best of luck in what ever you do.

As ever your loving nephew,
Normand

ADMIRALTY ISLANDS

Admiralty Islands
June 17, 1944

Dear Stan,

I got your letter of June 2nd, the other day and boy was I ever happy to hear from you, but it seemed that we've been so busy lately that I never got time till now to write. As today is Saturday, and I go on guard tonight, that takes care of my Sunday letter writing time, so I'm writing a few lines now, but I truly know that you have had very little time to write either. But someday we won't need to write letters to each other, to keep our old friendship.

The way the war news looks, it sure sounds favorable to the shorter end to all this mess. You spoke of how you'd like to be with us. I don't know of anyone I'd rather have than you. Just to prove it for some reason, in my dreams last night, I dreamed we got some new replacements and you were with them and boy what a happy day. Then the breaking dawn changed the whole scene. But we sure have thought a lot about you all the time and there never were or was a doubt in my mind that you can not take anything that's dished out to you.

We sure had some grand entertainment last night. They played some good records of Gene Autry, Roy Acoff, and some others. Then we got a rebroadcast of the Sons of the Pioneers. Then we had a real armature show of our own from some of the boys in our regiment, with guitars, banjos, a fiddle and a bass fiddle. Also one of the boys played left handed and could he really bring out the melody with a steel guitar. It sure was good and then there was another kid who sang alone and it sounded just like you. I sure enjoyed myself. I better close for now as it's about time, so take care old pal and we'll be seeing you again someday.

Your pal,
Merril

BEYOND THE BEND

Admiralty Islands
June 25, 1944

Dear Folks,

Well it is Sunday and I will write a few lines. We went to the Cavalry Services again this morning. The chapel is not far from our troop. I sure hope you went to church at home and are taking advantage of the opportunity that you have there. I sure wish I could be able to impress on some of the people at home the opportunity they have, for I didn't think they will ever know or realize until they get away from home and come up against what so many of the boys of the U.S. are doing away from home.

We are getting along fine here and hope all is well there. Aaron Attaberry just came back off of furlough the other day. You probably got a letter from him and a picture. So we have been doing some drawing. I have finished the picture I was drawing so I will send it. I am also sending one Aaron drew on a card. He also wrote the little verse. I sure think it's good. It sure has meaning behind it. Well there is very little to write about and I guess Merril told you all there was to tell. From the news we are getting and from what we know, the Japs are sure getting a raw deal here in the Pacific. Don't you think so? Well I will close for now as we are going swimming. Write more next time and write soon.

Love,
Normand

Admiralty Islands
July 1, 1944

Dear Folks,

Well I will write a few lines to you while I have time again, in answer to the last letter. It was an old one, the one telling of the fate of young Amos Terry, We had all ready got a letter from Mrs. Terry telling a little more about it, but that cleared it all up for us, though we are wondering just what anyone would do that to him for.

Well, one year ago today, we were really enjoying ourselves. I sure would like to be able to set down to a supper tonight like I remember of having one year ago. It's been over six months since I had any fresh milk. I've probably forgotten what it tastes like. Well, it seems time sure does roll fast. It's been almost a year since we left the U.S.A. and a lot has happened in the year and yet it seems that we had side stepped somewhere and part of that year has gone passed unnoticed. Especially this last six. Well, I'm wondering where we'll be and what changes we'll have come to pass in the next year.

Well, there is still no news from here and if there was, I couldn't write about it and I told you about the weather before. We're still doing a lot of swimming. When I get home, if I keep it up the rate I'm doing, I'll probably win the county swimming tournament. Ha ha.

Has Clint and those fellows left yet. Whose going to run granddads place, Don?

Well there is not much to write about. I am sending another picture Aaron drew and gave to me. He also wrote the poem underneath. I think it very good and very fitting. Its dedicated to mother from him, for us. It's supposed to represent a brief rest, just after capturing one of the toughest pushes we made. So, as I say, it is sure fitting to us here, who know both sides of the story. It represents both of us.

That Aaron has surely got a knack for putting such thoughts and scenes into a picture and words. I think that sometimes something like this can say more than I could in a letter, if I wrote all day. And as the saying is, there's more truth than poetry in that. I have other pictures, but I am sending this one. I hope you like it as well as I do. And if you can see the picture as I do, all I should have to do is say, let this be my letter to you Dear Mother. We'll I'll close for now, so write when you can and let us know how things are at home.

As ever, Love,
Normand.

Admiralty Islands
July 21, 1944

Dear Folks,

We got your two letters wrote July 2nd tonight, so I will attempt to answer them, also one or two old ones we got the other day. I hardly know how to answer or what to say or whether to say anything or not. It was a quite a shock to us when we finely finished our mail tonight. Of course you know why. I don't know whether you know how something like this hits us over here, or what it means. I'm not speaking of this one instance, but of the many all over the nation, not small ones but large ones, them that are sometimes hinders the war effort that we read about or hear of in some way or another. Nor am I speaking of Merril and I alone, but of us all over here, especially the more serious minded ones who are looking forward to a peaceful and happy world to return to someday. But this is closer to home, so I speak. It's like I told you before, I think, of some of the outstanding hero's of this war after many months of fighting, sweating it out and waiting and dreaming of home, finally getting a chance to go back for a visit, and then what a let down they got and what kind of a nation did they find.

They, like all of us here, were thinking, and are thinking, dreaming, hoping waiting, fighting, taking what ever comes up, sometimes not liking some things we have to do, and grumbling about it until we can return to the world from which we left, the home and whatever occupation we might of had. To return to a better world, a place where we can enjoy the freedom, peace and happiness we fought for. And as we perform our duties, what are we thinking about and often talking of? This. What a great day it will be when this is over and we can return to that Nation. What a joy it will be to return from the scenes of hatred, bloodshed and destruction where squabbles, fights between two forces is always going on. All for one thing, to stamp out such things and return to a place where that kind of thing is not going on. We're banking on that Nation and those people who are still there in that Nation, greeting us with such a place. And when we have won the freedom and price, we certainly will know how to enjoy and not abuse it. Though fighting is going on all over the world, there is still a place where people can enjoy peace, where people are united and being one is your friend, so to speak.

This war has brought us closer together. Brought a closer bond between us, or at least in the case of us over here. Fellows from every part of the Nation, from every walk of life, of every belief, kind and race. We are thrown together, live together, fight together and die together, all for the same thing. Perfect strangers from two extreme parts of the Nation and of two extreme kinds of characters meet and a bond of friendship is soon felt, though had they met in peacetime at home, perhaps they would become enemies, each trying to tramp the other under. But now, they meet both under the same circumstances, both with the same feeling that we're all in this together, all fighting for the same thing and we've got to pull together and be friends, not enemies, and get along. That is the kind of nation we're out here for and that is what we are hoping to return to.

So, like I told you before, those who had finally got the chance to return, what did they find? Things wasn't what they expected. It wasn't what they had been dreaming of, longing and waiting to return to. They meet a disappointment, and found themselves almost wanting to return to that which they had waited so long to get away from. Of course, it was good to be home and all, but down under they were disappointed and let down in those things they had fought for and had faith in. I don't know just why Uncle Vasco was so disappointed and wanted to be back over seas.

All I know is that in his letters he can't seem to be too satisfied and wants to be back out here again. Don't misunderstand me for that little instance you spoke of is a very small one compared to the ones I am thinking of and have heard of and that those whom I told you of before who had got to return were referring to. But, like you said, and it says in the books, such things would surely come and all that you know it says is coming the conditions the world would be in. And in the end, few there would be who would stand. It is nothing new to us, we have read about it. It's been preached and prophesied would come and it begins to look like it had come. But so many can't see it that way yet, so they continue and things get deeper. The outside world isn't looking forth to such. But to us of the LDS who have more enlighten on this sort of thing, who have something that others don't seem of these things are should be and whole lot clearer. We should set the example and should be thankful for the privilege of having what we have. And yet, I'm afraid something else has crept in. We are letting down or being maneuvered from the right course. We're being swept under with the rest. We've all, all of us, the whole world got to wake up. So it's such things as this and others you have spoke of, like those cattle and the owners, not trying to take care of them and others, it's something that is hard to know what to do. Such things make it look as though it wasn't the outside world only, but that it has crept in right close to home. And were we like some of those others, I spoke of, going to be disappointed when we come home. Life is a continual struggle for existence and a person has to sometimes stand up for his own rights or get trampled under. But it's like you said, there isn't as much unity as there should be, the brotherly love is going cold. But maybe someday we'll understand. But dear folks, I hope that by now things are patched up and forgotten for that is the first step to doing away with such things. Well I guess I have rambled on enough. And I don't want you to take me wrong, we all can do a lot better and me for one, a whole lot better. I've got to try harder to live what I have wrote. Well there is very little news from here. We are getting along fine and happy in spite of conditions. So I'll close for now. Write often.

As ever, Love,
Normand

P.S. Was glad you had such a fine crop of hay and that it's up now and hope we'll get a chance to come feed some of it up sometime for you.

Still Resting on Koroniat

The big sheltered Seeadler Harbor became one of the best sea ports in the western Pacific, accommodating a large dry dock where damaged ships could be brought instead of having to go all the way back to Pearl Harbor. We were able to see a lot of large battleships and carriers come and go, and even got invited out on some of them. I especially remember one time when a ship carrying our cousin Val Laub came to port and we were able to go on board and visit with him. We especially enjoyed the good fresh food, which was a welcome break from our K-rations.

One day the Captain or the 1st Sergeant didn't seem to have anything for us to do, so after reveille and breakfast, some of us men went out on the beach where the tide had gone out and left a bunch of blue and red starfish on the smooth, damp sand. We introduced the starfish derby. Each of us found a starfish and drew a circle in the sand and placed our racing starfish in the center. Then we laid down on the sand to wait and see which one would get out of its circle first. Some might move fairly rapidly, like a couple of feet in an hour, and some wouldn't go anywhere. It was okay to shout or stomp by the side of them to try and stampede or scare them into moving, but you couldn't touch or push them. We'd get tired of watching and waiting and would go for a swim out in the water or dive to the bottom to find a fresh fish and bring it back to try.

One time, Merril and I went down to the beach and saw a couple of other guys who had gone out in the harbor for something in a little rowboat. A sudden storm swept down from Manus across the south end of the harbor where they were. The strong wind and the waves kept driving the boat out to the little passageway between Koroniat and Los Negros, and try as they might they couldn't seem to buck the tide and wind to get back to shore. I could see them frantically paddling and getting nowhere but closer and closer to the pounding, crashing surf where the two tides met. I got worried and finally ran and got someone to take a landing barge and go pull them in. They were pretty nervous and were about to abandon ship and try to swim in, but only one could swim.

Thi s same little passageway between Koroniat and Los Negros at times was also helpful to us. When the tide was down, we were able to wade across it to meet with other LDS servicemen stationed on Los Negros. We would pack our clothes in a bundle and hold them over our heads so they would not get wet as we waded across. My brother and I enjoyed the occasions that we were able to meet with those men.

It was there that I had a little experience with a new 2nd lieutenant who had joined our outfit as a replacement. One night we were having a formal, full dress (in our fatigues) rifle inspection. Lt. Bailes told me to straighten up, a very unnecessary little request, I thought, for a combat zone, so I answered with a yes-sirrrrr. I really slurred the sir, which he didn't seem to like, so for my sarcastic disrespect, I got the privilege of digging a six by six. That's a little hole six feet square and six feet deep. This didn't make for the best of feelings or relations between us. I thought he was an egg-head from one of the prominent universities in the East who got caught up in the draft.

An interesting footnote to this little incident was that not long after it happened, we went on to the Philippines and Lt. Bailes was assigned to G2 after the Leyte beachhead. While we were holding the high passes of central Leyte, I was assigned to make a reconnaissance patrol behind enemy lines to see what his buildup and troop movements were. It was interesting that we should be working so closely and interdependent together. Because of the success of this patrol, Lt. Bailes recommended me for a military citation. This is quite reflective of the spirit of war and battle. You may be enemies but you are also buddies in a very interdependent and common cause and bond.

The comforting presence and concern of my older brother Merril during the Admiralty campaign was, in retrospect, immeasurable. When the campaign came to a close, we enjoyed more than ever our togetherness during the summer in this tropical paradise, in the lull before the storm of our next beachhead. We had so much to share and to talk about, to hope for, to dream of. We had never been closer. Our pride and gratitude for the land of the free and the home of the brave had never been higher. Our beloved family back home had never been more precious and dear to us, and we longed for the day when we could go back to Western ranges, good horses, and wild cattle. Like ever combat soldier, our love for peace had increased and our anxious hope to return to that peace was an ever-present obsession.

May 12, 1988

New Guinea and the Admiralty Islands were the highlight and most important and interesting part of another trip back to the South Pacific. But that part of the journey was also the most difficult. Those five days were by far the most physically challenging and draining of any we had ever taken. One might think that anywhere a modern jet airplane can fly had got to be pretty up to date, but it really wasn't. Some of the little airfields were like a cow pastures, but I didn't see any cows. And, of the members of the 1st Cavalry Division tour group that came to Australia and Brisbane, Bill Swan, Barbara and I were the only three to have made this expedition. But we made it, we survived it, and we were back in civilization again.

But we were all a bit sick to our stomachs and had a bit of dysentery. I thought it was quite easy to develop those conditions when you went to a place like that and ate and drank the food they have. We weren't too hungry in those few days, but we did drink some fresh coconut milk over on Koroniat, from some young green coconuts the natives provided, and I kind of remembered that could have contributed to our condition. Barbara's legs and arms were a bit sunburned from our boat ride and so she took some alka seltzers and went to bed. I gave Bill one too, and he went to bed. But I felt pretty cool and comfortable as I sat there and wrote. And that was good because I had a lot of writing to do.

It was good to write on paper again that didn't feel like a wet dishrag and to not be dripping and wiping sweat off all the time. In the islands you could take a shower with the same temperature water coming from either faucet, and you couldn't even get dried off before you would be wet and sticky from perspiration again.

Those were two places I had never expected to be again and certainly places not many people have even heard of let alone gone to. I had once thought if I ever got back to Australia and the Philippines that would be beyond my wildest expectations. To look back now, especially since being able to return to the primitive, difficult, unheard-of South Pacific islands was the fulfillment of an impossible dream. But we went. We visited, we saw, we reviewed, and I communed with the past, and already, looking back to that part of our journey, it seemed more of a distant, remote fantasy than a reality. In a way even today was somewhat of a journey into the past, into a world and part of society that was little known or scarcely existed on the great international highways and air ways of modern times. The interesting, but difficult part of my history, was that much of the history, the people, the places and the things we had seen, visited, and encountered were as interesting and enchanting today as some of those same things I had come to review and try to revisit in the past. The exercise showed us that the past was still beyond the bend, as it were.

Merril, Karas, and Normand on Koroniat, summer 1944.

Merril Laub, good soldier and good friend.

ADMIRALTY ISLANDS

Aaron Attaberry's drawing of the
Laub Boys, and his poem:

"A Mothers Welcome"

As I sit here to eat my bully beef
With the sun shining brightly above,
My thoughts travel back to the land of my birth,
To my home and the ones that I love.
I'm dreaming today of the friends left behind,
I remember my playmates again.
And the scenes of my childhood come crowding to mind,
As I puzzle old memory's chain.
But the best of them all is my dear mother's face,
With her fond eyes and smile full of joy;
Though another has come, she still has her place
In the heart of her wandering boy.
How often I wish I could turn back the years,
Say my prayers once again at her knee,
And see the war ended, its tortures and tears,
And to know mother's welcome for me.

Drawings by Normand and Merril while on Koroniat.

ADMIRALTY ISLANDS

Normand revists Hyane Harbor beach on Los Negros, above, and the beach on Koroniat, below, in 1988.

Chapter 6

Leyte Campaign

MacArthur's Return to the Philippines

There is some question as to the exact spot on Leyte that General MacArthur waded ashore and on which of the assault waves he may have come in. But one can still almost hear those proud, but prophetic words, "People of the Philippines, I have returned," followed by his question to President Osmena, "Mr. President, how does it feel to be home?" It's reported that the President of the Philippines had no words, but his eyes were wet. It must have brought a moment of sweet revenge to some of this little group when it was learned that part of the force that defended this Leyte beach were from the infamous Japanese 16th Division that had participated in the 1942 surrender of Bataan and the terrible death march of prisoners that followed.

I couldn't correctly report the exact wave on which the General arrived; however, it must have been the fifth or the seventh because we were in the first, and after we hit the beach we kept right on going. Fortunately for us, the south end of White Beach where we went ashore was quite undefended. (This may have been why it was chosen as the best place for the General to land.) This invasion, the biggest ever in the Pacific, hit the beach with four divisions abreast, nearly 100,000 men per 20-mile front. It was pretty hard for the Japanese troops to cover every beach and every point. This landing was a double triumph for General MacArthur. First, it fulfilled his pledge to return, avenge, and free a nation. Second, it gave him and the Pacific war its greatest sense of respect, recognition, and national support in terms of troops, equipment, and supplies, which had not come since the war began, having played second fiddle to the European war most of the time.

But here now was a full army, the 6th, backed by two naval fleets (the 3rd and 7th), all engaged at once. This made it a pretty exciting party, especially when you add the fact that the bulk of the Japanese fleet would try to steal the show. The 7th and 96th divisions were to the south, the 24th was in the middle and we, the 1st Cavalry, were on the north. Three regiments of the 1st Division went ashore that first day: the 5th, 7th, and 12th, and the 8th was there but held in reserve. A wise battle commander always holds a fair-sized force in reserve if he can to throw into the battle if needed. My unit, the 5th, was on the extreme south portion of our assigned beach, next to the north flank of the 24th. We went ashore not too far from where the MacArthur Landing monument now stands.

The Night Before

> "We came to Leyte just before midnight on a dark and moonless night; we laid and waited for dawn before entering Leyte Gulf. On almost every ship, one could count on infantrymen nervously inspecting their rifles. Late that evening I went back to my cabin to read again those passages from the Bible from which I have always gained inspiration and hope. I prayed that a merciful God would preserve each one of those men on the morrow."
>
> —General Douglas MacArthur

The only two Mormons in the 5th Cavalry, Merril and I were known as "the Brothers" or "the Mormon boys," and we firmly believed it was more than a mere coincidence that we were never separated or assigned to different units despite the army's indiscriminate shifting and juggling of personnel throughout our training at Ft. Riley, Kansas, our amphibious operations in Australia, and our reinforcement mission to New Guinea.

We had grown up together and loved and enjoyed our home, our family, our freedom, and our peaceful western land. We had been taught to believe in God and tried to obey His commandments. Being raised in the Mormon faith, we didn't drink, smoke, or carouse, and because of a special promise found in our Word of Wisdom, we even abstained from tea and coffee, so when they were the only liquids available, we didn't drink anything at all, and we repeatedly found that the "run and not be weary, walk and not faint" promise found in the Word of Wisdom (89th section of the Doctrine and Covenants) to literally be true. Many times we were able to keep going when others faltered, and we often helped carry the loads of some who claimed that were it not for that cigarette or cup of coffee, they couldn't take another step.

The night before our beachhead in the Philippines, October 20, 1944, was hot and stuffy, both a short and a long night. Sleep in the hold of the crowded troop ship had been light and fitful. For some this would be their first combat; for others it would be one more battle in that long and difficult journey back home. Judging from the size of our floating armada, however, this battle had to be something pretty big. We took it one day, even one hour, at a time. A buddy, a veteran trooper, standing in the crowded aisle of the dimly lit hold, held out his mess cup in sort of a joking gesture for others to see his hand shaking, on purpose or uncontrollably, who knew?

"Are you scared?" someone asked.

"Not really," was my reply, although we were all a bit tense and nervous because we knew in the next few hours some of us would be dead and others terribly hurt and wounded.

While waiting to go over the side, I opened my little pocket scriptures and read the last part of that 89th section of the Doctrine of Covenants. As I read the words in verse 21, "And I, the Lord, give unto them a promise, that the destroying angel shall pass by them," in that indefinable place where messages are born of the Spirit, there came an unspoken assurance to me that this promise would be fulfilled.

For the first time, and I'm not sure why, because I had never wondered, worried, or done anything like it before, I turned to my brother, leaning down to his bunk just below mine, and pointed to the verse I had just read.

"That may be true," he responded after a moment's hesitation, "but if it's your time to go then it doesn't really matter." The book and issue were closed, pushed aside and out of mind by the press of the moment's concerns.

The minutes ticked off slowly and yet all too soon came the command passed by word of mouth from one to another, "Prepare to debark."

We shouldered our packs, picked up gun or gear, and almost as if we were robots or mechanical soldiers wound and primed, we climbed the ladder in silence, doing the things we had been trained and drilled to do. We went up together; we were always together, it was almost as if we were linked by an invisible chain. Nothing was said, but there was kind of an unspoken feeling, an awareness and understanding. I don't remember that there had ever been any thought or concern in the past about this togetherness. It had been so long taken for granted, as though we always had been and therefore always would be together.

Though it was still a hot and sticky night, the air out on the deck was a little fresher and it felt good to be top side. There was a little time to relax. The deck, though swarming with men, was a scene of order and action. Where were we? What island? This, as with all military operations, was still top secret. But then, that didn't matter. What difference did it make anyway? None, really. This was hard, grim, routine business, curt, crisp orders being given and executed by veteran sailors whose every move seemed accentuated with speed. Landing barges and rope nets were being lowered over the side of the tossing ship. This could all have been part of some simulated training exercise, except off in the distance, in almost rhythmical sequence, could be seen sudden, bright flashes of light, followed by the rolling boom of big guns, as the navy battle ships pounded the nearby shore with giant exploding shells.

Leyte Beachhead

October 20, 1944

The big guns on the ships had opened fire at dawn, like rolling thunder all around us. The enemy defense of our area had been established further inland along a row of low hills beyond a wide swamp, which was a pretty smart move for the enemy when you consider the blistering barrage that was laid on the beach.

"Now hear this! Now hear this! This is it, D-day and H-hour has come. You will go over the side in the order and place preciously rehearsed and designated." The battle for Leyte had begun.

With a clang and rattle of guns, ammo and equipment, men like ants began going over the sides and down the rope nets. Leyte Gulf was filled with ships. It was getting quite light in the eastern sky. It was about 9:00 a.m. that the fleet of landing barges filled with crouching soldiers left their mother ships and, with the roar of engines suddenly set at full throttle, settled deep in the water on the stern with the flat bottomed bow slapping and bounding over the rolling waves, as a long gray line of invasion barges headed shoreward, splashing foam and salt water in fine rain back over the tense, silent, grim-faced soldiers, half sitting, half crouching in the bottom. On every side ships were riding toward the island. Soon the barges scraped sand, the ramps dropped down, and every soldier instantly sprang to his feet.

"This is it, hit the beach."

In a simultaneous rush, 30 men were down the ramp into knee-deep water and scrambling ashore. Our location was just another typical jungle island, with coconut palms, ferns, wide-leafed banana trees, and all the other jungle growth, but torn and shattered by the heavy ammunitions. The approach and landing was quiet, uncontested where we came in, but how could it have been otherwise, so intense had been the pre-invasion shelling and bombing? There was hardly a living thing left to greet us, including a tree or a bush. Carefully, but cautiously, we moved up the beach, picking our way through the fallen and shattered palm trees, shell holes and bomb craters. A short distance inland, the jungle became dense and thick, and then suddenly out of nowhere came a thin, ragged Filipino woman leading a little girl with a slightly bleeding arm. Where she had come from and how they survived that pre-dawn naval barrage, no one knew. But there was no time to talk or ask questions. We motioned her back to the beach where someone would take care of them, and we moved on inland.

We plunged into the swamp and tall grass and bamboo thickets single file, strung out for a long ways. Although not all that wide, I think less than a mile, it seemed like we made our way through this type of terrain for miles, and it felt like hours passed with very little change, sometimes wading up to waist deep through murky swamp. Wading in water most of the day, we couldn't find a place to rest or sit down. As 2nd gunner, in addition to the pack on my back I carried in my arms or on my shoulder the 40-pound weight of the 30-caliber machine gun, which I tried to keep from getting wet. It was a very slow and difficult order of march; we spent most of the first day in it. And except for a little sniper fire and a few scattered artillery shells, the enemy resistance still wasn't bad. But the swamp sure was.

Finally, late in the afternoon we reached some high ground and decided to dig in for the night. We were further inland into the cover of the jungle, nearer the first low hills. We took stock of ourselves and situation. "Whew!" All was well. Everyone was accounted for. That wasn't as bad as we had thought or expected. We loosened up and relaxed, at least for a moment. The battle wasn't over by a long shot, but the first stage was and that was good news.

It was during the night that our new C.O., Col. Drake, was killed in his foxhole inside the perimeter by a sniper. I didn't know if or how the Japanese knew he was the highest ranking officer in the area, but he was and he was dead. Then I later learned that he was actually shot by one of our own trigger-happy men, when he stood up to take a look around.

The World Came to an End
October 21, 1944

The next morning we came out of the jungle into an open field with the first low-lying hills beyond, moving in a generally westerly direction, the same as yesterday. Then we came to kind of a road, skirting but paralleling the hills in a north-south direction. As soon as we hit the trail, we turned to our left, south, and followed it for a short distance. The trees and jungle growth were quite dense and we couldn't see much or very far. We didn't follow this trail far until we took a hard right back toward the west and the hills which had to be somewhere quite close. I don't remember if the trail turned or forked or what, but anyway we headed west again. We were going up this trail when suddenly it opened up into a small clearing covered with grass about one to two feet high. At the far end of the clearing and just beyond were the hills, rising quite steeply from the valley floor, partly bare, that is, only grass covered and less jungle or trees.

And then came death, streaking out of the base of the mountain. We had got about to the middle of the clearing, maybe 50 or 75 yards from either side, when Japanese machine-gun bullets began to snap and crack, splitting the air all around us. Being the squad leader and always out in front, my brother was one of the first ones hit. As we all hit the ground, I saw Merril buckle and slump. *"NO!—NO—NO!"* my whole being cried out in shocked protest. *"Not my brother!"* Not that death or dying was such an unfamiliar tragedy anymore. We had learned to walk with him by day and he sat up with us at night. Only this time it was different.

The captain was killed instantly, but Merril was hit only once, right in the pit of the stomach, just below the navel. He was directly in front of me, so I crawled up to where he was and turned him over. He was still conscious and said, "I'm okay. Watch out for yourself." His wound was only a little round hole in the stomach, not even bleeding, but the bullet was lodged in his spine and I think he was already paralyzed from the waist down. There wasn't much I could do by way of first aid, so we sent word back along the line for our first aid men or litter bearers. We called the field EMTs who accompanied each outfit. But because we were exposed and very vulnerable, help was unable to come, because anyone that made much of a move was shot by the enemy.

The request by word of mouth was sent up from the rear by the platoon leader, Lt. Campbell, wanting to know who was hit and how bad. Of course Merril heard the request and said, "Tell the lieutenant I'm okay." But he was already going into shock and beginning to fade in and out of consciousness. I gave him the morphine tablets each of us carried in our little first aid kit, with a few swallows of water from my canteen, but he was unable to keep anything in his stomach, and they came right back up. This began to concern me. At first I had thought maybe he was going to be all right, but now he was beginning to slip in and out, to sweat profusely and to ask for a drink of water when he was conscious. I sat, holding his head in my lap, and gave him water, but it wouldn't stay down. I knew that we had to do something to get him better medical attention or he wasn't going to make it. Of course, we did make more frantic requests for medics or litter bearers, but none had yet come. So I asked a buddy if he would help me make a stretcher out of ponchos and rifles so we could carry Merril back to the rear and hopefully to an aid station.

The U.S. Army hadn't been totally out of commission all this while and the mortar and artillery personnel, through their little walkie-talkie radios, had called for strikes on the enemy position, which sometime along in here had silenced their welcoming party or else they had packed up and left. Anyhow, about the time we got ready to move Merril, a couple litter bearers arrived on the scene and did what they could, which was very little, but they put him on a stretcher and carried him back down the trail. I bid him goodbye, telling him that at least he wouldn't be in this hell anymore; there was a white hospital ship out in our convoy that he'd be taken to where everything would be fine. I've wondered since why I didn't go back with him, but I didn't, didn't even ask to.

I remember sitting there awhile longer, then our unit moved on ahead into the edge of the trees where we stopped again for a time. About this time, a troop on our right made a breakthrough and joined forces with us, and we fought the enemy to silence. With the enemy gone for the moment, I slumped at the base of a coconut palm utterly spent. The troop on our right had a jeep and a weapons carrier, and word was quickly sent that the dead and wounded could be hauled back to the beach instead of carried through the swamp we had crossed. My faith and hopes for my brother were suddenly shattered when the same two medics came back up the trail—for the stretcher they carried now bore the blanket-covered sign of death.

Unprepared for this unthinkable twist, my first impulse was not to see them, or even to run away. Sort of a subconscious logic I suppose. If I refused to look, he wouldn't be dead.

They went over near the vehicles and set the stretcher down on the ground. I had begun to have an empty, shattered, and dead kind of feeling, hard to describe. I thought, "Before they load that stretcher, I have got to go and see who or what is under that blanket." Deep inside my whole being shrank and objected to the idea of even entertaining such a thought of the reality, that my brother could be dead. But forcing myself to get up, I walked like a zombie the few paces over to the stretcher. A sudden hush fell over the fifty soldiers gathered around as I leaned down, turned back the blanket for just a second. Then with neither sound nor falling tear, I gently replaced the blanket and walked back to my post and sat down.

I think I had suddenly turned to stone. Probably not sure what they should say or do, none of my buddies said or did anything. Of course nothing was really expected. At first the silence was deafening. I realize now how a word, a touch, or any token of comfort could have meant so much to me then. I didn't have my brother to lean on. He was gone beyond the bend. Locking the hurt of that tragic day deep in the bottom of my troubled soul, I tried to never let it show on the surface, and somehow my buddies must have sensed that this moment and my brother's name had become a hallowed, untouchable subject and they never mentioned either in my presence again.

The world came to an end for me that day, but the war went on and I went with it. I suppose it's quite an understatement to say the next few days, weeks, or even months were pretty dark and difficult for me, and I guess many times and in many ways, the inward battle and grief, though kept very tightly locked within, was more difficult than the battle that was often raging around me on the outside. Yet deep in the wilderness of my grieving soul, a smoldering fire began to burn with a growing feeling that God had been unfair and failed to keep His promise. Up to this point I had never possessed any real desire to kill. Like most combat soldiers I did what I had been trained to do. From that morning on, my attitude changed. I was engulfed in deep, dark, brooding feelings. I lost all desire to return home. How could I go back and face my family alone? My brother and I had left home together and had planned to return together. If he couldn't go back, neither would I. No, I would follow my brother, but the price I fixed was high. I would avenge him first.

Battle of Leyte Gulf

The beginning of the end of World War II started the day after Pearl Harbor, but the nation still had countless deadly battles and beachheads to endure. One of those costly battles was the invasion of the Philippine Islands, and before it was over, it would include the largest sea fight ever known, the Battle for the Leyte Gulf. The two greatest navies in the world, the "terror of the Pacific" Imperial Japanese Fleet and the invincible, rebuilt American Navy, met in a final showdown spread over 500,000 square miles of western Pacific.

Far away in Tokyo, under the high command of Admiral Toyoda, one of the biggest gambles in naval history was set in motion. He divided into three separate task forces all that was left of his once mighty Japanese fleet: 4 carriers, 2 battleship carriers, 19 cruisers, 33 destroyers, and 7 battleships, which included the two largest and newest battleships in the world, the *Yamato* and *Musashi*, with their super speed, latest armor, and 18-inch guns. This fleet was still a pretty intimidating force, but quite small when compared to the numbers now in the American 3rd and 7th Fleets with their 32 carriers, 12 battleships, 23 cruisers, 100 destroyers and over 10,000 ship-based aircraft, nearly double that of the enemy's dwindling air power.

To offset this suspected disadvantage, Vice Admiral Takijiro Onish, in command of the 1st Air Fleet, suggested and promoted another desperate measure: "The fate of the empire depends on this operation," he said. "To assure that our meager strength will be effective to its maximum degree requires that our bomb-laden fighters crash dive into the decks of the enemy carriers." And thus was born the "kamikaze" or suicide attack.

The strategy of their daring, cunning scheme was to send a small decoy force north of the Philippines to lure Admiral Halsey's powerful 3rd Fleet away from the Leyte landing, while the other two units, in a pincer maneuver, went through the San Bernardino Strait on the north and the Surigao Strait to the south and closed in on the Leyte landing.

As the battle was joined, this daring gamble almost worked. With most of our big boys now far to the north chasing a decoy, Admiral Kinkaid's smaller 7th Fleet, with its older, slower crafts, ran into serious trouble right off. The limited range of its small 5-inch guns were no match for the superior range and effectiveness of the enemy's 18-inch guns, which began to take their toll and prompted a pressing call to Admiral Halsey for help. But when it was learned that the 3rd Fleet was too far north to give any immediate assistance, and even worse, was not patrolling the San Bernardino Strait as had been thought, an urgent message was sent to Admiral Kinkaid's flagship in the Leyte Gulf: "The worst has happened. The enemy fleet is only three hours steaming time from the Leyte beach."

Weary from days of shore bombardment and nights of battle, in some cases low on fuel and ammunition, the 7th Fleet was suddenly fighting for its very life. But with the help of heavy smoke screens and rain squalls, Admiral Sprague's task force was able to survive. Launching a desperate but courageous counterattack with destroyers and P.T. boats, the outnumbered, outgunned 7th Fleet took its own toll, even though it was nearly wiped out. Two destroyers, a destroyer escort, and a baby carrier were sunk. Two carriers, another destroyer, and a destroyer escort were also badly damaged as the running battle closed in on the now exposed Leyte Harbor.

From the silent depth of a grieving heart, on the brow of a nearby hill I watched part of that awesome battle of the Leyte Gulf unfold, especially the blazing gunfire at night. Temporarily holding the high ground, we were often entertained by the latest American hit tunes from Tokyo, via the seductive voice of the Orient, Tokyo Rose. Picked up on our little radio sets, she also kept us up-to-date on the great sea battle now going on. She even seemed to know who we were and welcomed the 1st Cavalry to the Philippines. She repeatedly invited us to lay down our arms and surrender while we still could, telling us that our navy was destroyed and we were stranded on the beach with no hope of rescue or reinforcements. We laughed it off at the time, but we didn't know until later how close to being right she really was.

It was a good guess, of course, that some of our ships had been sunk when we saw a stream of navy planes flock to land at the little Tacloban air strip we had just taken. Then just at dusk, from our lofty position we watched a Japanese Zero slip seemingly undetected into the circling line to land. Taking his turn, he swooped low over the runway, dropping a couple of bombs on the strip, then banking to the left, executed a kamikaze crash into one of the ships in the bay.

The battle at sea was going even worse at that point as it closed in on the crowded Leyte Gulf. The badly wounded 7th Fleet, part of it sunken, was now widely scattered as it tried to dodge the heavy shells. The baby flat tops had already lost 105 planes and some observers desperately concluded it was only a matter of time. Then on the eve of October 25th, a very strange miracle happened. Suddenly at 9:11 p.m., victory within his grasp, Admiral Kurita broke from the action and turned his ships back to the north. "Damn it, boys," a sailor quipped, "They're getting away!"

Kurita's action does have some logic, though mistaken. Due to the courageous and repeated charges of the American small boys, a very stirring episode in the long history of naval warfare, Admiral Kurita thought he was being hit by Halsey's 3rd Fleet. Of course, his losses had also been very heavy, including both of his giant "unsinkable" battle wagons. At one point in this raging sea battle, the skipper of the destroyer *Heermann* remarked to his second mate, "What we need Buck, is a bugler to sound the charge!"

In his final report of the greatest sea battle in history, Admiral Sprague made this interesting observation: "The failure of the enemy to completely wipe out all vessels of this task unit can be attributed to our successful smoke screens, our torpedo counterattack, and the definite partiality of Almighty God." So thus it was that we on the beach were spared.

Campaign Continues

The dark tropical sky suddenly flared red as the sinking sun found one tiny slot in the ceiling of heavy black clouds. It was then that I first really saw it, the ragged outline of a massive mountain range, as she stood in bold relief, silhouetted against that giant curtain of flame rapidly sweeping across the western sky. Then she was gone, swallowed by the black jungle night. This was one of those rare scenes you never forget. Yet, far more lasting in my memory was the scene that had played out near the mountain's base and that would send me up into that tangled black hell in search of something I could never really find and certainly never replace.

Stretching the length of Leyte Island, evenly dividing the east from the west like a ragged high wall, was a row of steep, rain-drenched jungle peaks and deep, nearly impassible canyons. The strategy of the Leyte campaign once the eastern beach was secure, was to take hold and patrol the passes of the ragged fortress wall and keep at bay any enemy reinforcements while a giant pincer movement encircled the island from either end. The 5th Cavalry was sent up into the mountains of central Leyte to hold and patrol those key passes and prevent the enemy troops, pouring in from the west, from getting through.

Thus began, in a modern age, a very primitive type of jungle warfare. Operating from a few isolated base stations, small units combed and patrolled these high cloud-capped mountain passes. For days on end, it was hit-and-run squad action where the hunter and the hunted stalked each other through the jungle, and only the living kept the score. This wasn't big-time combat with tanks and planes and artillery; it could be quite personal and very deadly. It was exactly what I wanted and thought I needed. Like ourselves, the enemy operated in small units and it wasn't hard for a lone man, hidden in one of those dark jungle corridors, to ambush an enemy patrol, shoot hell out of it at close range, and then vanish into the jungle unobserved. Somehow this type of action seemed to best satisfy my burning desire for revenge. This fight had taken on a new dimension and I often did more than had to be done.

Living conditions up there were the GI's worst enemy. The interminable rain and mud meant that clothes were seldom dry and sleep was broken at best. Rations were short and sometimes missing if the Filipino pack trains got intercepted by enemy forces. Disease and dysentery were prevalent. For these reasons troops were rotated ten days up and ten days down in a semi-rest area.

I had little desire for rest, so I transferred from one unit to another, always staying with the one on the line. Although this dark, sunless environment probably did little to help my troubled spirit, it did fill a certain need. Not only did it give me an opportunity to hunt the enemy, it also gave me a lot of time with my inner thoughts and feelings. My feelings were pretty base and hard, probably colored by this environment. Some guys thought that I had no human feelings anymore. But I had something, and quite often in the dead of a stormy, pitch-black night, I would let it come to the surface and wander about through the dripping jungle alone, brooding. I continued to question the justice of God and wonder why. I never denied my faith in God, but I allowed a bitterness to creep into my soul during the dark days which followed. Why was my brother taken? We had been good boys, and compared to the standards of most soldiers, our lives had been clean and honorable. Now deep in my heart I found myself hard put to understand the justice of God in taking my brother while sparing those I judged to be his less-worthy buddies. *Why? Why?* I cried in my heartbroken soul. Of the eight men in our squad, he was by far the most deserving to live. It didn't seem to help that most of the other eight were also gone by the time the Leyte campaign came to a close.

Mission Bagatoon

"We need an experienced jungle scout for this mission," Lt. Bailes explained. "G2 would like to know what the enemy is up to. We think they've been pouring reinforcements into Leyte's west side by night down at Ormoc, but we don't know how many and we don't know where they're going. Once they leave the beach and reach the heavy jungle interior, our spotter planes [Piper Cubs] can't tell us very much." G2 had sent numerous scouting patrols deep into the area to learn what was going on, but each time they were turned back by the impossible terrain and jungle conditions. After having spent almost two uninterrupted months up there, I had come to know part of the jungle pretty well, and someone suggested I might be able to help, so the next scheduled patrol recruited me to go with them.

Taking three good men from my squad with three map-reading experts and Lt. Bailes from G2, we set out for Mt. Bagatoon, an area the Piper Cub pilots thought might be an enemy staging ground. To get there, we had to intersect and cross a crowfoot pattern of three dense, deep jungle canyons. The contour maps provided by G2 indicated that the best route and possible trail was a huge half-circle loop around the tips of the crowfoot toes. But it would be a difficult, time-consuming journey at best.

When we finally reached the third canyon, we began to find fresh signs of an enemy presence. Cautiously making our way up the narrow stream, sometimes wading in waist-deep water (often the only trail), we came to a small waterfall. As I cautiously climbed the 12-foot ledge to examine the upper level, I heard a loud snort and a sudden swishing in the water. It was a water buffalo that had apparently been appropriated by the Japanese as a beast of burden and had evidently been beaten and driven to the limit. He had finally quit on them and resumed the life he had previously abandoned. And he wasn't about to let us pass without a fight either.

One shot from my M-1 could have quickly eliminated the obstacle, but we didn't really want to kill him, much less alert the enemy of our presence. So, using my cowboy experience with angry cattle, I maneuvered to one side of a little clearing, close enough to keep the bull's attention focused on me while the rest of the soldiers sneaked past.

A short distance further on, we discovered a large bivouac area recently vacated by the enemy. From the looks of it, a sizable group had been assembled there for some time. The number of small palm and banana leaf shelters indicated there could have been several hundred troops holed up there. As the trail became increasingly fresher, we became increasingly cautious. Already we were into a grueling three-day journey from our base camp, and the last thing we wanted was an open encounter resulting in some dead or wounded buddies to carry back.

Finally feeling we'd better stop and do some reconnaissance, Lt. Bailes told the others to wait and keep an eye out while he and I left the main trail to conduct a flanking maneuver. It was a good thing, too. We discovered an enemy out port we would have run into ahead. After appraising the situation and its overwhelming odds, Lt. Bailes whispered, "Contact made. Mission accomplished. Let's get the hell out of here while we still can."

With night descending, we retreated a good distance back down the trail and disappeared into the thickest jungle we could find so we could squat down for the night. A squatting position made our helmets and ponchos our tent, shielding us from the constantly drenching rain. Wet, weary, short on rations, and having an overwhelming enemy too close for comfort made us extremely anxious to get back to the security of our home base. The next morning I suggested that instead of taking the long way back, we make a beeline for camp.

"Do you think you can find your way through this mess and still find our camp?" asked Lt. Bailes. Drawing again from my cowboy tracking days and with a sense of direction like a homing pigeon's, I was pretty sure I could find the camp unless we encountered some unknown and impassible barrier. Following hours of tough and difficult going, sometimes having to literally hack our way through the jungle, the complaining began: "Why did we ever follow this jungle-happy Laub in his one-man war?"

Then, just before dark (although darkness didn't always matter—we seldom saw the sun or the sky anyway) we climbed a steep razorback ridge and stumbled into a well-used trail—one we all immediately recognized. The complaining instantly changed to cheers and thanks and praise—and eventually a military citation and medal for meritorious achievement:

> "While on a reconnaissance patrol to investigate enemy activity and terrain in the vicinity of Bagatoon, Private Laub operated continuously for four days and four nights as point and scout [meaning he always went first—the most dangerous position]. . . . [He] broke trail and sought out possible routes of advance in order to save unnecessary and exhausting steps for his comrades. His untiring efforts and dogged persistence in the face of such discouraging obstacles materially aided the successful accomplishment of the mission and greatly inspired his fellow soldiers."

End of the Leyte Campaign

Christmas 1944 came and went with rain, mud and dysentery. Time was no longer important. The Leyte campaign came to a close on New Year's Eve 1944 after 72 days of fighting Japs, rain, mud, and jungle. The great pincer movement that had circled the island from east to west was about to be completed on the west side in the Ormoc Valley. As the 5th and 12th Cavalry troops moved down out of their high jungle fortress where they had been holding and patrolling the high passes in the central mountains, they joined forces with the 24th and 32nd Infantry divisions closing in from the north and the south, in a final three-pronged meeting at Ormoc Bay.

By this time most of the enemy resistance had been destroyed, beaten, or dispersed, leaving only scattered resistance. The only living enemy we saw on our last push down out of the mountains were a few straggling Japanese soldiers sneaking over a bare ridge behind us back into the jungle. Too few and too far away to be any worry or threat to us, we didn't pursue them. But in my bitter zeal to avenge the death of my brother, I couldn't resist firing a few shots with my M-1 as they hurried to get over the ridge, out of sight and out of range. Except for venting my hurt and anger, my shots probably only hastened their retreat. One of the problems with jungle combat was that you hardly saw the enemy until he or you were dead. It was usually only a fleeting glimpse of movement or shadows, which was somewhat disappointing to me as I seemed to have a desire for a fully open target. I got my opportunity in our last push down to the Ormoc Valley.

With the Leyte campaign officially over, the year end midnight hour was greeted and celebrated with a burst of weapon fire into the sky nearly equal to a full-scale invasion, with nearly every gun in the area joining the jubilant celebration.

Loading on 6x6 army trucks the next morning, we and our weapons were transported back to the east side over a makeshift road around the north end of Leyte's high central mountain wall, to what was being established as a base camp and regroup area before being assigned to our next mission. On one of my wandering one-man patrols earlier in this area, I had stumbled onto one of the many supply dumps the quartermaster corps had established in the jungle as temporary supplies for our troop. So on New Year's morning over the vigorous objection of one of the guards, I found a gallon can of peaches, opened it with my trench knife, and gobbled most of it down in one sitting. I had become so hungry for fruit or anything besides the dry, tasteless army K or C rations.

Then, with an army buddy, Leon Felt, who was also from Utah and had joined us as a replacement just before the invasion, I paid a brief visit back to the beach where we had landed. I had heard rumors that my brother was still alive and wanted to believe them. But there in a small, temporary jungle cemetery near Tacloban with rows and rows of solemn white crosses was the supreme price paid for taking this jungle island. I found my brother's grave, with his helmet and dog tags attached. My first impulse was not to look at it, to run the other way, my mind and heart still not quite able to accept or deal with this bitter reality.

It's pretty hard to try and describe the pangs of hurt, sorrow, and emptiness that suddenly shot through my still aching heart and lonely mind as I knelt by this humble, makeshift shrine. Though I had taken some revenge, it failed to ease my hurt or bring me any real comfort. At that moment, that jungle island with its shredded, war-torn beach became a sacred, hallowed place to me, indelibly stamped in my grieving mind and lonely soul forever. It was a place it was hard for me to leave, because it was the place I had hoped and expected I would never leave.

Having somehow survived the Leyte campaign, I couldn't help but wonder what fate was in store for me. Officially promoted to corporal with another stripe on the way, I had now taken my brother's place as leader of our heavy machine gun squad. I found grim hate still burned in my breast. Cold, steady, and barren of love, my feelings now were a far cry from those which had torn me apart nearly three months before.

My feelings were deeply mixed as the Calvary quietly sailed back out of the Leyte Gulf two and a half months after our blazing entry, October 20, 1944. I was bitter and resigned. Since fate and destiny had willed that I go on—and I never expected to see that place again—I would always have a deep and haunting attachment to it. A lifetime of hopes and dreams had been swept away with the death of my brother, and my big, wonderful world had been reduced to an endless realm of ocean, mud, and jungle.

Two perspectives of the landing on Leyte Beach,
October 20, 1944.

LEYTE CAMPAIGN

Immediately ahead of the beach was a swamp.

Cavalry soldiers manning a machine gun of the type Normand carried through the swamp on Leyte and used in the Admiralty and Philippine campaigns.

Leyte Gulf, October 1944.

Filipinos packed supplies to the troops in the mountains of Leyte.

Normand visited Merril's grave on Leyte in early 1945.

Chapter 7

Return to Leyte

Into the Past

February 25, 1985

    I didn't know for sure how high we were, because we were in a heavy dense fog. But then, I thought sometimes real life was like that too. But as the dim and once-distant island of Leyte, once so mystical and far away in a mind and memory of deeply hurt and shattered feelings, rapidly approached, not only in fantasy but in actual if a bit unbelievable reality, I couldn't help wonder at the strange sequence of events. For how could I make the real, seemingly impossible trip and visit into the past, to pass through some mystic or invisible barrier separating the past and the present, and emerge, as it were, out of the present real world into the dim and distant world of yesterday? So there we were just as the shades of darkness closed down around the lonely island of Leyte. And there we came, literally out of the fog and mist of the present into a dark and waiting world of yesterday. And somehow, as from high in the sky we descended through the dark swirling mist for that rendezvous with the past beyond the bend, we may not have been alone in our return.

An Extraordinary Time

February 26, 1985

    This couldn't be real. It was a dream, a myth, a fantasy. Yet behind the little desk where I was seated to write was a mirror, and as I looked up, I looked straight into my own eyes. So this was real. There I was after all those years, sitting in that yesterday world, but it was not just a dream or a fantasy. Though it was still very dark, I could hear the heavy waves of the ocean crashing and breaking on the beach in front of the room where Barbara and I were staying, and somehow there was in that sound the very essence of eternity. A symbol of the timelessness of time itself. A mere 40 years washed away in a few rolling waves, and the past and the present sort of merged and blended into one, with very little between them. And as I stepped to the door and stood for a long moment, listening to the pounding surf and trying to see through the darkness, I could feel an unseen presence.

There, somewhere off in the bay, was a ship, a troop ship, crowded with soldiers. With no lights and very little outside signs of life, that ship was already bustling with activity. Soldiers clothed in full battle dress were quietly, if nervously, waiting in kind of a hushed silence. It was almost as if having met here by arrangement, he, my brother Merril, and I, now boarded that ship together and joined that jostling throng, and time, and distance, and existence all mingled and blended and faded into one great sweep of existence with little regard for dates....

It was approaching 6:00 a.m. at the Leyte Beach Resort where Barbara and I were staying. Outside, the constant roar and rolling sound of the pounding surf and receding ocean kept up a steady rhythm. It set the stage for this surreal but very real episode. And with the approach of daylight, I became anxious to go outside and see just exactly where we were and what it looked like.

To begin with, the place we were staying was right down on Red Beach. On the front porch facing south we had a 180-degree view of the Leyte Gulf to the left, and the first low hills where Merril was killed on the right. The ocean and pounding surf were only a stone's throw from my chair. The monument with statues of General MacArthur and his staff wading ashore in a literal pond of water, called "MacArthur's Landing," was only about 500 yards up the beach to the north.

I had no idea there would be a place to stay right on the actual site. Nobody we had talked to seemed to know about it, so we thought we would have to stay in Tacloban about ten miles north. We had tried to reserve a room in what was recommended as the best place to stay, but we didn't get it done. The unbelievable thing was that we met an Anglo at the airport, Paul Cherry, who mentioned it by chance and then arranged for us to be brought right to it. It was beyond belief or chance. As I told Paul, if I could have formed in my wildest imagination the exact location and kind of a place I would have wanted to find and stay in, I couldn't have done better than this.

Last night, after we had gotten unpacked, we met our new friend, Paul, at the covered patio restaurant for dinner. As we sat and visited and talked about the war and the landing, asking questions and trying to get a bearing as to exactly where we might have waded ashore, the waiter, a young Filipino about 24 years old, went and brought an extensive array of maps and charts showing the history and date of the landing and battle for Leyte in 1944. As we were telling Paul about being in Japan the week before, he said, "You must be friends with the Japanese now." So I dug out the teletype picture and the newspaper article that had been sent to the Tokyo office of Zen Noh, and which Amy, our guide, gave to us as we left Japan. We had attracted the attention of the waiters and several diners gathered at the restaurant. Paul commented that the newspaper article was written in Japanese, and I said that I needed to get someone who could read Japanese to tell me what it said. One of the waiters tapped me on the shoulder and told me that there was a group of Japanese tourists eating there. We hadn't noticed them, but they had noticed us. So I went over and asked one of them if he could read it for me and he said he would.

Though it was difficult to translate to English the exact wording, in essence it gave the data of me and Merril and the war and the taking of the flag in Manila and how I wanted now for the relatives of the Japanese soldier to have the flag. I couldn't help but think how strange and interesting it was that I should come down to the very scene of Merril's death and meet, mingle, and visit freely with some Japanese people, even asking them to interpret the writing.

The man gave me his card and told me he was representing a Japanese shipping company and had been there four months and would be there for over a year yet. He and his three friends were there eating again tonight, so I gave him my last pamphlet with our name and address on it and had Barbara take a picture of us together. Can you imagine, me having my picture taken in the very location where my brother was killed by their soldiers? It was very interesting, another of the singular incidents that kept attending us.

Our friend Paul arranged for us to get a private car and driver to take us around. We had wondered how we might go where we wanted to go, so a private driver was super. The driver met us at the main office and restaurant at 7:00 a.m. We weren't too hungry, so we didn't stop for breakfast. In fact, we didn't stop to eat all day until we got back at night. First we made a quick stop at the MacArthur Landing monument, an elevated cement slab or platform with a little square cement wading pond in the middle and half dozen statues of men, in nearly knee-deep water, striding across it led by General MacArthur.

Next, we went up through the city of Tacloban, probably a very normal Philippine city with its narrow, crowded streets, filled with pedestrians, and jeepneys, kind of an old open-sided, roofed, old-style car or mini-bus used for hauling people around. There were small motor bikes with a covered side cart passenger seat, kind of like the old white-top buggy of the horse-and-buggy days. We took some pictures, picked up a book about the Leyte landing, and visited a Catholic cathedral where people come to worship at all hours of the day. We also went to the memorial museum, built and furnished by the First Lady of the Philippines, who was originally from Leyte and a very impressive woman. We then had our driver take us up to the Samar Bridge, a long, high span bridge a few miles above Tacloban, where we crossed over onto the island of Samar. I didn't get on that island when we were here in 1944; the 8th Cavalry landed on it.

BEYOND THE BEND

We then came back to Leyte and headed for the south and west countryside. I wanted to get up into the high mountain range that divide this island east from the west, where I spent most of my time on Leyte, 60 continuous days in a dark jungle, high-cloud-capped mountain area. But they say there are still no roads into or very close to it, so we drove as close as we could on the road that goes up around the northern end, over to the west side and Ormoc. This was a very interesting drive, through Palo and several other towns where we got to see the Filipinos plowing their fields and planting, weeding, and harvesting rice and other crops. This was an area we went through shortly after our initial landing in 1944. This area, except for a few modern touches like cars and trucks, and signs in some of the markets, was pretty much the same as it was 40 years ago. They still farm and ride and transport using the traditional water buffalo, and they plant, harvest, thresh, and dry their rice by hand.

We saw in the distance the dark green, cloud-capped mountains, that haunting land of my deepest hours of sorrow and grief, and I wanted to go there. We drove past Alangalang, up to Jaro, the closest point, right by a large river. Leaving our driver, we took a hard left down a country street that crossed the boulder-strewn wide river bed. The water wasn't too high, and at one point where it narrowed a bit, most of the water was spanned by a coconut log. Native women down along the river were doing their laundry, beating the clothes on a big smooth rock with a flat wooden paddle. By now we had attracted a lot of attention, and we had quite a following of kids and younger people. With a little encouragement, Barbara crossed the coconut log (but one of the children took the camera across). We took the road a ways, then left it for a trail that led out through some small thatched bamboo huts of typical native villages, complete with the Filipino razorback hogs, chickens, caribou, dogs, and people of course. We were headed for the mountain jungle, but after taking some good pictures, we decided the mountain was still way too far away, so we had to turn back. We stopped on top of a small hill with a good view overlooking a small stream and ate some of the snack nuts and fruit Barbara had prepared and brought just for such an occasion as this. But we were somewhat like the Pied Piper, carrying our camera and little red attache case through the jungle with a following of laughing, giggling, curious children, so we didn't drink the juice, as we only brought two cans, but we did share the mixed fruit and nuts with the kids.

As we walked back through the villages, the word had spread and even more people were out to see and greet us. When we returned to Jaro, we had attracted a following of 80 or more people and were, as I told Barbara, the talk of the town. So we stopped and talked and took some pictures and told them who we were and that I had been here as an American soldier, and about my brother being killed. Also about being in Japan and giving back the flag and having love for all people. This also enhanced our stature. They wanted our names and addresses, so we gave them all the rest of the cards and pamphlets we had (and wished we had more), and they gave us their names and addresses, wanting us to write to them.

I asked if there was anyone who was old enough to remember the war and the American soldiers. We were invited into the home of an older couple who both remembered. She was 61 and he 72 years old. They sat us down and sent up to the corner store for a couple of bottles of pop and some cookies to serve us while we visited. I'm sure they didn't have the money but spent the last they had for us. It was a rewarding experience.

We then got our driver and returned back to the low hills and probably the most dramatic, impressive, and memorable part of our whole journey, the one place we had wanted to find, if possible, and come to visit and photograph. So it was that we got a picture of the back side of the low row of hills at the base of which Merril was killed.

BEYOND THE BEND

We came through the gap to the beach side of the hills, then around and back west on the road that leads directly west from MacArthur's Landing to the foot of the hills. The Philippine military base is along the base of these low hills, so it was a restricted area, but we got permission to enter past the weapons carrying personnel. We went around the base of the nearest little hill to the left or south, possibly in the same area only closer to the hill than 40 years ago, and into a small cove back in a bit where there was a small clearing, now a rice paddy, possibly the very clearing in which we were ambushed and Merril was killed. At the extreme west end of the little cove and clearing the road wound up over a low pass, over the near hills to the other side.

We drove up toward the low pass, only about halfway to the top of the hill, in a northwesterly direction. I decided if we climbed to the top of this particular peak, I could look out over the whole area and possibly be in the same place we had spent the next few days after Merril was killed, watching the Battle of Leyte Gulf and the Japanese airplanes trying to bomb the ships. Telling our driver to wait again, we took our little red bag and started up the hill. The first little ways wasn't too bad, but then the path faded to a very faint trail. The top and east side of this particular hill was quite free of tall trees, but the grass, vines, underbrush, and small trees were very dense, about ten feet high, so it was pretty tough going, and then when we got to the top there were a series of little ridges and points, so we kept going. We finally got to the very top, but I still couldn't see out over the beach area very well, so I left Barbara to rest and went on, out to the extreme eastern point.

There was no path at all, and it was very dense and tough going. I still couldn't find a place where I could see back down into the little cove below to the south, and the rice paddy clearing where I thought Merril was killed, but I had passed a tree and thought I could climb it. So I went back and climbed part way up so I could take a picture of the clearing from above, and also of the beach where we probably waded ashore. But then I discovered I had lost my glasses out of my shirt pocket. I had no idea where I might have lost them. They had probably got caught on a twig or vine and pulled out, but I decided to take a quick look, although their brown case would blend very well with the dead grass and leaves. I had climbed over tangled thickets of undergrowth two or three feet off the ground. If they had fallen out there and down through, I had better just as well give up. But I had only gone a short distance back when I spotted them, for which I was very glad, so then I turned around and went back to find Barbara.

When I got about back to where I had left her, I called to see exactly where she was and at first she didn't answer. But finally she heard and answered. She was in tears and quite nervous and upset to think I would leave her so long. I hadn't planned to be so long or go so far. She said it had been a half hour and she had thought I would only be a few minutes, so she was becoming quite alarmed, concerned for what might or could have happened to me, and she didn't know how she could ever find her way out of there. So my return was a welcome relief. She said, "I will go around the world with you, but don't ever leave me alone again."

On our way back down, I thought we might take a short cut straight down a small canyon to the road below, rather than follow the top of the ridge back. It looked like a trail might have gone that way some time. But after we got off the top of the hill, on the back or west side, the tall cane grass gave way to trees, vines, and genuine heavy jungle growth. In fact, the mountain got very steep, with several little ledge places to climb down. Again Barbara began to think we were lost and had made a bad choice. It was a real jungle experience, one I had wanted, and we did get some real good pictures, although Barbara didn't share my satisfaction. I was pretty sure we would come out onto the road down near the bottom and even told her about where we would come to it, but she began to complain and worry and wish we had never taken that route. I told her that she reminded me of my army buddies 40 years ago who complained on that scouting patrol to

Bagatoon, when I got my first medal and military citation for guiding a patrol through the jungle and finding a shortcut back. And sure enough, just about when and where I told her we would find the road, we did, only it was a little further north than I had thought, because the canyon had turned to the northwest. I assured her I had a good sense of direction and had rightfully won my medal 40 years ago. Barbara was glad to get out of that mess a bit scratched and torn, but I was elated. It was just what I had wanted and hoped to get a picture of, and I had given it up.

We walked back up the road to the south where our driver was waiting on the divide. We were paying him by the hour, so it cost us a bit for this jungle experience, but I was still very glad. We had been gone a little over two hours, but we probably had not been over a half mile away; maybe we had gone three miles at the farthest in kind of a triangular circle. We then were driven back down the hill, and now having seen the area from above, I stopped the driver near the bottom, about where I thought the Japanese gun placement might have been, and got out and took a picture of the place. It was now easy to see how we were sitting ducks 40 years ago and had walked dead into a very well located ambush. But in jungle fighting there were many times there was no other choice, if you were on the offensive anyhow. It was interesting to see the fatal location from the other direction after all these years.

We then went on to the bottom, and I was going to walk out in the middle of the place about where I thought we had been pinned down, but the military stopped me. After explaining what we were doing and why I wanted a picture, we were granted permission for Barbara to take one picture of me out in the clearing a little ways. After this very successful adventure, we had our driver take us back to our room.

Everything I Had Hoped
February 27, 1985

It was about 6:00 a.m., and I had been up for about an hour and a half reviewing and re-writing. We had a very good night's sleep. Being tired, we went to bed early, 9:00 p.m., and I didn't wake until 4:30 a.m. It was beginning to get light and I hadn't really noticed, but in addition to the constant roar of the surf, my ears caught another half-familiar sound. The porch was wide, but going to the edge, I discovered it was raining this morning. The steady patter of falling rain on the palm and other broad leafed foliage created its own low, muffled roar. It was a beautiful, if cloudy morning. A beautiful place for a mind and heart filled with memories and new thoughts.

I stopped writing to walk down to the edge of the water to take a picture of some little canoes out in the gulf, Filipino fishermen, I presumed. Yesterday the tide had been down and going north. This morning it was up and flowing south. The 6:50 a.m. jet roared by on its way back to Manila. We had thought once we would take it, but I was sure glad we hadn't. I wasn't done, wasn't ready to leave yet. It quit raining, and the morning sun broke through. Barbara got up and came out to join me and take a picture of the sunrise. The little fishing boats were closer and I could count about five of them, and on the distant horizon, the mast of a ship was either coming or going.

We had a pretty good breakfast. To confirm our flight back to Manila, we had to be driven into Tacloban and get the booking put on our ticket, so we got a MacArthur Park Resort driver to take us. We were headed back when it began raining again; in fact it had rained off and on all morning. So again it would seem this trip and the days were made to order. It would have been very inconvenient, difficult and maybe even impossible, to have tried today to take the trip we were able to complete yesterday. We changed into our beach and hill clothes, took our special little red attache bag containing our important papers, cameras, and umbrella with us, and went down on the beach for a stroll up to the MacArthur Landing monument and park.

It was our second day there and it was on our second day, 40 years 4 months and 7 days before that Merril was killed. We had decided to stay one more day, even though we did pretty well see and do nearly everything I had hoped and wanted to do yesterday. But this was such a beautiful, peaceful, serene and compelling place, so filled with overwhelming memories and thoughts, a place so desirable and attuned to the thoughts and memories that were stirred and awakened within me, that I wanted to stay as long as I could, just sort of living in close communion with the past. So while I had the time, I wanted to return once again to yesterday, both now and 40 years ago. On the second day of the invasion, by 1:00 p.m. it was all over, my brother Merril was dead and in a way so also was part of me.

Not that death itself was any big deal, in combat it was an everyday occurrence. You took it almost for granted. Death had become a grim, real part of life. "She walks with us by day and we sit up with her at night." Only this time it was different. This time it seemed almost as if part of me also died and was buried there on the lonely, hauntingly beautiful, tropical island, forgotten and so far away where the rolling waves of the blue Pacific idly fall and splash on these quiet shores, some of them almost unchanged, as if it literally were just yesterday that we waded ashore on that fateful day.

As we had approached and had tried to anticipate this return, I was not quite sure what I would find or what I even wanted or expected to find. But I wanted to come and really needed to come, though I never expected it might ever happen. But once it had happened, now that I was here and it was almost over, it had more than answered all my deepest hopes. It was so beautifully and peacefully fulfilling and rewarding, and so much freer and easier than I had ever thought it might be. They told me things would be changed, that it wouldn't be the same, that I might even have a hard time finding the same places. But except for those few buildings and the roads, things really hadn't changed all that much in 40 years.

We were able to locate very closely the spot where we came ashore, after a very careful study of the entire area both from the beach and from climbing to the top of the first low hills where I could see the whole area—many things may change or be moved, but not hills. So I was able to wade ashore, traverse the swamp and low lands, find the little clearing where my brother was killed, and take pictures, both from the beach and also from the top of the hill looking down, and then from a position near the base about where the Japanese gun placement must have been. And then I was able to stand out in the clearing, not quite out in the center where he was hit—not quite, because it's a wet rice paddy right now—but pretty close.

It was a very memorable experience, something I had long wanted and felt I needed to do, and even though quite touching and emotion filled at times, it was very good for me and opened some doors that had been closed and locked in my inner self for more than 40 years.

It was raining again, and I was seated under a large overhanging porch with a small table to write on, with an almost unbelievable view of the ocean, the beach, the coconut groves, and the first low hills in the background, a view that for the most part was unchanged from what it was 40 years ago. Only this time, it was not torn by the sounds and sights of war nor filled with the tensions and pressures of battle, of fear and hate of a lurking, deadly enemy. Nothing, for the most part, was changed we found, which only added to and made this sentimental journey into the past a journey of rewards, of feelings of peace, and of beauty beyond compare. It was truly a healing balm to sit there on that porch, on that beach, and to watch the rolling waves break in a never-ending pattern and then rush back down the smooth sand to meet and be engulfed in the next wave as it broke on top of the receding last one with a hiss and deep rolling roar, echoing all up and down the beach. More than that, it seemed to whisper, maybe a little sad and lonely, but also in a soothing way, a message from out of the distant past as well as the limitless future. A message of peace, of hope and tranquility, almost from the very bottom of eternity, which is kind of the overwhelming feeling I got as my gaze went from the dark green of the jungle to the blue green of the ocean and then the blue black of the stormy sky out where the sky and water meet.

It was almost as if I were permitted to peer into the very bosom of eternity where time and being itself began. It was such a compelling, deep, indescribable feeling, touching the very depth of my immortal soul. Yes, this had been a richly rewarding journey. One that I needed and wanted to take. A trip that really was a journey into the past and yet became a passport to the present and the future, like few things that had happened to me, tying, blending the past and the present in sort of a harmony and symphony of beauty and peaceful serenity. Yes, the sights and sounds of this beautiful setting were music to the heart and peace to the soul, and I couldn't begin to express my gratitude for this opportunity.

It would almost seem the very hand of destiny had been guiding, directing, and even guarding nearly every step of this unusual journey. And it would almost appear that some unseen person had been accompanying us almost throughout this journey, but particularly during these last few days. Was it possible that we had been assigned an unseen, but very real guide on this particular journey? One who prepared, and arranged, and cleared the way for the amazing things that kept happening to fall into place? Surely the unusual and appropriately timed incidents and events were not all a matter of chance. Would anyone care to speculate who might have been our unseen guide?

"Far on the deep, there are billows that never shall break on the beach
I have heard songs in that valley, that never shall float into speech."

The time was fast drawing to a close. It was a little after 4:00 p.m. and we had to leave at 5:50 to catch the flight back to Manila. Although we had only been there for two days, it was hard to leave. Of all the places we visited, I suppose I would say this one had the greatest fascination, and of course, it had a 40-year deeply sentimental attraction. I think if it had to stand on its own, it would still overshadow any other place we had the privilege of visiting on this entire trip. So we were quite sad at having to say farewell to the Leyte Beach Lodge.

Normand stands about where his brother was shot;
below are the low hills from which the ambush came.

Normand leads the way through the jungle; Barbara reminds him how he earned his medal 40 years before.

View of Leyte from near the top of the hill.

The river crossing near Jaro.

MacArthur Landing Monument on Leyte Beach

Chapter 8

Liberation of Santo Tomas POW Camp

Flying Column to the Rescue
February 1, 1945

The beachhead at Lingayen Gulf about 100 miles north of Manila had already been made by someone else, so we marched inland unopposed. We had hardly got moved in with our gear and equipment and temporarily bivouacked when General MacArthur gave the 1st Cavalry Division C.O. Gen. Mudge our new mission.

Through the Philippine guerilla underground the General had learned that as we closed in on the enemy, that of the 3,700 American and British civilian POWs held in the Santo Tomas University prison compound in Manila, the Japanese planned to kill the men and boys and hold the women, girls, and younger children as hostages. Our mission was to make a flying column a hundred miles through enemy lines and take the compound and rescue the prisoners. This was the only time in the entire war that we filled the famous and traditional "Cavalry to the rescue!" role.

"Get to Manila as quick as you can," was his order. "Go around the Japanese, bounce off the Japanese, save your men, but get to Manila."

As leader of a heavy 30-caliber machine gun squad, I was part of that flying liberation column. There are about 800 men in a normal Cavalry squadron or brigade, including the service, kitchen, medical, and staff personnel. There were four troops to a squadron. The 1st squadron was made up of A-B-C-D troops. The first three are rifle troopers, and the 4th, D troop, is a heavy weapons or support troop of machine guns and mortars. The 2nd squadron is made up of E-F-G-H troops, with again the first 3 being rifle and the 4th, H troop, being a support. The 2nd squadron, 5th regiment that I was in would have had about 400 line troopers (soldiers) and then extra or special support. The 1st Section, 1st platoon D troop that I was in was assigned to the 2nd squadron as a special support section in this operation. So in order of march, being a heavy weapons support group, we were toward the rear.

Mounted on jeeps and trucks instead of horses, with some tanks and half tracks from the 44th Wolf Pack tank battalion as our lead escort, elements of the 5th Cavalry headed south shortly after midnight, February 1, 1945. That first day, I remember passing through a banana grove where horse-drawn Japanese artillery were still tied to their banana tree hitching posts.

I think it was the second night just as darkness was closing in that the flying column was moving quite fast along a strip of highway well strung out for over a mile. The lead troops had come to a little town, I don't know which one, with a major intersection, and they had decided to hole up for the night. Some of the troops had set up in some buildings on the corners of the intersection. There was a small gas station on one corner with pumps. My D troop was back down the road a bit, just on the edge of town by a farmhouse. It was getting dark, so we set up right along the road on each side. We usually didn't travel at night, only on special patrols, night missions, or forced marches.

Not too long after midnight we could hear some trucks coming down the road from behind us, the direction from which we had just come. We were a bit mystified, for no one we knew should be on this road that close behind us, much less traveling at night, but here they came, quite a convoy of them. The little highway was a narrow two lanes, maybe 12 feet wide. We were set up with a machine gun on each side, but I don't remember which direction we were set up to guard. The land on each side was quite open, with rice paddies and fields, but we had only quite recently come out of a heavily wooded, jungle-like area. The engines didn't sound quite normal, but we were not sure until the first two or three had passed that the soldiers silhouetted against the evening sky were Japanese. I don't know where their garrison may have been, but evidently they had orders or had decided to try to join their buddies down in front of us.

After we discovered they were enemy, over half the convoy was past or even with us, traveling totally blacked out, but we could see their old Model T trucks piled high with equipment and troops. We couldn't shoot straight across because we would be shooting at each other. Nor could we safely shoot at those that had already passed because we had troops down the road at the intersection. We got our guns turned around and opened up on the last two trucks that were either stopped, stalled, or abandoned. One of the soldiers shot one enemy soldier off the last truck to pass us who fell on the road between our guns. But the convoy sped up and got out of control and created a traffic jam down at the little intersection. One of the trucks crashed into the little gas station, shearing off the gas pump and starting a gasoline fire and explosion that lit up the night sky and created a good deal of confusion, not only among the enemy, but among our own troops. We lost several good men in the fire and explosion. Then the enemy quickly scattered in the dark, and in keeping with our number one assignment, we loaded up and moved on.

For the most part, the road was good though narrow, the first paved road we had seen since leaving Australia over a year ago. Some of the bridges were damaged, but most of the time we beat the enemy to the bridges before they had time to destroy them.

Arriving at the outskirts of Manila just at dusk, our 72-hour dash appeared to have taken the Japanese quite by surprise. Col. Lobits led the prong of the flying column that I was in, and we encountered very little resistance until the leading elements entered the Manila City limits about 6:00 on the evening of February 3, 1945. Crashing the gates of the Santo Tomas University prison compound, our lead units were able to gain control of most of the compound in short order. This was reportedly the oldest western university in all of Asia, quite a large complex of Spanish design, with a stone fence completely enclosing its nearly two block area.

BEYOND THE BEND

When my squad reached the street in front of the compound, there were a group of internees gathered around. They were overjoyed, but mainly I remember a little English lad in knee pants, grabbing me by the hand and saying, "You got here just in the nick of time!" It was a common little saying back home, but I hadn't heard it for a long time, and it brought a quick pang with thoughts of my home and family, things I hadn't allowed myself to dwell much on.

Moving past the front gate with my heavy machine gun squad supporting some rifle troops, we were directed to move on down the street into the city a short distance and set up a guard for the street for the night. Setting up on the ground floor of a nearby building, we discovered it housed a half dozen big, long, sleek torpedoes. Some of my squad were a bit nervous about spending the night by these unfriendly kind of weapons.

Although our flying column had succeeded in rescuing most of the internees, 63 Japanese guards barricaded themselves in the Education building, still holding 261 men and boys as hostages. After two days of negotiating with the cocky little Japanese commander, it was agreed the Japanese would release the prisoners if they were permitted to keep their weapons and be escorted beyond the compound into the city and to their own lines. While I was not present when this deal was made, some of the soldiers who were there told me the Japanese colonel, wearing brass and pearl-handled Western pistols, spun them on his fingers Tom Mix style and put them back in their holsters as he and his men were escorted out of the western gate, without any shots being fired, and marched down the street into town.

Reunion Fifty Years Later

We were invited back to the Philippines to commemorate the 50th anniversary of the liberation of Manila and of the 3,785 POWs who had been held by the Japanese in the Santo Tomas University compound, where my army unit, the 1st Cavalry Division, participated in that very noble venture. Somehow my participation in that world-disrupting war as a young man not yet old enough to vote left an indelible stain on the fabric of my life and soul that time and a world of happenings have not been able to remove or even fade. Of course, war, death, and violent destruction inevitably leave their stain not only on those most directly involved, which I was, but on a much wider circle also, like a pebble dropped in a pool making the ripples extend out in all directions. World War II was more than a pebble, it was a huge boulder plunged into a pond, whose waves and backwash almost inundated the entire planet.

February 3, 1995

On a rainy afternoon over 10,000 people assembled on that same high-walled campus to commemorate that joyous and historic liberation. Seated in a covered grandstand with many of the city fathers, provincial and national officials, including President Fidel V. Ramos himself, were some of the original prisoners of war. The POW Children, they called themselves, and 50 years ago they would have all been just that, being from 5 to 14 years old when they were interned. One of them told me there was an old city dump in the compound with some old car axles, and they were able to get the ball bearings out of the wheels to use for marbles to play with to pass time. They said they were told when they were interned that they would be there only for three days, to take food and clothing for three days, and it turned out to be 37 months. One lady had a full-length, hardcover book titled *Santo Tomas*, a journal kept by one of the internees. It mentioned the many people who helped him keep and hide his record during those three years. I hoped to get a copy or some excerpts from it. It also contained a pretty good list of the internees and their hopes, their hunger, their struggles, and their despair. Stan Baker and his wife, June, were here from England. He was about 9 years old in 1941, and his family were already on the run, as they had fled Shanghai when the Japanese moved in there, and they had made it to Manila only to be overtaken by the same aggressive enemy.

Some of them had brought wives or children now to feel and share this most unforgettable moment. There were 27 survivors of the Santo Tomas prison compound and about half of them had been girls here. There were only three of the 1st Cavalry liberators here for the occasion. They were Major William Swan, on special assignment for the 1st Cavalry, Sgt. Henry Swindall, G troop, 5th Cavalry, and Sgt. Normand Laub, D troop, 5th Cavalry. Bill Swan was from Long Island, New York, Henry Swindall from Alabama, and my wife and I from Utah. There were a few of the old soldiers of the Filipino underground, some of whom may have participated in the liberation of this camp. One of them gave me a Cavalry pin that had been given to him by one of the American Cavalry soldiers 50 years ago.

One of the names to remember was a lady, Sascha Jean Weinzheimer Jansen, who was one of the tour directors and who helped put this tour together. She was a 12-year-old girl at the time of the liberation. She gave us the invitation and information that helped get us interested and registered for the tour and reunion.

This was a very special group and it was a special experience to be able to meet and share this moment with them. On our way there, the internees told stories of what they were doing when the U.S. soldiers came. One girl ran out to meet them, and her father jumped out of bed and followed, but her mother stayed to watch the beans so they wouldn't get stolen. She had just bought them with her wedding ring, food was so precious. One boy was thrown over the fence and a GI put him down in a tank to ride, but he got scared and cried, so they took him back out. When they first heard the tanks coming, they thought it was the Japanese until they heard a southern accent, and then they knew we were Americans.

It was a very emotional moment for many of them when our tour bus pulled up to the new university gate where a big poster read, "Welcome Home." It was also very touching and heartrending moment as these victims of war remembered and reviewed their past experiences and tragic ordeal here. "Interrupted Lives," some of them wrote in their own memoirs and histories. These were the children of the prominent and well-to-do pre-war Americans and British of the Far East, bankers, business heads, and government officials. As one lady put it, "It was a very drastic and sudden change in lifestyle to go from having five or six meals provided by house servants to living in want, fear, and poverty." Some died and others were beaten, bayoneted, and tortured often for the slightest provocation. They were made to stand roll call every morning and to bow in a very proper manner to their always-armed guards. Some remembered the fading hope and despair that ran through the camp when they learned of the fall of Bataan and of Corregidor. They had been able to hear a bit of the fighting, bombing, and shelling. One lady said her mother was very patriotic and had insisted the Americans would be back. But many of them, all the Filipinos, and even General MacArthur were bitterly disappointed when the United States didn't send supplies and help to the struggling little force trying to hold onto the island, but let them fight and die and be taken over without help or hope because the powers in Washington had already committed America to the war in Europe as their number one priority.

While their fears, hardship, and despairs were innumerable, their greatest single test was slow starvation. At first conditions weren't too bad, but as the Japanese began to lose the war, things got worse and worse. What can a mother say to a little 5-year-old boy who keeps saying, "Mommy I'm hungry"? By sharing her own portion with him, this five-foot eight-inch, 130-pound mother dwindled to 78 pounds, her daughter told me, and she surely would soon have died had we not gotten there. The K rations we shared with them were a special thankful remembrance.

Their endless thanks and praise for their Cavalry liberators was a very humbling reward, and when they repeatedly noted, "If it hadn't been for you, we wouldn't be here today," they really meant it. I was looking for that little British lad who met me at the gate of Santo Tomas, grabbed my hand and said, "You got here just in the nick of time," which the internees confirmed was true, as the Japanese planned to kill them and burn their quarters. I was sorry that I wasn't able to identify this little lad with anyone there.

We had had a special lunch there by the lake in the late afternoon the day before. We were entertained by a Filipino band, two guitars, a drummer, and a bass fiddle. They came to our tables and played and sang some songs. When they set their instruments down to have a drink, I asked if I could take one of the guitars, and with quick inspiration, got up and told our group I'd like to sing them a special song, written during the war by the GIs in our platoon, called "That Crazy War." It went over very well and even surprised me that I could remember all the verses.

1
Now I was just a country boy who lived down on the farm,
I never hurt a flea or done no one no harm
'Til that war, that crazy war.

2
The sheriff he walked up to me—said, "Come along my son.
Your Uncle Sammy needs you to help him tote a gun."
In that war, that crazy war.

3
They took me to the courthouse, my head was in a whirl,
But when the doctor jumped on me, I wished I'd been a girl
In that war, that crazy war.

4
They gave me a suit of khakis and a pair of GI shoes,
They said, "Young man, you wear these and you'll never have the blues."
In that war, that crazy war.

5
I grabbed myself a rifle—went on the rifle range,

I shot a box of cartridges and never hit a thing.
In that war, that crazy war.

6

Now when I reached the Philippines, I looked around with glee,
But rain and water buffalo was all that I could see.
In that war, that crazy war.

7

A cannon ball flew overhead, I started home right then,
The corporal started after me, but the general beat us in.
In that war, that crazy war.

8

The Captain said, "Why did you run, was you afraid to die?"
I said, "Captain, the reason I run, I didn't have wings to fly."
In that war, that crazy war.

9

Now I went through the Philippines a fighting for my life,
Before I go to war again, I'll send my darling wife
To that war, that crazy war.

It was a special opportunity to share with the POW Children that glorious day of deliverance, when the tanks and jeeps and trucks of the flying Cavalry column came down the street and crashed through the gate just about dark. Earlier, an airplane had flown over the university grounds and dropped some leaflets which read, "Santa Claus is coming," sort of a disguised message of hope. Many of the prisoners were already aware of the change in the status of the war, as American planes had begun to dominate the sky, unlike the dark days three years earlier.

The prayer at the opening and the talk by the American Ambassador to the Philippines made reference to rising above the bitterness, of hate and war, and trying to be at peace and live in peace with all men. On that rainy afternoon, February 3, 1995, when the Filipino army staged a very realistic re-enactment of that historic moment 50 years ago, and a group of cheering university students played the roles of the jubilant internees welcoming their liberators, I couldn't restrain my tears. In response to some questions by a news reporter sitting nearby, I said, "I didn't cry then, but I did today."

Unfortunately and rather sadly for me, when I led my squad past that gate 50 years ago, I was still quite hard, cold, and bitter, still brooding over the death of my own brother, who had been killed a little over three months earlier, and I was still pursuing my own personal revenge and score.

So, remembering now the inhuman suffering and atrocities of the Bataan Death March, the slow starvation of Santo Tomas, and the futile and total destruction of Manila, let us never forget the tragic cost of winless war.

> Feb. 3 [1995] marks the 50th anniversary of our liberation from Santo Tomas internment camp, Manila, Philippines. I am writing to express our deep appreciation for the members of the 1st Cavalry who effected our liberation.
>
> For 37 months we had endured hardships, hunger, sickness and innumerable petty torments inflicted upon us by the Japanese. We welcomed the return of Allied planes, which bombed Manila steadily from September until the end of January, 1945. Food became increasingly scarce until we were reduced to 600 calories a day. Starving is not easy but it is 10 times worse when you watch your children cry for food.
>
> The story of our liberation is so fantastic it reads like a book. The official camp interpreter was an English missionary cordially hated by everyone, as he was so friendly with our captors. None of us knew, of course, that he was a British Intelligence officer.

The Japanese were so desperate as the Allied forces pushed them back that they had determined to put all men into one building, destroy it, and use the women and children as hostages. Our interpreter saw the orders, and got word to the guerrillas to tell General Douglas MacArthur. The result was that 750 members of the 1st Cavalry fought their way 60 miles South and burst into the camp at 9 p.m. on Feb. 3rd.

Not only did they give us every scrap of food they carried, but these gentlemen were the most gallant and humane soldiers. They showed us unbelievable courtesy and kindness. We owe them a debt we can never forget.

God bless the 1st Cavalry and God bless the United States.

Kathleen C. Watson, Pasadena, CA

The Cavalry's Flying Column fought their way to Manila.

Santo Tomas main building on February 4, 1945.

LIBERATION OF SANTO TOMAS POW CAMP

The Anniversary 50 years later in Manila, February 1995:

Maj. Bill Swan standing far left; Normand kneeling at left; Sgt. Henry Swindall standing far right.

Chapter 9

Retaking Manila

A Building at a Time

February 5, 1945, 6:00 A.M.

From my seventh floor guard station I had a reasonably good view of the city. Except for several fires still burning and an occasional burst of small arms fire, the past 12 hours had been pretty quiet. The calm before the storm. Taken by surprise, the enemy had retreated south across the Pasig River to regroup.

"Hey Powell, it's your turn on guard," I called, "I'm having breakfast in bed" (from my personal supply of K rations). Then I took my morning shave and shower with a half cup of water in my helmet. And what to wear wasn't a real heavy decision either. I'd just wear the same green business suit (a wool herringbone twill) I wore yesterday with hat (helmet) and shoes (jungle boots) to match. Same suit I'd worn every day for the past week. In fact I liked it so well I hadn't taken it off once, even to sleep. Of course, sleep hadn't taken too much of our time anyhow.

After 395 days of nothing but ocean, islands, and primitive jungle wilderness, the sights and sounds of civilization, even though war torn, brought me a fleeting moment of homesick reflections. But even that did little to change my feelings or resolve.

Our entry into Manila was only the beginning and not the end of the battle for that city. Still held by 20,000 die-hard Japanese marines now trapped in its inner section, the battle for the city took a full thirty days as we had to take it one block and one building at a time. Nearly all 20,000 defenders had to be killed as very few surrendered, and it cost over 1,000 American lives. The street fighting and building hopping was a whole new experience in warfare for me and even provided some new opportunities to fill my unsatisfied thirst for revenge as we were now often able to clearly see and observe the enemy before he was dead. But the greatest single price in the liberation of the city was paid by the civilian population themselves, with nearly 100,000 lives. We continually found dead Filipinos, raped, beaten, and shot or bayoneted in the back, scattered around yards and houses. Next to Warsaw, Poland, the beautiful city of Manila was the most ravished and destroyed allied city of World War II.

Philippine General Hospital

In the fourth week of February my heavy machine gun squad, supporting the A-troop of the 5th Cavalry, had finally gained access to and control of the main building of the Philippine General Hospital. We were assigned to hold the building with our gun pointing down the street through a missing panel in one of the big double doors. During the day, the enemy periodically sprayed the front of the building with machine gun and rifle fire from a building across the street, along with lobbing mortar shells on the roof and patio. But we weren't too impacted, so we held our position and waited for some other supporting elements to move up to help us.

Under cover of darkness, however, that night an enemy runner slipped undetected across the street and lobbed a satchel charge through a broken window into a little corner room off the main lobby where we were guarding. The explosion was powerful enough to blow out the walls of the little room, blow the big double doors off the front of the hospital, blow our machine gun over, blow the helmets off some of the squad, and injure most of us with flying shrapnel and shattered debris. Not sure how bad we were wounded, the rifle troop company we were supporting further back in the rear of the building ordered us to fall back and join them in a new line of defense.

But after getting my men and gun back to the new position, I told the lieutenant I couldn't see letting the enemy get into the building if we could help it, because from the main front lobby they could go upstairs or out through the inner court and get behind our line. So I would take my rifle and go back and try to guard the front entrance. A close buddy, Merle Kincaid from Arizona (who had been with my brother and me since the Admiralties), volunteered to go back with me. "You don't have to, but you can if you want," the lieutenant said.

We barely got back to the main lobby when we heard the enemy start to come in, like I knew they would. Passing between us and a small fire still burning in the corner room, we could see them but they couldn't see us. With our rifle fire and grenades we were able to stop most of them. Only one man got past into the patio before he was killed. Realizing we were still there and pretty much still intact, the main force stalled out on the street. We could hear them calling and shouting to their comrades inside, but with no answer, that first group was all that tried to enter. Things pretty well quieted down for the rest of the night, and Kincaid and I took turns standing guard until morning. Awhile before daylight, we heard the enemy singing and chanting in their building across the street, followed by a series of hollow booms.

The next morning on the ground floor of that building, we found about 80 enemy dead soldiers, who in some type of ceremonial order had linked arms in a huge semi-circle, with a live grenade held to each of their breasts. Evidently when their counterattack failed, the rest of the force decided to quit the battle on their own. This seeming mass disregard for life, especially one's own, suddenly left me pondering my own clouded goals and sense of values.

Although the C.O. I had told I was going back to hold the fort was killed the next day, someone turned me in for a citation and I was awarded another Bronze Star and a Purple Heart for the slight head wound I received when the blast that blew off the front door also blew my helmet off. The most serious injuries to my squad appeared to have been popped ear drums of a couple of the guys, and they had to be pulled out of combat. The rest of us were sent for a check up to a front line aid station, where they kept me overnight. I remember spending the night on a stretcher beside a handsome young 1st lieutenant who had been seriously wounded and who died that night before they could get him the help he needed. I remember feeling sorry as I visited with him, and thoughts came of my own brother's death.

Horrors of War

The next day while we were waiting around, two pretty little 12- or 14-year-old Filipino girls came with an older guy who may have been their father. He played a guitar as they visited with and sang to us. They were so sweet and pretty, I remember thinking. Their little voices blended so beautifully as they would sing and then laugh and giggle. I can remember only a few words of one song that they sang, though they must have sung many. It went something like this: "Parting is so much fun. Let's you and I have another one, before we can say good night." The man with them also had a good, rich, deep voice and I remember him singing, "Give me some men who are stout hearted men, and I'll soon give you ten thousand more." This was one of the songs of the time, and pretty soon everyone would join in the chorus. This was kind of a refreshing switch from the experiences we had been having in the middle of this city.

The next day in this ruthless, soul-destroying war, I was invited to go with Herris, the young Filipino native who had been assigned to my squad as an extra, to the Philippine underground headquarters in Manila, where a very impressive lady and some others held a Filipino collaborator who had helped the Japanese and had caused some real problems and misery for his own people. They held a trial in their own language, convicted him, and passed sentence on him—death as a traitor. Their feelings were quite bitter and some of them got in a scuffle with him, and while I sat there and watched and did nothing to interfere, they beat and kicked him to death right there on the upstairs floor of their Manila headquarters. I guess war, under any banner, or condition, is always hell and often brings out the worst in us human creatures, or maybe more correctly stated, war is a demonstration of the worst traits of men, allowed to rule or come to the surface.

I remember making a one-man patrol out to the old walled city where the Japanese had holed up in a last stand in the city. The wall had been blasted by artillery in a couple of places. I climbed up on the crumbled wall with the wind and mist blowing in from the bay, with some deep, sad, melancholy feelings which are hard to explain, standing with my rifle in my hand as I gazed into the distance, seeing nothing in particular, my thoughts back in Leyte.

An incident that took place just before or just after we crossed the river that runs through the middle of the city showed the baser side of people in wartime. It was quite early in the battle, and as we moved down this street we cleared or retook what must have been a warehouse of food supplies. The Filipino civilians in great numbers rushed and crowded into the building and came out with boxes and bags of some kind of flour or rice or both. Some would break on the ground and the people would be pushing, crowding, and trampling on top of each other to get a handful of that food, men, women, and even little children. It was not a pleasant sight. Here these people had been deprived and mistreated for two or three years, but here they were, fighting and pushing one another now, in a very ugly way, to beat each other and get some of that food. It reminded me of animals, hungry cattle or starved dogs.

One time a soldier was out scavenger hunting and was stirring through a burned-out, destroyed part of town when he flushed out a lone Japanese soldier. The GI's .45 army automatic pistol jammed, and evidently the Japanese soldier only had a sword, which he had drawn. The GI turned and ran, the Japanese guy right after him slashing with his sword, almost clipping his coat as they rounded the corner of a building where some other U.S. soldiers were.

Another incident happened toward the end of the battle for Manila. We had worked our way down to the old walled city and then were out in the southeast part toward Hickem Field. We were still among some buildings on the edge of the city where some enemy airplanes had been parked in dirt revetment bunkers, but they were crippled, shot up by our pilots before they could get off the ground. But off in the distance along the field, we could see some people moving around. It was too far for good identification without field glasses, but with our binoculars we were able to identify them as enemy, and though nearly a half mile away, we opened up on them. They in turn opened up on us and we exchanged fire, with very little effect on either side, bullets skipping along the cement around us. This was still a new experience for us, after months of jungle fighting where you seldom ever saw a thing and usually couldn't see more than a few feet most times, to be out where you could see the enemy almost a harmless mile away was very different. We had with us an artillery liaison officer, who capitalized on this opportunity. Like us, the artillery had fired most of their bullets at a target they never saw, so when he saw what looked like a lone soldier riding a bicycle down the road away from us, the artillery officer called back on his walkie talkie to his battery of four or six 155 howitzers and called for battery fire, opening up with every big gun he had on that one, lone Japanese soldier, fleeing on a bicycle.

We holed up for a while there, and while there I climbed over and into a Japanese "Betty." I think it was a twin-engine bomber, and I sat in the pilot seat at the controls and mock flew it.

In Manila in 1945: above, Normand's crew in a street barricade.

Below, makeshift hospital in a former school, and a bit of the widespread ruins of the city.

Above: Normand in Manila in 1945.

Below: Normand in the "hallway of death" in the restored Philippine General Hospital, 1995.

Chapter 10

Southern Luzon Campaign

Moving South from Manila

With the city pretty well taken, part of the 5th Cavalry moved south and east to join with the 7th Cavalry in trying to take the hills of Antipolo. We headed south in our final drive for the liberation of Luzon. It was quite hot, but we were not plagued too much by rain, though we did have occasional showers. For the most part our line of march followed a narrow concrete highway winding its way south through the jungle, or a narrow-gauge railroad track, or both. We moved steadily southward since leaving Manila. We moved in kind of a leap-frog formation; first one troop would take the front line and point and push through the jungle rice paddies, small villages, and barrios, and then it would stop or slow down and the rear troop, mounted on trucks and jeeps, would take the lead for awhile. I don't suppose we were totally clearing the area of enemy as we went, but rather driving a wedge down the lower section of the island. While this was merely another in a continuing series maneuvers I participated in, I pursued it as a matter of course, not knowing or realizing at the time that this would be my final march. I had come to take life one day at a time, not planning or even thinking too much about the next day or what it might bring or where it would lead. We were trained to act and obey, not to question or think. Someone else planned and worried where we would go next or how we would get there. "Yours is not to wonder why, yours is but to do or die."

First we moved to the east, toward Antipolo and the mountain area, where the enemy had dug in and were terrorizing the civilian population, as well as us sometimes, with some kind of a buzz bomb or rocket that was being fired out of some tunnels up in the hills. It was usually at night. I never did learn exactly what they were or how they worked. But they evidently devised some kind of a crude launcher that they would wheel out at night and use to fire the crazy thing. It was referred to as "the crazy bomb" because neither we nor even they ever knew where it would go or who it would land on. It reminded me of some giant fireworks, about as erratic or unpredictable, making sort of a swishing, sizzling sound as it went off and zoomed through the sky. Our reconnaissance couldn't track it down or detect it. Anyway, we were set up on this little hill facing the main mountain and had been there a day or two. I had been given a couple of new replacements for my squad to bring it back up to strength. (One thing the Army did was try to keep the troops up to fairly good battle strength. So as soon as possible after a squad would lose a man, they were given a replacement. Almost like issuing more ammunition, equipment, or rations. I guess that may be where the real term *GI* is drawn from when referring to soldiers—Government issue. It may seem rather cold, but that is really the way it was. I needed a replacement and the army sent me one.) One was an older man, married, with a family back in New York. We called him Pop; I think he was maybe 40 years old.

Quite often at night we would try to dig in on top of a little hill or some other commanding point and set up our machine gun covering a road or trail, and then, if there wasn't too much happening, take turns keeping watch or standing guard. I don't remember just which shift it was, but it would have been one of the earlier shifts on guard that we had given Pop. We had just got to sleep when a grenade went off, right out in front of us. We were in quite dense growth, so you didn't see or throw very far. Instantly, everyone was awake and whispering, "What's up?" Well, Pop had thought he heard something coming up the trail in front, so he had pulled the pin and tossed a grenade at the sound. We waited a bit and nothing happened, so we went back to sleep when "Pow!" another grenade went off. Again everyone was awake and wondering. Again, it was just a noise he had heard. I waited and listened a bit and down in front, every now and then, you could hear some mice or rats or some small animals of some type scurrying or digging around in the leaves and underbrush. It wasn't always easy, but a combat soldier needs to learn to distinguish the varied and many sounds of the jungle. All too often you could give away your well-concealed position if you got too jittery and fired at the wrong sound. Anyway, I cussed him out good and told him not to throw any more grenades, and we all settled down one more time. Shortly after, "Pow!" another grenade went off. By this time, all of our patience had run out and I really got on this rookie. His shaky and apologetic explanation was that he had already pulled the pin on the grenade before I had given him the strict order not to throw any more, and he had sat there and held it in his hand until he began to get numb and he was afraid he couldn't hold it any longer, so he threw this last one just to get rid of it. The rest of the night passed without incident, but there might have been a few less rodents in that part of the woods the next day.

We were advancing down a little narrow-gauge railroad through some quite open territory when the enemy from a building down the track opened up on our scattered troops with 20-mm anti-aircraft guns. The first thing I knew was AA bullets skipping down the railroad track and exploding among us, and soldiers falling off the grade on both sides into the rice paddies. The little station was so effective, we called for planes and artillery, but before our support could go into action, the enemy beat us to it and began dropping artillery rounds on the fields we were scattered in. Our section (two squads) was right near a bridge, and we were able to get down under it for protection. Then we set up our own gun and returned the fire back down the tracks.

It was decided we would break for the trees and jungle about a quarter mile to the left, where we could advance on the station undercover, or bypass it. As we tried to make our way through the open field, the artillery round began to rain down on the scattered and running soldiers. We couldn't run too fast carrying our heavy 2-piece machine gun. Our troop commander, Captain "Mustache" Brown, in a jeep, began ferrying soldiers to the side and back. We had an ex-

SOUTHERN LUZON CAMPAIGN

sergeant, an older peacetime soldier named Cass in our platoon who kind of froze up with battle fatigue and refused to leave the shelter of the railroad to make the dash for the jungle, so we left him there. Capt. Brown went out to get him in his jeep with the mortar shells dropping all around. I recall he stopped to pick me up twice, but I waved him on to someone else both times. One time a round dropped nearby, blowing up a soldier. There didn't seem to be too much of him left, but we loaded him in the jeep. Another was almost a direct hit and there wasn't anything left to gather up. It was almost like you see in the movies, rifle, helmet, and pieces flying in all directions.

Cass must have come into my squad as one of those replacements as we moved southward. He had been in the Philippine peacetime army shortly before the war broke out and had been returned to the States. I don't remember just exactly where or when he came into my squad. He came in as a private, having been a sergeant or corporal but somewhere along the line getting stripped of his military rank (usually that happened for some irregular or disorderly act). He had known a family that lived in Manila when he was there before; the mother was Filipino and the father was French. He wanted to go visit them, so I went with him back to Manila. He found their home, a pretty nice home as places in Manila go. The father was dead, but the mother and two teenage daughters still lived there. The girls were very pretty, with lighter skin and dark hair. They had gotten along surprisingly well during the occupation, I remember thinking. They had a piano and the girls played for us. The mother fixed us a very delicious chicken dinner with biscuits, country gravy, and all the trimmings. Cass, as I recall, was from the country, south Texas I think, and was always talking about chicken and biscuits, especially during some of those times when we would be tired and hungry or low on rations. Anyhow, this was a pleasant experience for me.

As we moved on south with my squad bringing up the rear, we got word from some local people that there were some Japanese in a nearby village. Leaving the main group, I took three men with me and

BEYOND THE BEND

went to check this barrio out. We divided up, two on each side of the street. Pushing or kicking the doors open, we checked the houses one by one. Entering a street-level, junk-cluttered room, my ever-alert eye caught sight of a long-barreled Japanese rifle leaning in a corner behind a small waist-high divider. Quickly stepping around the divider, my M-1 at the ready, I encountered a Japanese soldier crouching on his haunches in the corner. I'm not sure if he was as startled as I, or whether he started to get up or raise his hands to grab his gun or maybe surrender. But whatever it was, he never lived long enough for me to be sure which. My reaction was instantaneous and I probably expended a full clip of bullets. The firing brought my partners and some Filipinos in a hurry.

When we reported back to our command post, the C.O., a lieutenant and late war draftee replacement just fresh from an O.C.S. in the States, was very interested in our report. This was probably his closest contact with the war so far, so he had a lot of questions. One of them, though ignorant, was quite innocent. "Sergeant," he asked, "could you have taken him a prisoner?"

Me, take a prisoner?! Of course, he didn't know me or my brother and his death nearly six months before, so he couldn't be blamed when, almost insulted, I turned and walked away. The guys that were with me told the officer, "Sgt. Laub doesn't take prisoners." But in the days and weeks that followed, that question came back again and again to haunt me, especially on guard duty during the long dark nights alone. Thinking about it, I could probably have taken this guy prisoner. He may have even been wanting or trying to surrender instead of wanting to join his honorable ancestors like that group back in Manila. If he had wanted to join them, he could have taken us both. He still had some grenades, and surely he knew I was coming long before I knew he was there. I couldn't help but wonder if the family members he really wanted to join may have been the woman and two small children in the photo the Filipinos dug out of his pocket. So it did bother me more than I cared to admit, as I pondered what one spared life, just one, especially if it had been my brother, could have meant to me and my family. Just one spared life, and it did bother me.

I Will Fight No More

Throwing his rifle to the ground in 1877 on a Montana hillside, the great Nez Perce Indian leader Chief Joseph made his noble and final surrender to General Howard, the one-armed army general. After successfully out-maneuvering ten army units pursuing him and his 700 people for 105 days on a grueling 1,700-mile chase toward freedom in Canada, to his hounded, weary, sick, and hungry followers he said, "Hear me, my chiefs! I am tired. My heart is sick and sad. From where the sun now stands I will fight no more forever." And he didn't.

I had a similar experience in the Philippines in 1945. I had begun to feel that I had gotten my revenge and then some, but it hadn't brought me any comfort or real peace. My personal and emotional battle surrender, commitment, and declaration took place alone in a Catholic cathedral on the island of Luzon in the closing days of World War II.

A few days after my experience in that village, further south near the famous and still-active Mayon Volcano, on one of my one-man patrols I came out on a ridge overlooking a small valley and village. Although a large enemy force was dug into the side of a nearby hill, the barrio itself, graced by an ancient Catholic cathedral, seemed quite peaceful and deserted. Drawn to it by a strange urge, I'm not sure why, I had to enter that church. Slipping carefully out of the jungle, I entered this holy shrine through a small door in its side. After I had gotten safely inside, my ever-watchful eye caught sight of a life-sized crucifix hanging on the wall, with its half-naked figure of Jesus. Although I wasn't Catholic, I knew what this was. I had been taught who the Son of God was and what He had done for the world and for me. Automatically, I took off my helmet and dropped to a knee in a token of humble reverence.

But then it really hit me. The questions I needed to ask that had probably been troubling my mixed-up soul for some time came to the surface of my mind. Is war and killing the only reason and purpose left in my life, the only thing for which I could live and die? Or somehow, somewhere, wasn't there something bigger and better in this world than death and killing? After two islands, three campaigns, and 160 days spent taking back the Philippines, I was finally beginning to be sick and tired of fighting and killing. It was time I should be. Surely revenge was a very poor reason for living. In fact, were it not for the message and mission of the Savior depicted dying on this crucifix now before me, those possibly unnecessary acts of war would probably haunt me forever. And so my thanks to Him whom this crucifix represented should be forever too. He had died that others might live, I remembered, and in a small measure wasn't that what my brother too had done? And I realized Merril wouldn't have wanted my vengeance, and then I couldn't help thinking what one spared life, just one life, would have been worth.

Then as I still knelt there, my life—the past and the present, the war, my anxious and grieving family back home, my brother and my shattered dreams—all flashed by in a quick, confusing review. Somehow in that dark jungle of sorrow, hate, and deep despair, I had lost sight of life's real purpose and value. Looking on this hand-carved symbol of the dying Son of God, I was struck with a strange and touching feeling there was much more here than just some object of wood and stone. He too had died a violent death, I remembered. But He hadn't been bitter or sought revenge. In fact, according to holy writ, looking down in His agony on the cross at His executers, He had even said, "Father, forgive them; for they know not what they do" [Luke 23:34].

And suddenly, the innocence of my last war victim hit me, and I couldn't help feeling his only reason for being there was because he too had been sent. I had failed the test. Clearly remembering what the Savior had done, I found myself torn with feelings of guilt. Could the

Lord forgive me? Even though I had taken so much revenge? Somehow, if my feelings were right, I finally felt that He could. Wasn't that why He came and why He died? "To this end was I born, and for this cause came I into the world," He had declared [John 18:37]. With my dark and heavy burden beginning for a moment to lift from my sad and troubled mind, I felt to rejoice and give thanks, almost to sing: *Shout it to the sky above. There is more to life than dying. There is faith and hope and love.*

So slowly I got up from my knees, and carefully I walked down the silent aisle until I came to the dusty little treadle organ. It probably hadn't been played for months, but it still worked. Leaning my rifle against its side, I took my seat and began to pump the pedal. I remembered a song my mother used to play and sing, "Whispering Hope," which brought back more long-buried feelings. As I tried to pick the melody out with one finger, some of the beautiful and touching words began to run through my searching and anxious mind.

> *Soft as the voice of an angel breathing a lesson unheard,*
> *Hope, with a gentle persuasion, whispers her comforting word.*

Hope, angels, soft words and comfort—had anything ever been more welcome to a sad and troubled heart?

> *Whispering hope, oh how welcome thy voice—*

Surely no words or song ever came with greater meaning and comfort to anyone than these did to me. Could the soft voice of the angel be my mother, breathing a lesson that needed to be heard, a lesson for me? That hard, bitter, angry soldier who had wanted nothing but revenge melted and crumpled, and I could almost hear my mother's voice, something I hadn't dared hardly allow myself even to think about now for months, whispering and singing to me across 7,000 miles. In a flood of tears that had needed to come but had been suppressed up to this point, I heard myself saying, "Mom, Dad, I'm alive, I want to live, and I want to come home."

From the time my brother had died up to this point, my family back in Utah had received no letters, no word, no news from me. All they knew for sure was that one son was dead, and they expected any day to receive word of the tragic fate of the other. Can anyone begin to imagine how comforted and glad that family would have been, could they have had a quick peek into that distant Catholic cathedral at that moment, to know what was taking place there?

Making my heart in its sorrow rejoice.

The words continued, and their meaning was beginning to come true. I really did rejoice, something I hadn't done for a long time.

When the dark midnight is over, wait for the breaking of day.

I remembered all those dark and lonely nights when I would watch and wait for the breaking of day. Those nights were always sad and lonely, even if there wasn't a battle raging. In fact, a raging battle used to help distract my mind from those lonely, empty hours when the breaking of day brought me no relief from the darkness inside. Now it was different.

Reluctant to leave the peace of this sacred shelter yet, I climbed the unkempt stairs and couldn't resist pulling the frayed rope and ringing the bell. With a newfound hope and lease on life and living, I rang and rang and rang that bell, sort of a physical release for pent-up emotions. I filled the surrounding countryside with the clarion sound of ringing bells. Looking down, I could see faces peeking out of the jungle on all sides, wondering, I suppose, what was going on. But for the moment, I didn't care. At last I was at peace with myself, the world, and my God. My heart was rejoicing for the moment and I couldn't keep it in.

And so I made a personal surrender. From the time I left that Catholic cathedral standing in no man's land, I would fight no more forever, and I didn't. Even though at that very moment on either side of the valley and village, two armies stood poised for their next great

SOUTHERN LUZON CAMPAIGN

battle, my aggressive part in that war pretty much came to a close that day. I had no more need or desire to hunt or pursue the enemy anymore. I let the war and battle take its own course. And the soldiers in my squad couldn't quite figure out the change that had come over me.

"What's happened to you, Sarge?" they would ask. "You're not the same." They couldn't understand why I was content to play low key for the rest of the Luzon campaign. Herris, my Filipino buddy, asked one day what was wrong with me and why wasn't I going into town with the rest of the guys. I didn't drink or gamble, but I had sometimes enjoyed the music and had tried to dance with the pretty dark-eyed girls. I guess a pass to town didn't mean that much to me anymore.

As the Luzon campaign ended, we set up a base camp in the Batangas area. While the fighting went on for a few more weeks as our troops continued their mopping-up operation, fortunately for me, my squad wasn't all that heavily or directly involved in this final part of the Luzon campaign, and I never had to fire another shot.

It was toward the close of our campaign, in a military update that we were given, that we learned we had reached one of the last battle lines where the enemy was attempting a defense and that some famous Japanese general had retreated nearby somewhere and had made a stand. A force of enemy soldiers were tunneled in some hills or mountains also nearby. One of the last things I remember was some of the soldiers going on a little hunting expedition into some caves and tunnels in the Legaspi region near the famous Mayon Volcano and inviting me to go along, but I wasn't too interested anymore and declined the invitation, which was a real switch for me. At this point, I was undergoing some real upheavals in my mind, feelings, and thinking, prompted by the incidents and events I had recently undergone, and my whole position, my goals, my determination, and my desire or lack of it, were all being reevaluated and restructured.

BEYOND THE BEND

SOUTHERN LUZON CAMPAIGN

Cleaning out caves on Luzon while moving south from Manila.

Below: Jungle patrols on Luzon.

Two of the young women Normand got to know at dances towards the close of the Luzon Campaign were Estrezza and Rubeja.

Above: Estrezza, Normand, and Herris, the Filipino who joined Normand's squad in Manila.

Below: A group of young people with whom Normand was friends.

Chapter 11

End of the War

With the Luzon campaign winding down, we were again pulled out for a brief rest period before the final great battle, the one for the Japanese homeland. And from past experience most of us expected that battle to be by far our worst yet.

Last Letter from the Front

Philippine Islands
June 6, 1945

Dear Uncle Vasco,

I sure was glad to hear from you. I received your letter, wrote from Brisbane yesterday. Glad you got a church to go to in Australia, for I think its worth a quite a lot, to of been there, and see for yourself what its like down under and also add one more nation to the long list of places you've already been. If you keep up you'll have been everywhere. I quite liked Australia myself. We met some very nice people there. We made a lot of friends and sure had some swell times. Those people there sure treated us fine. I'm glad you got to see them. I didn't know if they would still remember us. I got a letter from one of the girls, Naomi Shurman, she told me of you being there and what a fine guy all of them thought you were.

No, you never told me about this guy Keith. I can't place him. What's his full name and where did he say he knew me?

I sure hope you do come on up here and it can't be too soon to suit me. I'm getting along fine here. We have at last settled down in a rest camp again, and I believe it will be a little longer this time. For we have only had two short rest camps, one 15 days and the other 10 days, since we started in last October 20th, so I think they figure they can give us a little more now things are settled down a bit. Also to let us get ready for the next one.

I don't know where, but it will probably be the toughest yet, from what's left to work on. Of course, you probably know more about that than I do. Though I would rather be where we were and doing what we were doing before we came to this camp. It was quite a ways south of here. I had my squad and another with us were set up in a small town, not far from a larger town. We were by our selves and not bothered by the higher ups much. We were kinda on our own, had a nice place to stay, beds, chairs and all. And our job was easy, for it was a stationary job, and in all the time we were there, we only had interference once by our little yellow friends.

They had three dances, while we were there. We really had a nice time. I never expect to have it that nice in the army again. And to be considered combat too. We had a lot of Filipino and Chinese friends and they were mostly girl friends at that. Ha Ha

Well, as I guess you know, the rumors about the point system is really going around. But they are making it look good so we filled out cards and tallied up our points. They have picked out some with the most points to go home already. By a lot of good luck, I guess, I barely made the 85 mark, counting a couple or three little old decorations. Of course, I haven't built up any high castles for I am still figuring on being here quite awhile and seeing one more major campaign.

Well I guess I'll close for now. I sure hope to hear of you up here next time I hear. And let me know and I might get off, for I sure want to see you as soon as I can. Write again soon.

As always, a loving nephew,
Normand

Waiting to Go to Japan

While we were still on Luzon, I recall some quite pleasant memories while waiting to go home or to Japan or wherever. In the afternoon, the soldiers could get a pass and a GI truck would take us to the little railroad station, and for a few pesos we could catch the old-

END OF WAR

time narrow-gauge train which ran down through the country. We'd ride to town, where soldiers were welcomed as heroes and treated very well. While many of the soldiers drank liquor and caroused and visited the houses of ill repute, I drank lemonade or pineapple juice, listened to the Spanish type music, and even tried to dance with the very attractive girls, or watched with real interest as they did the tango or rumba and tried to teach me. I enjoyed it very much.

It was around this time that another replacement joined our unit that I should not overlook mentioning, because he was the only other LDS man in my outfit. His name was Gus Hansen and he was from Joseph City, Arizona. He was married and had a family back in the States. I'm not sure just when he joined us, but it was right near the end of the war. He was a good guy and a good friend and I appreciated being with and visiting him.

About the first of August we were once again loaded aboard ships and were out in the China Sea preparing for that last beachhead when we got word that a powerful new bomb, the atom bomb, had just been dropped on Japan. It would end the war and change the world forever. Although we didn't really understand or begin to comprehend the magnitude of this powerful new weapon, we were happy to be sent back to Luzon to a base camp to await further orders. We didn't have to wait long before the day the whole world had been waiting for came—Japan had surrendered. THE WAR WAS OVER!

While some have lamented the horror and mass destruction of dropping the atom bomb, many of the soldiers in the field viewed it as the lesser of two evils. I was glad for more reasons than one. We didn't have to make that last beachhead on the Japanese homeland. Knowing the disposition of our enemy, we were well aware that it would have to be men, women, and children. Anyone and everyone would be the enemy. The Japanese policy had dropped the age of soldiers in 1944 from 19 to 17 years old, but then they went down to the age of 8, training boys to defend the country in case of an invasion. Whom could you trust?

Troop Celebration August 1945

Surely few people welcomed and appreciated the end of war and declaration of peace more than the combat soldiers, so the celebration in the Philippines was no small affair. A free beer ration along with free cigarettes (government issue) was often provided overseas troops when in rest camp, so there was plenty for everyone this time, and the celebrating lasted more than just a night.

Not being a drinker, I didn't get too involved in the celebrating. Over the months I had acquired both respect and a bit of resentment because I didn't indulge in any of the parties, drinking, and carousing binges most soldiers engaged in. I had had some small clashes and provoked some resentment partly because I kept to myself and remained somewhat aloof from the rest of the group. Somewhere in the midst of that gala celebration, someone noticed that Sgt. Laub wasn't there. "He's probably down at his tent," someone said. "If he won't come drink with us, then we'll go drink with him, even if we have to pour it down him," someone else boasted. And then I heard them coming, about eight or ten guys, mostly the cooks, clerks, rear echelon and motor pool personnel, guys from the east coast, New Yorkers, who for some reason had never been that close or friendly with me, a Mormon and westerner.

My squad tent was about halfway down the company street. It was late and I was already in bed. It was a pretty rowdy and vocal group of drunks that staggered down the street to my tent. Though I heard them and knew pretty much why they were coming, I hadn't decided yet what to do, but I still had my rifle and I'm sure they knew that. They stood there, shouting insults and cussing, inviting me to come out. After some more discussions which I couldn't quite hear, they turned around and headed back down the street to continue the rest of the party back at the mess hall. They knew something I didn't until the next morning.

At the same time this group came down the street in front, Hansen and a few of my other buddies came out from behind my tent. Unbeknownst to me, they had also heard the commotion going on and had come down and gathered just behind my tent, ready to come to my aid should the front group try to carry out their loudly proclaimed boasts. Among this group were Hansen, Buckmier, Fink, and others, I'm not sure who all, who told me about it later.

My Courage Failed

It was hard to believe that the war was really over. The shooting and killing had finally stopped and we hadn't even got to Japan yet. But as grand and glorious as August 14, 1945 was, nothing could ever compensate for December 7, 1941, not for me. Where do we go from here? I wondered. While I was glad the war was over, its personal toll cast a dark shadow on my joy.

I had mixed emotions. I wasn't sure I was quite ready for the challenge of going home without my brother. I would sit for hours by a small stream that ran by our camp, pondering the mystery of some words I once read as I watched the moving water come to a quiet stop before moving on, "Still water runs deep." Though I didn't fully understand its meaning or my own feelings at the time, it did bring me a measure of melancholic comfort.

Called into the office a short time later, I was informed that even though General MacArthur had selected our division, the elite 1st Cavalry, as one of the special units to go on to Japan as part of the army of occupation, I wouldn't be going with them. In compliance with the military point system, I had accumulated enough points, through my overseas time, beachheads, battle campaigns, medals and citations, to qualify me to be among the first to be sent home on the rotation plan. I learned that Merle Kincaid, the buddy who had volunteered to help me hold the Philippine General Hospital back in Manila, and I were the only two in our troop to make the cut. We were to be put on a troop ship being booked right then, and together we would sail back to America.

I really wasn't a coward, yet how could I face my family alone? How would I act? What would I do? What would I say? Of course, at first I had planned not to go back, hadn't wanted to go back, and hadn't even expected to go back. How could I? But now that it was about to happen, I wasn't sure I was equal to the test.

I spent some long hours the next few days trying to reshape and rebuild my life, my thoughts, and my future. I sat again by the small stream that ran down the little draw behind our camp, watching its clear water run into some deep, quiet, murky pools, which much like my life and thoughts now, which didn't seem to have any bottom or clarity. For over two years, this jungle wilderness had been my life, had been my world. And for nearly half that time, I had been alone with my hurt and sorrow locked up deep inside. No one had ever shared it; no one had ever put an arm around me and said, "I'm sorry." Of course, that wasn't their job and I didn't expect anything, so I had built a protective wall around myself which kept others out and fenced me in. And I wasn't sure I was ready to come out or let anyone else in.

It was about the 1st of September 1945 that I came to Manila from down south, was cleared, checked out and hauled on a GI truck to the port in Manila Bay where I boarded a ship bound for the USA. We sailed up the west coast of Luzon, somewhere around its northern end and then headed for San Francisco.

A lone, lost, battle-weary soldier sat on the deck of that ship, and watched Manila Bay and the rock of Corregidor fade into the night as we sailed out into the South China Sea. That long-awaited day was not the joyous and jubilant occasion I had once thought it would be. Instead, I found myself quite sad and very lonely, even though the boat was crowded with more than 2,000 soldiers. There was nothing but the wide, wide, blue Pacific between us and home, the land we had left so long ago. The land we had fought for, lived for, and died for—that was why I watched the islands fade into the distance and into the past and found myself torn.

How could I leave, or even think of leaving the land of eternal jungle and ocean that had been my place of wandering residence for almost 24 long and desperate months? This strange and difficult land had been my home, though foreign in a way, and had become part of me and I felt I had become part of it. It was here I had experienced my greatest fears, fought my greatest battles, both without and within. I both learned and paid for life's greatest lessons and that price was not easy or cheap. It was here I had met the greatest trials I ever had been asked to face. It was here I was called to prove myself. It was here, an entire lifetime may have been lived in a few months, a few weeks, or sometimes even a few minutes. It was here I grew up overnight.

My return journey was slow, burdensome, tedious, hindered not only by the wind and the waves, but by the deep, sad, and clinging memories of that which I was leaving buried on a jungle beach along with my brother; part of me seemed to have been buried there too. So at best, I was only half, and half-heartedly, going home. And like the ship I was on, my journey back was beset with many dark and lonely nights before it would reach those golden shores.

For a moment, I see again that lone soldier seated far on the bow of a ship, plowing through the inky black waters of a midnight ocean, churning eastward, carrying the precious load of American soldiers back to their homeland. As the ship rides the tossing waves, he wonders what he will do and how he will act, how he could ever bring himself to meet his family and loved ones at home. They had left home together, so proud, so young and full of assurance. Now he must make the long, sad journey back alone. He is at times still troubled with the thought that maybe it would have been better and easier if he too had fallen, if he had stayed by his brother's side. In life they were never parted, should death now separate them? But fate and destiny had ruled it so, and nothing could hold back the dawn.

The afternoon of September 26, 1945 was a beautiful clear day, filled with the warm sunshine of autumn as the *S.S. Brazil* sailed under the Golden Gate Bridge into the San Francisco Bay. The *Brazil* was laden beyond capacity with U.S. servicemen being sent home on rotation. It would be pretty hard to try to describe the scene of wild joy and ecstasy that burst from these GIs, who had spent months in the steaming, enemy-infested jungles of the southwest Pacific. Now at long last they were getting their first glimpse of this land they had fought for, longed for, dreamed about, and were finally now returning to. An unmistakable din of glee vibrated around the deck of the ship as men cheered, yelled, screamed, and even wept.

I must confess I was numbered with those who wept. I had not wanted to find myself still physically whole and safely aboard that ship, knowing that I was headed home. It didn't make my task any easier to know that of us two, my brother had been the considerate one, while I was selfish. He had been reserved and modest; I was impulsive and cocky. If only one of us was to return, why me? He was the most deserving. We were supposed to have come back to our family together, but if only one of us was coming back, why was it me? For this reason my part in that triumphant landing at Frisco was overshadowed with deep foreboding.

As we docked, I found myself violently torn between joy and sorrow, though my cheeks never knew the warmth of a hot tear, nor my eyes the refreshing mists of visible emotion. Mine was the silent kind, buried deep inside. I suppose to most of the soldiers on that ship, the land whence we came was even now growing dim and had begun to fade into the past and would gladly be forgotten. But to me, that trackless blue waste dotted here and there by tiny specks of green could never be forgotten. Part of me would forever linger down where those rolling waters splash on lonely quiet shores, shores which once rang with the haunting cries of war. Shores stained by the blood of friend and foe alike, who now peacefully sleep together in the suns of perpetual summer, where the ruins of death and destruction lay bleaching in the sands of time.

As we disembarked from the ship, I tried to close that chapter of my life. But I tried in vain. Already seized by a mounting feeling of uncertainty and a deep, different fear than I'd ever known, I began to wonder what I'd do. I knew if I carried through, I would of necessity have to reopen that dark night of the past, and I wasn't sure I was equal to that task. While my courage, both physical and mental, had met many a bitter test, this would be so different, so very, very different.

"Come on Laub. Let's go phone," called Kincaid as soon as we were given the opportunity to call our families.

"Thanks, you go ahead. I will later," I replied as I sat on my bunk. Unable to face the task yet and too restless to sit very still on my first night in the States, I took a stroll down to the camp canteen where a gala party was in full swing. The music was inviting and the American girls really looked good. I had to wait in line, but thanks to some gracious gal, I finally got a dance. To be so close to a real white girl again after all those months was a very pleasant experience in itself, not to mention the dreamy music and dance, and for a brief moment this activity claimed all my attention.

"You don't have much to say, soldier." It was the girl speaking. "You're not like the last one I danced with."

"Who? Me? Oh, I'm sorry," I blurted as it dawned on me I hadn't spoken a word since I asked for the dance.

"Aren't you glad to be back?" she asked.

"Oh sure, sure it's just—say, what's that line over there?" I said, groping for words to change the subject.

"That one?" she said, pointing. "That's where, if you wish, you can make a recording of your impressions and reaction to being back in the States. It's free to overseas veterans, courtesy of the Pepsi-Cola Bottling Co."

"Sounds interesting," I replied, toying with a sudden idea.

"You should make one," she encouraged, "they make nice souvenirs."

"Maybe I will," I said, as I thanked her generously for the dance. That was it. That was the thing to do. I could talk to my folks much easier this way and then send them the recording. Everything was set and the operator flashed the signal, "You're on."

I gulped and swallowed my tongue, but no words came. After a sickening silence I finally stammered, "Hello folks. Well, we're back. I didn't think we'd ever make it, but we finally did." There is no need to say this first attempt, even at an indirect contact, was a miserable failure. I never sent the recording.

For once the army was really on the ball and there weren't any of the usual long, tedious waits. We were shipped to the separation center nearest home and discharged in a matter of days after stateside arrival. I was sent to Ft. Douglas in Salt Lake City, where I was honorably discharged from the United States Army on October 1, 1945.

"There you are Mr. Laub," said the Major as he handed me my discharge papers. I was a free man, a civilian. I could go home or do as I pleased. But I didn't go home, at least not then. I didn't even call and let them know I was out. In fact, it was a long hour before I even left the fort. I spent that hour on the side of the hill by the gate. It had been at this very base just three years before, lacking one month and six days, that my brother and I had entered the army. We were pretty young and inexperienced. How well I remembered our words as we stood before the induction officer and swore to uphold the Constitution of the United States and defend its flag. "Sir, we have enlisted together because we would like to be able to remain together." How these words mocked me now as I stood at the gate alone.

My feelings were poignant as the momentous happenings of the past three years, like a rushing mighty torrent, swept through my mind. How trivial now were the thousand and one fears we had experienced in the first four months before we were finally assigned to a line outfit. Fears born of the total disregard for name, rank, or serial number, so manifest in troop movement, as tens of thousands of men were run like mass production through induction, training, and replacement centers. The blast from a whistle, followed by the sharp command, "Fall out!" brought our hearts to a stop a dozen times a day. "John R. Jones, William A. Black, Isaac David Zimmerman, etc., go pack your things, you're shipping out." And so it went.

Then there was that day, after we had been assigned to a line outfit, when there came the rumor of a really big move, the one at which all the previous training and preliminaries had been aimed. Amid the excitement and bustle of that scene, my brother had been called into the office of the troop commander and invited to stay on as cadre.

"Thanks for the honor, Captain," he had said, "I'd rather not. My brother will be shipping. We enlisted so we could be together, and I joined this man's army to fight. Thanks, but I'd really rather go." That had been a long time ago. If he had only stayed then, maybe now . . . . But an eternity blotted forever that wish. Oh how I wished that those years had never been.

> *Turn back, turn back, O, ye sands of time*
> *Let the fleeting years cease to fly,*
> *Let memory bridge the fateful past*
> *To those who fell, but never die.*

How these words surged through my mind and I would that I could shout them to the world. For like my brother, there were 400,000 other brave Americans who would never return. My thoughts went out to them also, and to their homes and their people, and though those people didn't and never would know me, yet I felt a kinship with them. And from my thoughts of them and their sorrow, I drew a bit of strength to help me to do what I had to do and should have been glad to do—return to comfort and tell my people.

But somehow, I still belonged to another world, and though the traffic and bustle of a busy city filled my ears, a silent call from the distant islands filled my heart. I finally mustered courage enough to contact some of my relatives living in the nearby city, and in company with some of them, I gently eased back into the civilian social circle. There was the customary round of visits, a party, a dance and so on. But no one dared to mention my brother, and I was thankful for that.

My Uncle Vasco, also a serviceman with the rank of a lieutenant colonel, finally persuaded me to call my folks down in the little town of Enterprise, Utah, some three hundred miles away. That is, he got them on the line and I finally took it after much hesitation, which ran up a fifteen-dollar bill. I don't remember what I said in this first conversation, but it was quite brief and formal. It was decided that I would stay in Salt Lake City and they would drive up and get me.

In my family there were my father and my mother, my two sisters, and then three brothers much younger. I didn't meet them when they arrived in the city, and though it was hardly excusable, several hours elapsed before I did. It wasn't that I didn't want to see my folks and talk to them, for deep down that was the thing I wanted more than anything else, but I got pretty shaky and weak when I thought about meeting my family face to face. I had that wall around myself, and my deep hurt was locked inside. My emotions had been bottled up and never allowed to show. My brother's name and his death had become an untouchable subject, never mentioned or discussed aloud. This was the barrier which now stood between me and my folks, and I lacked the courage to face them for I was afraid of the moment when they would tear my barrier down.

Fortunately or unfortunately, when our first meeting finally took place, it was in a hurry and in a crowd. It was Sunday and we were all on our way to church. Somehow I managed to keep that barrier up, so our first meeting was cool and formal, even a bit mechanical. I suppose my beloved family experienced a misgivings about this meeting too, because of my actions and behavior, though I never meant to hurt them in any way. I did kiss my mother, but social etiquette would have called for that anyhow.

The real meeting with my folks, the one I had feared so much, took place several hours later when we were finally alone. Nobody had to tear the barrier down—it suddenly crumbled and fell and was washed away in a flood of tears, as my pent-up grief found release from the silent prison. Like a mighty torrent, the bitterness in my soul poured out, and the dark door of the past opened to the only people in all the world I could open it to, those I most needed to open it for. Yes, my courage had failed, but it was the best thing that could have ever happened to me. My healing, badly wanting and needing, finally began.

I thought of all of the families whose sons, brothers, fathers, or husbands would never return, those who would never know but would forever wonder and long to hear what really happened to their loved ones at the end. I realized what a blessing and comfort it could be to them to have any kind of a last word, message, or report from or about them. Sort of a message from the dead, if you will. I suddenly felt my obligation to my own family. How could I ever have thought not to fulfill this special privilege for my own beloved family?

THE COMMANDING GENERAL
FIRST CAVALRY DIVISION

Takes pleasure in commending

Private First Class NORMAND D LAUB 19171808,
Troop D, 5th Cavalry
upon receipt of the Bronze Star Medal

CITATION:

As announced in General Orders No. 22, Headquarters 1st Cavalry Division, dated 23 February 1945, Private First Class NORMAND D LAUB 19171808, Cavalry, United States Army, for meritorious achievement in connection with military operations against the enemy at Bagatoon, Leyte Province, Philippine Islands, from 5 December 1944 to 8 December 1944. While on a reconnaissance patrol to investigate enemy activity and terrain in the vicinity of Bagatoon, Private LAUB operated continuously for four days and four nights as point and scout for his patrol, constantly pushing ahead seeking a route through the desperately difficult and unreconnoitered mountain terrain which had stopped the previous attempts of other patrols. Unmindful of the danger of moving through this enemy infested area, he broke trail and sought out possible routes of advance in order to save unnecessary and exhausting steps for his comrades. His untiring efforts and dogged persistence in the face of such discouraging obstacles materially aided the successful accomplishment of the mission and greatly inspired his fellow soldiers.

Verne D. Mudge
Major General, U.S.Army

Normand's Bronze Star Citation.

END OF WAR

His second citation, for an Oak Leaf Cluster, read as follows:

"Corporal Normand D. Laub 19171808, Cavalry, United States Army for heroic achievement in connection with military operations against the enemy at Manila, Luzon Island, Philippine Islands, on 24 February 1945. When an enemy demolition charge blew out a section of a wall of a building held by Corporal Laub and his squad, many of the men were seriously injured and their machine gun was damaged beyond repair. The squad was forced to withdraw to an adjoining room for protection. Corporal Laub, together with a comrade, returned to the original position to guard it for the night. During the night a force of approximately twenty Japanese attacked their position. Corporal Laub and his comrade, despite overwhelming odds and though armed only with rifles and grenades, held their position and killed a large number of the enemy, forcing them to withdraw. The courageous act of Corporal Laub was responsible for the repulse of the enemy's counterattack and enabled our troops to accomplish their mission. Hugh Hoffman, Brigadier General, U.S. Army, Commanding."

The "high point" men, including Normand, were deployed home from Luzon before the rest of the 1st Cavalry went to Japan.

Chapter 12

My Mission and My Marriage

So Much Guilt

> *Empty saddles in the old corral.*
> *Where do you ride tonight?*

These words of a sentimental western ballad we used to sing became a striking reality when I finally got back to the home ranch. Even our favorite horses seemed to sense something amiss, especially Merril's big bay, Diamond, a blooded horse we had bred and raised, and my little pin-eared Snipe, a western mustang I had caught as a colt and raised on a bottle. While it was good to be home, things would never quite be the same anymore. All those cowboy plans and dreams didn't seem to fit after the war.

I found it hard to settle down and difficult to adjust. I also returned feeling a lot of guilt. I had felt so much hate after Merril was killed and had taken so much revenge. In the jungle and street fighting, I had seen, face to face, many of the Japanese I had killed, and I still wondered if I could have taken some of them as prisoners. The bishop had me meet with our stake Patriarch Jones, and he told me that I should not feel guilty, that this was war and that I had to do my duty. I had overcome my revenge and had paid my price. My life had been preserved for a reason and that I should go on with my life trying to fulfill that purpose.

Though never quite at peace, I allowed myself to become caught up in material things. I found a girlfriend who began to fill an empty void in my life. I was thinking seriously of getting married. I avoided the question of serving a mission for the Church as long as I could. When my bishop approached me about going on a mission, I wasn't sure I wanted to leave home again and said, "Bishop, I'll go because that's the way I been raised, but I want you and this Church to know I'm making a great sacrifice for it."

Home Together

I was called to serve in the Central States Mission, which at that time in 1947 comprised all of the states of Missouri, Kansas, Oklahoma, Arkansas, and a small part of Illinois. I hadn't been in the mission field very long when I began to realize that this was not a sacrifice but a blessing. The unseen hand that had watched over and protected me in spite of myself during the war was not only still there, He knew exactly what I needed most and had a mission for me to perform. I frequently fell to my knees and gave the Lord my humble thanks. Going on a mission was not only the best thing that could have ever happened to me, it provided a spirit and opportunity I could not have received in any other way. To go from a mission of wanting to destroy life to one of trying to save it was a contrast and blessing beyond compare, and one I was reluctant to leave.

Because my mission was such a rewarding and fulfilling experience, I sometimes found myself feeling bad that Merril couldn't have lived to enjoy some of these beautiful experiences also. He would have been a great missionary and had planned to go if the war had not come. Then one early morning in Poplar Bluff, Missouri, in kind of a vision he came to my room and said, *"Don't feel bad for me. I'm on a mission. I'm doing exactly the same thing you're doing, teaching people the gospel, and I've been granted permission to stop by and tell you."*

I got the impression it was the same kind of mission mentioned by St. Peter in his first epistle, 1 Peter 3:18–20 and 4:6, where he explained that the gospel was being preached to those who may have died without hearing it. When I remembered the thousands of soldiers killed during the war, including many in our own outfit who may not have heard of or known the gospel, I had at last the answer to that question, why Merril was taken, that I so desperately sought and prayed for. I couldn't contain my tears as I rejoiced, thinking in the words of another most meaningful hymn:

> *Unanswered yet? The prayer your lips have pleaded,*
> *In agony of heart these many years?—*
> *Say not the Father hath not heard your prayer;*
> *You shall have your desire, sometime, somewhere—*
> *Amid the wildest storm, faith stands undaunted,*
> *Nor quails before the loudest thunder shock.*
> *She knows Omnipotence has heard her prayer,*
> *And cries, "It shall be done," sometime, somewhere.—*

So I learned that God is not unfair, nor does His word and promise go unfulfilled, but He does have His reasons and purposes which we can't understand. I also learned to love and appreciate this beautiful truth from these comforting words of another very understanding poet:

> *Not 'til the loom is silent and the shuttles cease to fly*
> *Will God unfold the pattern and explain the reason why.*
> *The dark threads were as needful in the weaver's skillful hand*
> *As the threads of gold and silver in the pattern that he planned.*

This story of faith, of sorrow, and of love would not be complete, however, without noting one final miracle and Divine blessing of fulfillment.

In the fall of 1948 while I was still serving my mission in Missouri, the War Department sent my brother's body home for burial in America. The Mission President, Francis W. Brown, agreed it would be good for me to attend that memorial service in southern Utah. He obtained permission for me to leave the mission. For some reason I missed the through train I had planned to take to St. Louis and had to take a later train. This later train met a baggage car from the west coast in Ogden, Utah and added it to our train. As we headed south for Modena, the little rail station in southern Utah where my brother and I had bid a tearful farewell to our family six years before, I learned from some of my relatives also on the train the almost unbelievable but overwhelming news that my brother's body was now on this train. I couldn't contain my emotions or the spirit that filled my soul and the unseen presence I also felt was there as we approached the rail station where my unsuspecting folks were waiting.

So at last, after an amazing procession of events, and because of the love of a just and caring God, my brother Merril and I did return home together like we had always planned—even if it was during temporary leave from our separate missions for the Lord—one in a flag-draped casket, representing the supreme sacrifice of service to country and fellowmen, the other standing, gratefully acknowledging the gift of a love-filled mission of service to God and fellowmen.

Of Spoons and Blood

One of the special experiences during that mission came when we were asked to do "country tracting," where we traveled through the rural area on foot during the summer months without purse or scrip, like they did of old, depending on the people we traveled among to feed us and give us a bed for the night. We were promised that if we were faithful we wouldn't go hungry or have to sleep out. To avoid being picked up for vagrancy in our modern world, however, we did carry some money with us, but we were encouraged to depend on the Lord and the people for our sustenance. This was a very humbling but also a very rewarding experience, and we met and baptized some great people. Many of the people who took us in and treated us the best were often some of the humblest and poorest in the country.

As we were tracting, we would explain to the people who we were and what we were doing, and we'd carefully try to hint our needs. But then as darkness came, if we hadn't got an invitation, we would finally start asking if they could put us up for the night. This was really quite hard for me at first and made me feel like a beggar until I came to realize how dependent we were on the Lord's help. We often met people we might never meet or see, and we were granted some experiences and opportunities few people seldom have.

On our first day out of Poplar Bluff, Missouri, we visited several homes and farms along the way, but none took the hint or invited us to stay. Late in the afternoon, a typical Missouri summer storm began to build in the north with heavy black clouds and ominous flashes of lightning. As darkness came, realizing what was about to happen, I finally humbled myself and told my junior companion, "We need the Lord's help," noting He had called us out here and promised us shelter. "But I guess we need to ask."

So we knelt down by the side of that country road and made our needs and wishes known, though it was now dark and not a very good time to ask a stranger for a bed. At the very next place, the man was about to say no and shut the door, like all the others had, when something seemed to stop him. He hesitated for a moment, opened the door back up and said, "Oh, come on in. We will try and fix you a place." We had barely gotten inside when the storm hit with terrible winds and rain. So we did give the Lord our thanks that night in the small room they gave us to sleep in.

Most of the people in this area were sharecroppers, and often the women and children had to help hoe cotton, so I helped the little girl with the dishes the next morning after her mother had gone to the field. While we were working together, showing the apprehension they had, she looked up at me and said, "You didn't have a gun in your briefcase to shoot us with, did you?"

Another evening as we were walking down a typical country road a bit farther on, we came to a very prosperous looking farm surrounded by a neat white board fence with a big, nice two-story house. There were also some well-built barns and sheds with a herd of fat, white-faced cattle grazing in the pasture. A well-graveled quarter-mile lane led from the main road to the big house with its well-kept yards and lawns. The middle-aged lady who answered the door was polite but cool, and when we told her we needed a place to stay for the night she said she was sorry, but they didn't have any room.

By now it was getting dark and there weren't any other places in sight, but we started on down the road because there wasn't much else we could do. A little farther on we saw a dim light through the trees on the other side of the road. Finding the path that led to that light, we came to a small, one-room, rough lumber cabin. The young man who answered our knock invited us in. After briefly explaining who we were and what we were doing, he consulted with his young wife and said that if we didn't mind sleeping on the floor we were welcome to stay. They took a rope and stretched it across the room and hung some sheets over it to divide the room for us and them and their two little boys. On finding out that we hadn't had any supper, the gracious young mother warmed up some leftover soup and gave us a glass of milk and a slice of homemade bread, for which we were very grateful.

The next morning this special family also invited us to have breakfast with them. As I remember, among other things we had oatmeal mush. My companion and I were seated on a bench together on one side of the table. Of course, their dishes weren't all that fancy and it pressed them, I'm sure, to put together enough silverware for all six of us. My companion had a knife and a fork, but no spoon. Sensing the possible lack of utensils he tried to make the best of what he had, awkwardly trying to scoop his cereal with his fork. Suddenly our hostess noticed his dilemma, and bless her innocent, unselfconscious reaction, she looked over at him and exclaimed, "Oh Elder, you didn't get a spoon. I'm sorry. Here, take mine." Then licking hers off, she handed it to him. He took it graciously and finished eating his cereal, not wanting to offend her. What else should he do?

It was about then that the thought suddenly hit me and I wondered, "What kind of table setting could my mother provide if she should have some unexpected company to feed?" As I thought back, I realized that I really hadn't ever paid much attention to what kind of table setting we had in our modest little home. I'm sure it wasn't all that fancy, and for sure not many pieces matched and some were strained and tarnished even if we had enough. Having added a bit of culture and a little more etiquette to my own country manners by now, I suddenly was aware that here was something my own family's home might be needing.

When fall came, my companion and I were transferred from the country to St. Louis for the winter months. Now an aging 23, this would be my fourth Christmas away from home. The other three of course had been spent in the armed services during World War II, two of which had been in the steaming jungles of the south Pacific where my brother Merril was killed. This would be the first time I had the opportunity, now that I had the maturity, to purchase something I felt my mother really needed and that was worthwhile as a special Christmas gift.

In St. Louis, for one of the first times since the war, stores were able to splurge and spread their Christmas wares in their sidewalk windows. As we often walked past this big department store to catch a downtown street car, one of the things that caught my eye was the most beautiful sterling silverware set I'd ever seen, six-piece place settings with service for eight, 52 beautiful pieces. The price was a modest $35.80, but back then, that was more than half my total December budget.

It's funny how in all of my growing-up years, something like a silverware set, and probably many other household items, had never caught my attention or really meant that much to me before. I suppose I had either never even noticed or else had taken things like table settings for granted. But this was extra pretty, an 1881 Rogers sterling silver set with a beautiful rose pattern in a nice gray case lined with pretty blue velvet. The knives were neatly tucked in their places in the lid which was open for display, and I couldn't help but remember that breakfast in the country during the summer every time I passed this window display.

It was now late November, and with Christmas coming soon, this beautiful set in its fancy case really caught my eye, and I went in and admired it several times as we passed the store. The same friendly clerk noticed this and asked some questions about my compelling interest. Because of my not having all the money to buy it then, she became quite sympathetic and suggested that I could pay a deposit and she could hold it for me for a while to ease my fear that it might get sold while I tried to figure out how to get the money to pay for it. There was no way I could get money from my folks, as they were having a hard time even getting together the money that was keeping me in the mission field, and I didn't want them to know anyway.

About this time, a well-known physician, a Dr. Keller from Utah who was quite involved in the famous Barns Medical Center in St. Louis, who was also a member of the Church and in our little branch, mentioned that the medical facility was short of whole blood and was paying around $10 a pint to anyone who would be interested in selling, not donating blood.

Both my companion and I were definitely interested, and so Dr. Keller set it up for us to go the next day to do so. We were tested and qualified, but there was a waiting period between each drawing. I was able to pay a deposit to hold the silverware set and the clerk took it out of the window. Then after the waiting period, I sold another pint of blood to make another payment, but I wouldn't have enough to finish paying for it until after Christmas. The sales clerk had by now learned my story, including a bit about my brother in the war, and so she was very sympathetic and let me have the set on the 20th of December so I could get it mailed to Utah. We had agreed for me to make the final payment between Christmas and New Year's after I sold another pint of blood. Surely this was how I learned to better understand and appreciate this famous little quote:

He who gives money gives much,
He who gives time gives more,
But he who gives self, gives all.

So, thanks to a humble, country family's poverty, this became a real opportunity for me. Although it literally did cost me some blood to get my mother a nice silverware set for Christmas, it was well worth it. My wife and I now enjoy this same lovely set in its pretty silver and blue-lined box, and it stirs some very special memories of a Christmas many years ago.

Home from My Mission

To leave home to serve a mission so soon after my return from the war hadn't been all that easy. Yet once I was out there and began to be blessed and comforted by that beautiful missionary spirit, I often thanked the Lord from my knees for this special blessing and call. And my mission became such a beautiful experience that I didn't want it to end, so I asked for an extension and was granted an extra three months.

I finally began looking forward to going home and trying to pick up my life where I had left off after the end of the war. My very rewarding and fulfilling mission to the Central States Mission for The Church of Jesus Christ of Latter-day Saints came to an end in early March 1949. My life and world had undergone some major changes and adjustments in my views in the past 26 months. There was a future, a very important and glorious one to be pursed with hope and gladness.

I had learned, taught, and come to firmly believe that the utmost purpose and fulfillment in this life was to find and marry the right person in the right place at the right time, and that this really was the essence of the gospel. I had been preaching and come to love that this really was the will of the Lord and His divine plan for all of His children. In fact, a pretty popular saying at that time for all the soldiers whose marriage dates had been postponed because of the war, and then for some of us delayed another two years for a mission, was "If you are not married six months after you get home, your mission has been a failure." Not just marriage, but to marry the right girl was the most important thing one could choose to do in this life.

Elder Stan Staheli and I served in the Central States Mission at the same time. We went out together and came home together. As the first returned missionaries to return home to Enterprise, Utah after World War II, we were kind of celebrities, quite welcomed and respected in the area and by most of the people. We were accorded many of the same honors, being invited to speak in several wards around the area, Cedar City, Milford, Gunlock, and all of the Uvada Stake wards. Looked up to as heroes of sorts, we enjoyed a bit of extra attention from many of the local girls.

It might seem strange that I didn't go back to my cowboy life when I at long last got the chance. Soon after I arrived home from my mission, one of the famous local cowboys came to see me. He invited me to go with them on a big cattle drive, one that would last several weeks. But serving the Lord, going to church and worshipping on Sunday had become my number one priorities. So I told him, "I have a new range boss now. I won't be able to go."

Courtship and Marriage

I seemed to have always had a pretty strong interest in and feeling for members of the opposite sex, especially some of the nicer, attractive, and more friendly females, so I wasn't too hard to convert to the idea of marriage. But who and where was that special girl for me? I had had a few casual girlfriends over the years, and after the war I had associated with a number of girls in the southern Utah and Enterprise area, but because of the war and my mission, I had really had limited exposure to girls and dating over all.

After the war and before my mission, I had become quite attracted to and serious with a fairly close relative (a cousin) from Gunlock, Blythe Bowler. Her folks, the Henry Bowlers, felt the family relationship was a bit too close and I probably didn't have much in material goods or education to offer either, so they were not too interested in this match continuing. But we did get pretty serious, sharing and enjoying quite a bit of time together, and we even thought and talked of getting married after I got back from my mission. We had even driven down by the St. George Temple and talked of the day we would be married there.

Time and feelings do change, and by the time I had been on my mission six months, Blythe had found another beau, Dean Terry, son of one of the more prominent and well-to-do families of ranchers in Enterprise. Her letters to me, which at first were very sweet and faithful and which I so looked forward to, became fewer and fewer and finally stopped. It was her mother who finally wrote and told me she was engaged and going to marry Dean. I presume the more distant kinship and seemingly greater share of material things made this match more acceptable, at least to Henry, but Dean's commitment to religion wasn't the best and he couldn't take Blythe to the temple to be married as I had thought she wanted and had planned. For a brief period this was sad and disappointing for me, but thankfully, by that time my love for and involvement in my missionary work for the Church quite filled my life and world, so it wasn't all that hard to accept it and get over her. Besides, there were plenty of good LDS girls in the mission field as well as some lady missionaries who were interesting.

About the time that Blythe got married, a slightly younger girl back home whom I had gotten acquainted with earlier and had casually dated a time or two, Rose Elise Lund from Modena, started writing to me. I had dropped her and she wasn't quite as affectionate and serious as I had hoped. But once I was coming home, however, I wondered, was she a possible prospect? But when Stan and I stopped in Provo to see Rosie and her sister, who Stan had also been interested in, Rosie was out on a date with a boyfriend. This was a bit of a disappointment to me right off the start, making the field still pretty open for me.

Shortly after my return home, my Grandmother Bowler told me about a new girl in town, Barbara Jensen (Page), whose family had moved to Enterprise while I was gone. Grandma probably knew that a returned missionary who had also spent three years in the army would be looking not just for a girlfriend, but a wife. Grandma was very impressed with this young lady as she observed her because of her sincere love of the Church and testimony of the gospel Grandma had heard her give. Was it merely by accident, or was it fate or design that I was able to meet and be introduced to this fair, golden-haired young lady the very first Sunday I was home? She was the Sunday School secretary and was going down the stairs to the basement of the old church for prayer meeting as I was going up the stairs, having been invited to speak to a priesthood group that had met in the basement before Sunday School. I don't remember all that much about the meeting except that she was quite pretty with her long golden-blonde hair.

Destiny wasn't through with us yet though, and on the next Tuesday after MIA (Mutual Improvement Association) as was the custom, they held a dance. During the dance they had a broom dance where you can take a broom and give it to the boy dancing with a girl you want to dance with, and he has to let you have her. I decided I would like to dance with Barbara, so when I got the broom I laid it down and went over to where she was sitting and asked her to dance. I welcomed the opportunity to hold her as we waltzed around the hall.

In the next twist of fate, the MIA officers were asking for more couples to practice the MIA dances for the Gold and Green Ball and June Conference Dance Festival in Salt Lake. Wanting to support the Church, Stan Staheli and I volunteered. I asked Barbara if she would be my partner although we hardly knew each other, and Stan took Lila Huntsman. Although neither of us remember this being anything but a normal social friendship and participation in a Church activity, Bishop Leland Huntsman, (Enterprise only had one ward at the time) said later that he saw sparks flying that night and knew this was going to be more than just a casual match up. I drove her up to the high school gym where the dance practice was in my dad's little stake rack pickup, the only vehicle we had. Most of the other dancers were young married couples, but we joined them and started learning the dances. After the practice I took her home, and as I said good night to her on her front porch, I gave her a very generous missionary handshake and thank you. And thus for the next few weeks this very casual, almost routine, relationship and association continued, nothing more. We did become a little better acquainted, but I was still quite open and looking.

The next twist of fate was that somewhere about this time the city of Enterprise was looking for a new sheriff. The old one, Carl Emmett, retired. The mayor, Alma Truman, approached me and asked if I would take the job. The city had just moved uptown and joined the modern world, having installed several stop signs along the main street, and they wanted someone to help enforce the new regulations. To make it more of a fulltime job and justify the city wage of about $75.00 a month, the new sheriff also became the city water master, running and regulating the city water for family lots and gardens in their extensive, open-ditch system from a city well. This well was right by Barbara's stepfather's and mother's place, the Geary Page residence, which made another convenient follow-up to our social arrangements.

In April I was very desirous to attend the General Conference in Salt Lake, as well as the Central States Mission reunion which was held in connection with the conference, where I could see many of the former missionaries and some of the saints from my mission field, many of them, particularly the young women, longing to gather to Zion. The folks took me up but didn't stay, as conference in those days lasted over three days. Stan and I stayed and enjoyed the reunion and visited with many of our former companions as well as the saints.

I even double-dated a former sister missionary, a Sister Olsen from Salt Lake who was now home, with Elder Hallmark, who was also dating a former sister missionary. We four went to a dance. Sister Olsen was probably in her mid- or late 20s and had either been married or lost a boyfriend in the war. It was on this date that I bravely but carefully indulged in my first real goodnight kiss with a girl, after those two years of mission restrictions. I'm not sure if it was she or I who initiated the action on her back porch, the thing I do clearly remember was that it wasn't quite what I had expected. It was what some call a wet kiss more than a tight-lipped smack, something quite new to me. I thought that maybe she didn't know how to kiss, but maybe it was actually me. There was nothing serious there and I was still looking.

There were some prospective girls from the mission field probably looking too, but no real attractions, although one young lady convert, who even moved to Salt Lake and got a job, later told me she wore her heart on her sleeve, but I didn't seem to notice.

Stan Staheli and I stopped in Provo on our way home after the conference to visit Stan's sister Ann and family who lived there. While there I saw a pretty blue 1947 Plymouth sedan that I quite liked on a used car lot. The salesman made a real good sales pitch of course; this car was already two years old, and I fell for it. I had planned to get a car, but they were still not all that available after the war as they had just started making new cars again. By calling home, which wasn't easy in Enterprise as they had to call my dad to the one local phone, we were able to arrange to make a deal, made some promises, signed some papers, and Stan and I drove that new blue Plymouth home the next day.

As the new sheriff, I needed a patrol car and the city didn't furnish one, but they installed a little fender combination red light and police siren on my new car when I got home, and I became a modern sheriff and patrolman. Besides that, I now had a car to spoon or sport in, along with an official job and position and an excuse to be on or stop by the Page street nearly every day. Barbara and I became good friends and she even accompanied me on some of my Church speaking invitations as well as on trips checking and regulating the water, and at times catching those who didn't stop at the new stop signs. (I finally started turning my head so I wouldn't see so many not stop.)

The dance practices were continuing on a regular basis, and Barbara and I became pretty regular partners, with me now taking her to and from the dance practices. We were seeing more and more of each other and seeming to like and enjoy what we were feeling. She was a lovely girl, with her long blonde hair, fair skin, blue-green eyes, cheerful smile, and pleasant personality. I have to admit that her pretty long blonde hair attracted me, and her apparent interest in and love for the Church and the gospel was a quality any good returned missionary would desire and look for in a wife. This was one of the things we enjoyed together and often talked about. As the season progressed, so did this budding romance and we began to think and talk seriously of our future.

Barbara's mother bought her a pretty blue formal dress for the dance festivals, but unfortunately some of the married dance couples couldn't get away the last minute, so the Enterprise Ward didn't take a group that June. She looked real good in blue and I really liked the dress but jokingly told her mother it was the wrong color (referring to the need for a white wedding gown). There was a bit of a problem here, however. As an A student in school, Barbara had earned a scholarship and planned to attend BYU to continue her education. Her folks, particularly her mother, felt she should go on to school and not get married yet, and she was still only 17, so she was not quite of age either. I remember spending hours debating the pros and cons of life, education, and purposes with her folks. I was sure I wanted to marry her, and finally I said it was a good thing I had just recently returned from a mission where I had been quite often involved in and got pretty good at debating my views or I'm not sure I could or would have hung in there arguing my case. I might have decided this argument was going nowhere and just given up. But I didn't give up and in the end I won.

It was a difficult time for her too. She had grown to love me and was pretty sure she did want to marry me and become that eternal companion I had dreamed and preached about. She did want to please her mother and had planned to go on to college, but since at my age I didn't really want to wait and she didn't want to lose me, it made a pretty difficult decision for her. But the firm, friendly, missionary handshake had been replaced with a very warm and affectionate goodnight kiss and sometimes even a couple or so. And so in due time she consented to accept a modest engagement ring which I was able to purchase from a traveling salesman on the installment plan.

Barbara received her patriarchal blessing in June and the patriarch told her she had chosen or already promised someone in the spirit world that she would be his eternal companion, so she needed to be sure. She had also promised certain spirits that she would be their mother on earth. She did have a special calling and heritage to fulfill. Years later this same Patriarch, aging Brother Arthur Jones, told her one day that she had made the right choice, which was comforting and good to know, since we had been married some time and had a family by then!

We set our wedding date for November 30th, after her 18th birthday on November 5th. Of course we had hoped to win her mother over by then, but I'm not sure even by then we had totally convinced her. But by then we had long since decided we knew what we felt and wanted.

Besides planning for a fall wedding, which Barbara did most of, we started designing and planning to build a home. My father had given me a lot north of their house and had given my sister Ruby and her husband, Leo Stewart, one next to it to build our homes on. Building basement homes was quite common during this period and certainly more economical for young couples just trying to get started to move into and then build on top later. Both Leo and I had basements dug, and with some good volunteer help from the townspeople, we were able to pour the walls and floors.

My sisters had showed me a pretty complete home furniture set advertised by Standard Furniture of Salt Lake City for $500. So when we went up to October conference, we also looked at and picked out the entire set with a nice cedar chest added as a bonus.

The Central States Mission held its missionary reunion in connection with the conference as usual, and quite a few of the members and saints from the mission field came out for it. With potential Church-member husbands pretty scarce in the mission field, many of the young ladies were always interested in the elders. When I introduced Barbara to them as my fiancée, some would kind of ask why I should need to rob the cradle.

Being the local sheriff, a pretty respected Church speaker and returned missionary, I found that our forthcoming wedding had the prospects of being a pretty big event for our little town. Some of the rowdy, wilder group of war veterans and men were already bragging about the special chivareeing they were going to give us, so we decided to out-wit them. We delayed our wedding reception about ten days after our marriage, after we returned from the honeymoon we had also quite carefully planned.

The Most Important Day

This most important of all days, our wedding day, November 30, 1949, dawned bright and clear in the little town of Enterprise as I went to pick up my special bride, Barbara Ruth Jensen, at her folks' home up by the town well. That long looked-for, waited-for and hoped-for time had finally come. As some great thinkers had declared, it was probably the single most important day in our entire life's span according to a perceptive evaluation of the three greatest events in our mortal lives, the day we are born, the day we marry, and the day we die. And since we personally have very little say about our birth and death, the day we unite with another person in marriage and begin our own special human social unit is the most important choice we make, besides being life's most beautiful occasion.

Probably the only sad note to this very sacred and joyous occasion was the fact that she was the only member of her family who could go to the temple. Quite sadly her mother still wrestled with some mixed feelings about Barbara's getting married instead of going on to school, and maybe she wrestled with our marriage a little because her first marriage didn't take place in the temple and had already ended in an unhappy divorce.

So Barbara went alone with me to St. George to the temple where we were to be married and sealed together, not only for this life, but forever. My mother, father, Ruby, Leo, and LaRee were at the temple to be with us. Barbara's younger sister, Sherlene, and a friend caught a ride to St. George where they did a super job of painting and decorating our car to fit newlyweds and to be there to throw rice on us as we came out of that beautiful and sacred temple.

We didn't quite get our new little basement home finished before the wedding, but rather than move into the post-war city housing complex that many of the veterans and young couples were moving into, we moved into a little one-room pioneer cabin my father and his brother had built on the old Enterprise Reservoir Ranch nearly thirty years before. When my folks lost that ranch, they moved the little cabin to Enterprise on the back of their lot. We fixed it up and it became our honeymoon cottage for four months while we finished the little four-room-and-bath basement home enough to move into.

Elder Normand Laub, missionary.

"Home Together,"
the funeral for
Merril Laub
in Enterprise, Utah.

MY MISSION AND MY MARRIAGE

Normand and BarbaraLaub
November 30, 1949

Chapter 13

Life Goes On

Starting a Farm

Now I was ready to settle down and be somebody and do something worthwhile. In view of my high ambitions to serve my fellowmen, it amazed some that I chose the role of a farmer. I might have gone to school; indeed, I thought seriously of doing so, having suddenly acquired a driving thirst for knowledge, but that would come later. For one thing, the spirit of the great outdoors still burned deep in my bosom, and having now married, I wanted my children to have the privilege of growing up close to nature. Then too, I had witnessed hunger and starvation among the peoples of the world and had learned what the absolute necessities of life really are and where they came from. To help produce and provide these necessities for myself and others seemed not beneath the dignity of human nobility.

With nothing but my bare hands and the vigor of youth, I set out to achieve this goal. Starting from scratch, I purchased a tract of 80 acres of desert wasteland on time. By drilling a well and installing a pump, I soon had underground water gushing forth on the thirsty desert, and after much determined labor, it became green and productive. But my little enterprise consumed huge amounts of time, energy, and money. The first two I had, but the third became an increasing problem. And then because of an economic condition known as the price-cost squeeze, this first hill became a towering mountain. But my philosophy was, "Once one had set his hand to the plow, he should never turn back." There was only one thing to do—climb.

This I did, despite the fact that during that first year of trying to make a farm, once again the hand of death parted its dark curtain and snatched away our oldest son.

A Journal Entry

Although a good way off, the summit finally came into view. With a long-awaited GI loan, a new home graced the farm, which had also doubled in size, and sleek horses could be seen contentedly grazing among well fed cattle. When we first came out and started farming here on the desert, there were those who said, and with good reason, that we wouldn't last three years—that was 50 years ago.

After our first few struggling and shaky years, a banker told a supervisor that I was the only person acquainted with my farming venture who didn't know I was washed up, finished, and beaten. When a national civic organization honored me by voting me one of the outstanding young men of Iron County, I said, "I guess I'm a success all right. I've doubled my farm, doubled my production, and doubled my debts. Having started out with nothing ten years ago, I've even doubled that."

I had long wanted to be a writer and had been plagued with an overwhelming obsession to write, but I also had a strong feeling that writing fell short of meeting men's physical needs, and I wanted to be a producer, not a parasite. I had an urge to build and make a farm, which we did, starting from scratch, until becoming a full-fledged dirt farmer, but for years I walked in the shadow of a distant and revered peak which I hoped to someday climb. I had done quite a bit of writing along the way, often even stealing time as it were to pursue this pressing desire. But I had often reflected and wondered why I, with little learning and no letters, should have had such an overwhelming thirst to read, to study, to write and reflect. Is it because, in my more meditative moments, I heard, as it were, voices in the wind, the mountains seeming to talk to me, the trees to whisper; the universe at times seeming to be alive with messages and communications from the past? There is music in silence, there are discernable sounds in the stillness of a quiet valley or the wilderness of the wilds. Somehow and sometime, it seemed, I communed with the intangible, invisible world, and yesterday passed in review, but not without pressing or crying for expression. So that was part of why I needed to write.

An Unexploded Bomb

The war was over. Had been for fifteen years, but there were still some unexploded bombs. One of them almost destroyed me. The trigger was a sharp knock, a frantic cry, and a cold December night.

It was nearly midnight on December 3, 1960 when the knock came. When I answered the door, a frantic, bathrobe-clad Navajo woman burst through it, our neighbor. "Oh help me, help me!" she cried. "My husband just shot himself. Please hurry. Call the doctor."

We lived out in the country where places were few and far between. A long mile stood between us and their place. "Where is he? How did it happen? How bad is he hurt?" I asked, rapid fire.

"I don't know, I don't kno-oow," she sobbed. "He's lying out near the well."

"Call the doctor," I told my wife. "You wait here," I told the woman. "I'll go see what I can do."

It was a clear night and a round moon high in the sky illuminated the stillness as it glittered on the white patches of snow. Dark shadows falling away from their creators in motionless forms were an eerie prelude to what lay ahead.

As I hurried past our neighbor's house, I caught sight of another dark blotch on the desert floor, only this one was not a shadow. Still partly propped up by the small rifle he had used, the unconscious form of my neighbor slumped in a pool of rapidly thickening blood. When I turned him over and saw where he had placed the muzzle of the gun, I knew he couldn't live. The nearest doctor lived 40 miles away and it would be at least that many minutes before he arrived. The only thing I could do was straighten him out, cover him up, and wait.

It was probably this prolonged wait, coupled with the involuntary sounds and physical contractions that sometimes accompany a body dying a violent, but lingering death, that must have lit the hidden fuse. During the fate-filled hush of this tragic wait, a similar experience, painfully buried and long since forgotten, suddenly flashed back across my memory screen.

It was 16 years and 1 month before that as a young soldier I held my dying brother, who had been shot, in my helpless arms on a jungle beach while I waited for a medic who couldn't come. Somehow, this incident must have somehow stirred those buried memories. Even had it been an accident, this sudden reminder was not a pleasant experience. But this present struggling death was not an accident, it was planned.

Why? Why? my soul cried out, *when most of us fight tooth and nail, sometimes against impossible odds to cling to life, would anyone want to deliberately end it?* A person's mind must be running in reverse to want to commit suicide. Somewhere along the way, the light of hope must go out. Jesus referred to this terrible condition in Matthew 6:23, when He said, "If therefore the light that is in thee be darkness, how great is that darkness!"

As I was soon to learn, it can be very, very dark. And even though I had fought a similar battle once before and won, it did not mean the enemy was dead or that he would go away and let me live happily ever after. Yet it was hard to believe that after years of solid faith and successful readjustment, this disturbing incident could turn my peaceful would into such a bizarre nightmare.

Of course there was also the recent death of a childhood buddy, a suicide. Also a veteran, he had experienced the misfortune of battle fatigue during the war and had suffered an off-and-on emotional disturbance ever since. It was barely two months before that he finally lost his battle with reason and shot himself. The details and effect of his losing battle had raised some searching questions for me.

Added now to my neighbor's sudden suicide, it brought my own world crashing down. Seized with a sudden surge of fatalism, I was carried to the very brink of destruction. Just before Christmas, in the middle of the night, the bomb exploded. I don't know what woke me. Everything was quiet, the room was dark, and all was still. Suddenly I was wide awake, but in a very frightening world. My wife stirred and asked, "What's the matter?"

"Nothing," I lied as I stared at a haunting ghost which seemed to imply I would follow the guys I knew who committed suicide. Cold beads of sweat began forming. Getting out of bed, I went to the bathroom, but my mind went to the closet where I kept my guns. There was a riffle there, a big one, that would be the one. I didn't say it, but something did. I suddenly felt myself drawn toward that closet. But something inside resisted this wildly throbbing impulse. I stopped. I decided to wait. Not tonight, later.

At that point, I became a split personality, a house divided against itself. I have never known such utter wretchedness. Was I crazy? I didn't think so, but people I had known who were, didn't think so either. I remember standing in front of the mirror looking deep into the eyes of the person I faced in a vain effort to discover what was going on behind them. Sometimes things seemed pretty normal and other times they were very abnormal and I didn't seem to have much control over either. But always lurking in the background was the ominous threat of the guns. Sometimes I hardly dared walk past the closet where I kept them. Other times I was drawn there with an irresistible urge. I even considered giving them away, or like Tolstoy, "Placing them under lock and key lest in a moment of despair I turn them on myself." What was even more confusing, I didn't have any good reason to be depressed. Happily married, I had five wonderful kids, a new home, and the desert waste I was trying to make into a farm was showing the fulfillment of a well-planned desire.

Finally sensing that something was wrong because of the changes in my eating, my sleeping, my anxiety and tension, my wife suggested I see a doctor. Half skeptical and half hopeful, I finally agreed. What could it hurt? I felt kind of foolish and embarrassed, confessing my problem to the local M.D., and I probably gave him such a modest account that he didn't realize how serious things really were. Quite interested and concerned with my war experiences, however, he asked a lot of questions. Then doing a little psychological arithmetic, he explained that locking the incident of my brother's death inside and not talking about it had not been good and had probably created an emotional wound or scar inside that never really healed. Like a delayed time bomb, it had lain dormant for all these years, waiting for something to touch it off. He said I should talk it out. It sounded reasonable and I did feel better. He gave me some tranquilizers and said I would probably be okay.

For a while I was, then boom, another violent death, another friend killed. Death and violence, the world was filled with it. It didn't seem to matter who you were or where you were, it was all the same. It was no use, I was doomed. Try as I might, I couldn't shake it. I sometimes felt it was all in my mind. But wherever it was, it had me trapped, or so I had come to believe. Sometimes I felt I barely clung to life by the tips of my fingers, and the only glimmer of light on the dark horizon was a knowledge that I had once known faith and hope and God. Was this some kind of test?

One beautiful Sabbath morning I went to feed the cattle. It was spring now and the whole world seemed to be bursting with new life and hope and the joy of living, all but me. Leaning on the corral fence, I remember thinking, *Why does my world have to be filled with such gloom and despair at such a beautiful time of year?* Perched on a nearby post, a little gray thrush tipped its beak to the sky and filled the air with his rich throaty gladness. For one wistful moment, I wished that I might feel again the joy of just being alive. Closing my eyes, I asked the God of that tiny bird if He would please give life back to me. Oh, I had prayed before, many times, but this time I pleaded with all my heart and soul.

Faith to Live

In a world still cloaked in gloom, I went back to the house. Someone was talking on the radio, a preacher. He was giving an account of accompanying a friend to the hospital for a very serious operation. Impressed with the calm assurance with which his friend approached his critical hour, the preacher asked how he could be so peaceful. The answer came, he had prayed and was confident all would be well. The preacher then asked his radio audience, asked me, "What wouldn't you give to have that kind of faith?"

Was this the answer to my prayer? Could faith cure me? Somehow the very thought began switching on lights. What happened next is almost as hard to explain as what happened in the beginning. In some amazing way, my thoughts changed from negative to positive. Both the fear of the guns and the pull of the closet were gone. "Faith," literally was "the substance of things hoped for, the evidence of things not seen" (Hebrews 11:1).

Like that lucky little bird, I too felt to sing. Suddenly the world was beautiful again. It was great just to be alive. I don't suppose we will ever know why people sometimes take their own lives, but one thing I had learned: the power of darkness and the loss of hope is very real and can be very terrible. And while the mechanics and sequence of a delayed time bomb is still a mystery to me, there is one thing I do know—that the word and promise of Jesus in Luke 17:19, "Thy faith hath made thee whole," is real and beautiful.

* * *

This article was written about six months after it actually happened, and while I usually kept a record of most ongoing events, during this particular period I couldn't bring myself to write anything, so dark and fearful was the gloom I seemed to be caught up in.

Looking back now, it's pretty hard to conceive that such feelings or thoughts could ever have happened to me. But they did, and I remember thinking and even asking the Lord once, "Why must I forever tramp the dark streets of hell?" It was more terrible and frightening than anything I ever faced in battle. The thought and fear that sooner or later I could and would shoot myself and was utterly helpless to prevent it plagued me both night and day.

I wondered and have since come to feel that this was possibly a test and an experience the Lord allowed me to go through as part of the price of my own extreme bitterness and vengeance after my brother was killed, because I did react much more than was necessary, even in war. "Vengeance is mine, saith the Lord." The test included the interesting fact that there were some very striking similarities to that experience I had had sixteen years earlier. Almost a replay, it would seem, of its most difficult part. And it was that part that probably awoke the long-buried memory deep in my inner soul and triggered those violent reactions inside.

This trial did give me a peek into that bottomless pit and world of outer darkness that the Savior referred to. And it also helped me realize that for reasons maybe even they can't explain or escape, some people can get caught or stuck in that hopeless broken-record syndrome of self-destruction and shouldn't be totally to blame for what they do or why they do it. But it's true, it's real, and it can happen, and it almost happened to me, a person who had no cause, no reason to want or even think of committing suicide, and yet I came within a breath of doing it. Something that even today makes me shrink and shudder at the very thought of it.

I thank heaven it's over, and I hope I have paid my terrible price and debt.

The Laubs' ranch in 1955–56, with the tar-paper cabin that was the Laubs' home in the first years there. Janet and Craig are out front.

The Laubs' home in the 1970s
on the same site as the tar-paper cabin.

Chapter 14

Sentimental Journeys

Turn back, turn back, Oh ye sands of time,
Let the fleeting years cease to fly
Oh let me return to yesterday,
There let me find the reason why.

A Date with Destiny

February 13, 1985

This entire journey from the very outset, as shown in numerous instances along the way, was much more than just a trip to the Far East, a vacation, a business or sightseeing trip, as perhaps it was for most of the other many travelers we saw. Rather this journey, with its opportunities, experiences, and places that each fell into place one by one along the course almost as if placed there by some divine and carefully guiding influence, was a journey of destiny.

In a way it started with an ironic twist. As a southern Utah rancher and farmer now successfully producing alfalfa hay cubes, who but Japan should become one of my best customers, often sending buyers to the farm to examine and purchase hay? Then in the fall of 1984, a former Cavalry buddy, Leon G. Felt, and I planned a trip back to the Philippines with our wives. When this trip was mentioned to visiting Japanese hay buyers, a special invitation to come to Japan was made by Nagami, one of their executuves. About that time, however, a family problem required my buddy Leon and his wife to cancel out. But with passports and plane reservations already made, plus an unexplainable but unquenchable urge to go back, I and my courageous wife and traveling companion Barbara decided to go anyway. Of course, most of the bitterness and hate that had once provoked my own personal battle against the Japanese, sometimes all by myself, had pretty much mellowed and vanished.

It was with both feelings of longing and interest that we found ourselves finally on our way. I had for years, in my more reflective and meditative moments, thought, dreamed, and written about this moment. This journey that for me would roll the clock back over 40 years and take me back into a somewhat dark and troubled world of the past. A journey that would reopen some long-closed doors. Some doors, that in a time and period of deep personal sorrow, hurt, and questioning were closed and locked, burying some feelings and emotions of love, hate and lonliness that few people may ever know or experience, occasioned by the world-shaking events of World War II and the death of my brother Merril in the invasion of the Philippine Islands, 40 years 3 months and 23 days before.

It was late in the afternoon as we dropped over the Cajon Pass from the dry, high desert to the green coastal landscape of southern California. It was a surprisingly clear day for the Los Angeles Basin, and we could see in the distance the setting sun, the vast unseen wilderness of the great beyond where two years in my battle for life and death and self and meaning and purpose were both fought physically as well as mentally.

Visit to Hawaii
February 14, 1985

This morning we caught the shuttle bus for the airport, arrived, got our boarding passes, and then proceeded to the boarding station for the Korean Air Lines. We were seated on the plane (ship). It was not quite as large as a troop ship, but this was a pretty big bird. There were 13 rows of seats, 9 seats across with aisles down each side. We were right in the center of the plane which seated 402 passengers. We have sailed on smaller boats.

While waiting for our plane, we met a man and wife, Bill and Helen Adair. When we told them where we were going and why, he told us he had been in the Philippines on December 10th, 1941 when the invasion of the Philippines started. Bill had only been in the Philippines six weeks at that time, a new infantry captain sent to Luzon to help train the rag-tag Philippine army that was being formed. He said he knew Gen. MacArthur and was a close friend of the colonel who was MacArthur's personal aide, who told him the night he was picked up that they were leaving and he wouldn't see him anymore. Bill became a POW, forced to participate in the Bataan Death March in April 1942. He survived the Bataan Death March by somehow getting on an ambulance. When I referred to it as a delaying action, he laughed and said, "Delayed? We ran like hell trying to get out." As we talked of battles and places of common interest, he mentioned the Caganatuan prison compound that we liberated on the way to Manila, and also the Santo Tomas University compound in Manila. He had been to both, also the old walled city, although he said most of the American and Australian POWs were moved to Japan and kept there. He had been taken to Japan and it was the 1st Cavalry Division that came to their prison camp in the back country of Japan and freed them at the end of the war in 1945.

By comparison, this departure from the USA was much, much faster, much smoother, and so much nicer than our 1943 departure. This ship was not crowded at all; in fact there were only about 30 people in our 100-seat section, most of them Oriental. But except for a few islands and the blue ocean below, there was very little to bid goodbye to, no parting farewells, no fanfare, no noticeable significance to this departure. No, this was not like that departure in 1943, with soldiers lining the rail, waving, cheering, and wondering. While flying was quite a different experience than sailing, there were some very similar sensations. The gentle rise and fall of the ship on the ocean or air waves that rock or tilt a vessel in motion, coupled with the low steady hum or vibration of the engines, all seemed quite similar. But the low, constant roar of the wind streaking by at 550 mph was different from the foaming splash and swish of the water being sliced by the ship at 25 knots. The sensation of movement was much more noticeable on a ship than on this plane; except for the few little bumps and ripples, the flying sensation was one of standing still, suspended as it were almost motionless in space.

Suddenly, we were coming down. I saw land ahead. The rugged blue outline of a mountain range splashed with billowing clouds. It was somewhere in this same vicinity in December 1941 where it all began, as Japanese planes came out of nowhere and started dropping bombs on Pearl Harbor. And so there we were in company with some Japanese on this very flight, circling over the Hawaiian islands, swooping low for the final run and landing. Yes, it was quite different.

Pearl Harbor
February 15, 1985

The most interesting attraction to me in Hawaii was our visit to Pearl Harbor and the *USS Arizona* Memorial. As we came to the national memorial, we were given a little review by Bill Speers, who was a sailor on the *USS Phoenix,* a cruiser berthed in Pearl Harbor at the time. He reviewed the attack and some of the things not written in many accounts, including the fact that some of the survivors were quite trigger-happy or nervous and shot at some of their own forces and planes. The U.S. Park Service has built a nice visitors' center and memorial where information, books, and a short movie were available. It was interesting to hear and learn the other side, the Japanese side of the plan, the strategy and the attack which succeeded in many ways beyond their own best hopes, and which without doubt had to have been one of the most brilliant and successfully executed war maneuvers of modern time.

Then we took a short boat ride out to Ford Island in the center of Pearl Harbor and the Memorial Monument which sits astride the *Arizona,* where over 1,100 men are still entombed in the sunken ship. This part of our trip began to touch the deep and hidden memories, thoughts, and feelings that, like the battleship *Arizona* buried in the harbor, had been buried inside me for decades. To see and read and relive that tragic day of history on the actual site where it took place was not only a walk through the past, but a hallowed link with the dead. As I stood over the hull of that sunken ship and read the names of the men entombed below, I not only felt a sacred hush of reverence for them but experienced a strange feeling of kinship to them and to that sleepy Sunday morning when the clocks all over the world took note of an event that would change the course of history.

To many of us, Pearl Harbor came to symbolize much, much more than a strategic harbor on the southwest side of Oahu. It became a moment in history, etched in our minds and lives with flaming pens of fire. An unbelievable moment both to remember and to regret. From here the vial of war dumped from the sky by those first Japanese planes spread like a plague until it held the entire Pacific locked in the cold grip of death. That grip would uproot many of us from our quiet homes to places and lands we had never even heard of before. Island after island rose to fame, Kwajalein, Saipan, Tarawa, Tinion, Muna, Buna and Lai, Luzon, Iwo, and Leyte, plus scores of others known only to geographers or mapmakers and the few souls who may have inhabited them. Even the tiniest, unknown island made headlines and became a well-known point of history as American soldiers, sailors, or Marines, along with the Australians and others, sought, fought, and drove the Japanese back to their homeland.

We went through the museum, saw the pictures and reminders, maps, notes, and other mementos, and bought a duplicate copy of the Dec. 7th Honolulu paper. Its stunning headline and pictures of the attack at first didn't begin to survey the total damage, only listing a small portion of the total casualties which finally came to nearly 2,500, nearly half of which, 1,150, were on the *Arizona* alone. Yet in retrospect, it was amazing that in that first three of four hours of the war a lot more people were not killed. A miracle when one reviewed the number of Japanese planes and bombs and bullets that were flying around on that fateful Sunday morning.

Journey to Japan

February 17, 1985

We were on our way, the pilot released the reins and this mighty bird with an unbelievable burst of speed raced down the runway right along the beach and then up, up—our liftoff was smooth and beautiful. We had no sooner gotten into the air than we banked sharp to the right, out over the ocean, before we were much over 150 feet up and still climbing. We made a half circle to the right, back past the narrow gateway to Pearl Harbor with the high rises of Waikiki and Honolulu in the background. Leaving the white shoreline and cloud-capped mountains of the blue-green beautiful Hawaiian islands behind, we headed out over the deep blue ocean below. We were soon up above the clouds and still climbing, but again with that deceiving sensation of standing still.

In that ocean crossing 40 years ago we spent days and days and saw miles and miles of nothing but blue water and sky. At least the water was tangible and one could see, hear, and feel its passing even if it did seem like we were in exactly the same place the next day. On that voyage, the sun came up, crossed the sky and went down many times. We had some clouds, rain squalls, and even some very heavy seas with ocean waves, sometimes nearly as high as the ship, breaking on the bow, where one could be walking down the deck and have the ship almost drop out from under you as she settled in the trough of a giant swell. It was quite a new and interesting experience and by the time we were over halfway through our journey, we were getting down into the southwest Pacific where the real war was going strong. And so with some wonder and concern we would sit on the deck at night and peer into the dark and try to think or imagine what lay ahead, what uncertain destiny awaited us. Where we might be going or how long we might be gone. By that time, home was a long way off, but our dreams and desires and plans to return began to become the ultimate idea of paradise, not the tropical islands for which we were headed.

By contrast, our flight was kind of a race with the sun, which we could not win, but ere the sun set over the vast land of China, we had crossed the wide Pacific, having gone from Sunday afternoon February 17th to Monday night February 18th in broad daylight, without it ever getting dark, crossing the International Dateline in the mid-Pacific. In 1943 we crossed the International Dateline too, but we also crossed the equator, going from the Northern to the Southern Hemisphere, referred to as the land down under.

> *I remember sitting on the bow of the boat at night, fascinated as we plowed through the inky black water, watching the nose split the sea into white phosphorus ripples that streaked and played along the side, listening to the hiss of the waves and foam. At night we would locate the Southern Cross, which takes the place of the Big Dipper as a celestial landmark. How we would sit and watch the darkness as we plowed through it on our date with destiny. We kind of sensed this and talked about it as we gazed into the southern sky, seeming almost a million miles from home, family, and old familiar scenes and things. As we talked about and longed for the yesterdays, I think that there were times way out in mid-Pacific that we began to feel the loneliness of our distance from home and all we once knew. We talked about our family and our love for them, and we began to really miss them and wonder what they were doing and wonder if they even had any idea where we were or what we were doing or going to do. In spite of the intrigue of new places and experiences, there was a deep undertone of emptiness that came at times, with a sudden pang, to those youthful hearts.*

We Land in Japan

The pilot cut the power and we made a long descent into the world below, heightening our anxious anticipation of this new land. The unknown and uncertainty as well as excitement and interest probably in no way compared with that of 1943, since this time we knew, we planned, we had met some of the people, and it was only a few hours away from home.

> *Last time it was a whole new world, almost a whole world apart. After days at sea, we saw birds and signs of land and everyone eagerly looked for and awaited the landing. Traveling in total secrecy, we didn't know where we were going. What and where would this new land be? It was the green coast of central Australia, up a wide river to the city of Brisbane. Interesting, exciting, and different, so very different from the good old USA. And with the teams of horses and men working on the docks, it was a step back in time also.*

It was a new experience, in keeping with the many such we had already experienced so far on this journey, to suddenly find ourselves all alone in a country of 100 million people, not being able to read or speak the language. Fortunately, there were some signs in English and some attendants who spoke English. We made it through long lines through check stations, customs, and baggage claim. We found our way to exchange some money, 250 yen for $1.00, and we made our way out to the bus depot, where for 5,000 yen we purchased a couple of tickets to Tokyo, about an hour's ride away. The bus we took did not take us to our hotel, but only into downtown Tokyo where we would have to catch another bus to get to our hotel. But where and when to change buses was a real concern. What we didn't know was that we would arrive at a central point where everyone got off.

There, to our welcome surprise, was Nagami, one of the Japanese buyers who was at the farm the November before and who had invited us to come to Japan and said that he would meet us. He was there watching and had recognized us before we did him. We were really glad to see someone we knew and who knew us. Barbara asked him, "How did you know we would be here?" He replied that this is where everyone met those flying into Tokyo. Again, it was a very strange and interesting experience to walk down the streets of Tokyo after all these years and in connection with this unusual journey, and our welcome was quite different than it would have been 40 years ago.

The Prince Hotel, Tokyo

I was in Japan, the home of a once bitterly hated enemy. I found that time, as in nearly everything else, wrought changes in me too. I thought that change might have started about 40 years before in a small village south of Manila, and it might have been about to find a desirable, if belated conclusion in this visit to Japan.

I had sometimes thought and even dreamed of maybe someday going back to the islands and the Philippines. But my thoughts had always been more in terms of going to Australia and then retracing my steps up through the islands with sort of a Philippine rendezvous. That was my vision of the journey into the past that I wanted to take. But when it finally happened, by chance or by fate I found myself going in the opposite direction.

On our final approach to Japan, as I tried to analyze it from 30,000 feet up, this would certainly be a different landing on the enemy fortress, the Japanese homeland, the final destination. To find myself suddenly dropped in the very heart and midst of these people. Maybe, even to meet and stand in line or rub shoulders with, real close range, without weapons, some of those who may have even been met or encountered in other places, under other conditions 40 years ago. It was indeed a strange moment in my life. True, things had changed. True, I had made my peace with myself and my Creator, but could I now make my peace with them?

There seemed to be one little part still missing. One little part still left undone. Granted it had crossed my mind at times, and for this reason I was prompted to bring back with me a small Japanese battle flag, taken in the Philippines General Hospital in 1945. I had showed it to some of the visiting Japanese people in recent years and they told me the writing on it was the names of some Japanese people. At the time I took it, I couldn't have cared less who they were, but now I couldn't help wondering about them. As a conscientious Christian, I found springing from somewhere deep within very different feelings and desires, some long suppressed and buried, pushing themselves to the surface with kind of a pressing desire for expression. In this step back into the past those desires made a kind of a bridge to bring together the past and the present. In and through a personal apology and gesture of peace to Japan and her people, I desired to personally return this flag.

Meeting and doing business with the people from Japan for several years had been a stepping-stone in my journey back into the past. The evening of our arrival, as I walked the busy streets of Tokyo, my mind flashed back to a snapshot, found on a soldier 40 years ago, of a Japanese woman and two small children who suddenly became real people to me.

As I continued this journey, I began to realize and sense, with some very deeply stirred feelings, that two long and widely separated parts of my person were about to be reunited—the one that was partially killed and buried on a distant jungle island was about to meet its other half, the one that sadly, reluctantly went back home just short of that final landing in Japan. Now, the one coming back via Japan from the north to the Philippines was about to meet the one coming up from Australia and the south, a meeting which in its own small way would be kind of a moment in destiny. What would they find? What would it be like? These were still some deep, haunting questions, and would it be a meeting of more than one?

At this writing I was not sure I could answer or even quite explain what I felt or what I expected, but deep within as I tried to analyze and place in perspective the many years, the changes, and different aspects of my sentimental journey into the past and into present-day Japan, I knew that when the two, or maybe three, of us met in a few days on that distant beach at Leyte, I would be glad it first included this visit and moments of insight in Japan. I hadn't planned it that way, but something or someone must have.

Kyoto

It took us less than 3 hours to travel the 300 miles to Kyoto. It was a very beautiful and historic city, the ancient home of the emperors and had many interesting and historic temples and gardens. I sat by a large window, seven floors up, overlooking a wide river with neatly laid, man-made rock banks with numerous little waterfalls, which gave the beautiful soothing sound of running water. There were dark green, heavily wooded mountains just a short way across the river, forming a beautiful backdrop with the city and some of the castles rising in tiers up the slope a little ways. It was a beautiful, picturesque and peaceful setting. The dark, storm-swept mountains in the background lent a very stirring, or thought-provoking feeling to our very, very impressive, much-needed and helpful visit to Japan. Our pretty guide, Amy, met us that morning as we were taken by special bus on a guided tour of the historic temples, gardens, and palaces in the ancient home of the emperors, Shoguns, and rulers of Japan. At first, we wondered why our host, Nagami, sent us out here, but soon we knew and appreciated why.

This tour was a very interesting and even helpful step along my journey, because it gave me a much deeper understanding and appreciation of and for the men and people who were my bitter and hated enemy 40 years before. That foe I viewed and regarded with very little respect or concern for who he was or where he came from or what his own history and background was. So it helped, even 40 years later, to have a better understanding of the fiercely dedicated and committed enemy soldier with whom we matched our powers and skills and abilities in that very deadly dual of war. That enemy we had come to know as a superb jungle fighter, one who fought bitterly, who had often unadmittedly won our deep respect and even fear, which often gave him the advantage. Now, I thought I understood better why he often did what he did or reacted the way he did and why it was at times so different and foreign to our own ways and thinking, albeit in war it is always kill, destroy, or overpower the enemy, no matter who, where, or how.

Returning the Flag

We had an interesting experience when we met with a reporter, Jun Harada, from one of the local papers, *Asani Evening News*. I had asked Amy where I might find a public relations office, explaining that I wished to return the battle flag to the Japanese. She suggested the local paper, so we called the *Asani Evening News,* and Jun Harada answered. Again, I briefly explained the flag, my part in the war and desire to return the flag. "Do you have the flag with you?" he asked. When I told him we did, he asked where we were and said their downtown office was only a block and a half away and invited us to bring it over. We gave him the flag, a copy of my story "Revenge is a Poor Reward," and some other thoughts and feelings I wrote our first night in Tokyo. I posed for a couple of pictures, and he said they would try to find some relatives. He explained, however, that this flag was not a unit banner but only the personal memento of an individual soldier, and the writings were names of friends and well-wishers who had signed it when he went off to war. Then pointing to writings near the bottom of the flag, he said, "This line says, 'We must win.'"

After the day's tour of Nara, Nagai and his wife, Sanae, invited us to their little apartment for dinner. This was a very special experience to go to a private home and visit and see the Japanese lifestyle. They are a very modern Japanese middle-class, business-type family. Their little four-room apartment was quite modern for Japan, built in the last five years. The rooms were like ours except the bedroom had only mats on the floor. In the closet were large fluffy, pillow-like mattresses they put on the floor for beds. The table in the living room is small, 3x4 foot, on legs about 18 inches high, with legless chairs around and a large ruffled quilt over the top. Under the table is an electric heater so in cold weather you can scoot in the chairs, pull the quilt over your lap, put your feet and legs under the warm table, and relax. And in our case it was doubly welcome as we had been out all day in Nara and the weather was cold and blustery, and they had no central heating in their apartment. It was about 6:00 p.m. and while Sanae finished fixing dinner, we visited and relaxed, very modern Japanese style. They had a lively two-year-old son who at first was very frightened of us but by the time we left was sitting on Barbara's lap.

This was probably one of the highlights of our whole trip to Japan as far as the people go. Sanae was very outgoing although she didn't speak any English, and I told her she was very brave to invite two total strangers, foreigners at that, into her home, but she was handling it quite well and had been cooking and preparing all day for us. The banquet she spread before us would have been a royal dinner in the USA. She had beef, pork, a special chicken, fried fish, pudding, two kinds of beans, and numerous other Japanese dishes, I don't remember. She said she didn't know for sure what to fix, so she fixed many things. Barbara tried everything, but I had a hard time with all this new food. We tried chop sticks again but didn't do too well, so she got us knives and forks. Nagai had stopped at a small delicatessen on the way to buy a special bread ball especially for me, as he discovered when we had lunch that I couldn't eat without bread.

While we were eating dinner, the reporter from the paper called and told us he had written an article to see if they could find the owner of the flag, and if we would stop by the office in the morning, we could get a copy of the paper and some pictures he had taken. Nagai had arranged for a friend who had a car to drive us back to our hotel, about 20 miles back into Nara. We were staying in the same hotel that the U.S. occupation forces stayed in, 1945–1946.

Nara to Korea

When Nagai met us the next morning at the Nara hotel, he gave us a letter his wife had written after we left. In was in Japanese, so he translated it to English.

Mr. Laub, Mrs. Laub,

Thank you very much for your coming to my house to have supper when you were tired. I was little bit nervous because it was the first time to invite foreigners. But I was relieved because you were gentle and kind. I'm afraid whether you were satisfied [with] Japanese food, but please try again in other places you go, unless you have had enough of it. If you have another chance to come back to Japan, I hope you will come to our house again. I'm not sure how long we can live in Nara (because my husband has to be transferred some day to another branch), but even if so, we can guide you to another place. I promise you to learn English and cooking more until then. Please be careful while [on] your long journey to America.

2/22 Sanae

Because of their warm and generous welcome, we felt a special attraction for them, so we had also written them a letter and put it with a "Joseph Smith" tract and a "Life Before Birth" tract.

Dear Mr. Mrs. Nagai,

We would like to write you this letter to express our deepest thanks and appreciation, to both of you for the very warm and special way you have accepted and entertained us. We have been well treated and received by everyone in Japan and we are very happy for this. We would like to tell you, that of all the people we have met, you are outstanding. We have traveled much and met with many people, but we have never met with anyone who we feel has became our more instant and true friends, than were both of you, so we feel you are very special people. We cannot say thanks enough for our privilege on this trip of meeting you and being so graciously invited into your home.

Because we feel you are very special we would like to do something for you and have wondered what can we do in return for you. The thing we thought of, is the most precious to us in this world, and has meant the most to us in our lives is our understanding of the true meaning and purpose of life. So we would like very much to share with you the thing that is most precious of all gifts, the gospel of Jesus Christ. We are sorry now to be leaving and not have the opportunity to tell you about it ourselves, but we are sure that if you will contact the Mormon church in Nara or the mission headquarters in Tokyo and tell them that Mr.& Mrs. Laub from Utah very much wanted them to send some special missionaries to teach you about it, they will. We feel, from the very bottom of our hearts, that this would be a special message to some very special people, that would be a gift and blessing to you for the rest of your lives.

We hope that you will accept this special gift of thanks we would like to share with you because of the special love and feeling we have for you.

> Again our deepest love and thanks,
> Normand and Barbara Laub

As we mingled and visited with the Japanese and particularly visited their own ancient political and religious shrines in Kyoto and Nara, I began to see and understand these people, this former enemy, in a much, much broader perspective than I had before in my own little, small and limited world. The culture, the long shaping history of these people, the unusual nation in the Far East, yes, the old enemy suddenly took on a new color, light, and meaning. Hate and scorn changed to respect and appreciation and a strange kind of warm feeling, even love. The tragedy, my emotional trauma and personal bitterness took some strange turns after being sealed in my breast for 40 years; they found a surprising but long overdue release and expulsion through being a personal guest of the Japanese on a sentimental journey back to the Philippines by way of Japan and the return of a Japanese battle flag.

My Return to the Philippines
February 24, 1985

We met and talked to quite a few people from the Philippines who told us a little about conditions there now. We had a young lady volunteer to help us when we got there. She was married to a Japanese man and lived in Tokyo but was returning to the Philippines for a visit. Her mother was from Leyte. She invited us to go with her to the Catholic church and then to visit her family at their home. She said her father was 61 years old and would probably like to talk to me. We learned that Grant and Nellie Clove, who were on a mission [for the Mormon church] in Luzon, were quite a ways south of Manila, which was where we wanted to go anyway, so we thought it might work out the best for us. The green island of Luzon appeared below us. First the mountains, then the broad green plain with its fields. We could have followed somewhat the same course as the flying column the 1st Cavalry made just over 40 years before in its race to Manila to free the Santo Tomas University POW camp and civilian prisoners. We banked sharp to the left and came down fast, hitting the dirt in a different way than 40 years before *I was back in the Philippines.*

Downtown Manila, February 25, 1985

"Hey Laub, wake up, It's your turn to stand guard." It's been a fairly quiet night, the streets are now dark except for the amber glow off in the distance toward the bay, where some fires are still burning.

SENTIMENTAL JOURNEY

It was not hard to let my mind wander back to the night of February 25, 1945. I'm not sure exactly just where we were 40 years before on this morning, but I thought daylight would have found the 2nd Squadron, 1st Platoon D Troop, 5th Cavalry regiment, 1st Cavalry Division camped somewhere in the war-torn, smoldering city. It might have even been on the top floor of some office building, in the Philippine General Hospital, or it might have been in a warehouse near the beach, where three large, silver Japanese torpedoes were still stored. All three nights in those places suddenly come back to mind.

So there I sat on the 12th floor of the Century Park Sheraton Hotel in downtown Manila, with a view out over Manila Bay on the left and a sweeping view of the city back to the north. It had been a fairly quiet night. I don't know what woke me, but the city was dark and quiet, except for a string of amber colored lights off in the foreground. If you half closed your eyes, let your mind wander just a bit, it was not too difficult to turn the clock back 40 years. But as for my companion and quarters, that was quite different, the understatement of the day. Barbara was still asleep in a queen-sized bed. For some reason, not by our choice, we had been given the large, left-hand end suite on the northwest wing of the Sheraton triangle. It was the largest, plushest room, thick carpets, plenty of furniture, and sweeping 180-degree view of the north part of the city. Could I have ever dreamed of the place and conditions I now found myself in?

Take our arrival then and now. In both cases we did come streaking down from the north, but the one took minutes, the other took days. We didn't meet too much opposition coming either time, a few clouds and rough air pockets this time, a few blown bridges and muddy rice paddies before. Our first point of arrival or destination was a little different too. This time it was the Manila International airport. Before it was the Santo Tomas University compound. We were not the first off the airplane, nor was my squad the first soldiers at the gate, but in both cases we were suddenly engulfed in a throng of anxious people and faces from many lands.

We stood in line to be admitted and processed through customs yesterday. Forty years ago we quite often moved in columns and did a lot of waiting, but nobody checked our papers or questioned where we were from or what we were doing. This time we had a small welcome party to meet and pick us up and see us safely to our quarters—two LDS missionaries from the Philippines Manila Mission arranged, unbeknownst to us, by President and Sister Grant Clove greeted us and drove us to the hotel. Before, we were met by two groups, the Filipino people of Manila who really cheered and welcomed us, and the troops of the Imperial Japanese Army, but the greeting and welcome was not the same.

It was at this point that our two arrivals lost their similarities. Yesterday it only took us a few minutes by air-conditioned car to get to our peaceful and beautiful, comfortable, air-conditioned quarters. Forty years ago it took us days, even weeks, to cross the city, and it wasn't beautiful. Some of the buildings were air conditioned, but not cool, nor by design, it was just that they didn't have any doors or windows or even part of their wall may have been missing.

It was beginning to get light. Always a welcome sight, 40 years ago I could relax a bit. I didn't so much mind the daylight activities, when I could see, but the nights were always a worry and a problem.

We took a trip around the city. To me, the drive down along the old Manila Bay highway, with the rows of palm trees along the beach and the buildings on the other side, brought back memories of riding down that stretch in army trucks. So did the busy streets of Filipino street venders and peddlers, the hot, sun-filled, muggy afternoons, the smell of the sea, the same place, the same people, merely 40 years later. I found it very easy at nearly any given point to turn the clock of time back. It really didn't take too much imagination or eye squinting, nor even thoughtful meditation. In fact, surprisingly, in spite of the 40 year time change, I found myself almost walking in a time capsule. But it would seem that each day, each place and experience had been a step-by-step walk back beyond the bend into the past. Can one really walk back into time?

Tour of Manila

Santo Tomas University is in the northern part of town, the first place we hit when we got to Manila on February 3, 1945. The walls and buildings were still about the same as they were 40 years before. The tour bus usually didn't stop, usually just drove by, but I got the driver to stop and let me take some pictures, one of me pulling on the iron gates, trying to open them. The university compound covers a larger area than I remember.

The Philippine General Hospital is a little further south, downtown. The tour bus was not scheduled to go to the hospital, but I asked if we could go by so I could see it and get some pictures. Except for being repaired and fixed up, having some trees planted in the front yard, and having a drive-through ramp up to the front door instead of the big porch and front steps, it was still the same old place. The big front waiting room seemed smaller than I thought it was, where we were set up and where the Japanese runner threw the satchel bomb in the front window that nearly blew us out. And then I got a look at the hall leading off the main foyer, where I came back and met the Japanese as they started to come in.

Well, it was a hurried visit. Each of these places brought its own special recollections, some pleasant and others not so pleasant, all with a note of sadness.

Looking for the Catholic Cathedral

We were on a little dove, really small, compact, and close to the ground compared to the giant eagles we had been flying on. We were right close to the front of the left hand side, right behind the cockpit. This was quite a different flight and experience for at least two reasons. One, we were flying over mostly land and lower down. Though it was only a matter of minutes, I think we were soon over the area, southeast of Manila, where the incident took place with the last Japanese soldier with a snapshot of the woman and two children in his pocket. Also, it wasn't too far from there where I found the Catholic cathedral. Then we climbed above a heavy cloud bank and we were high above an area which held some dark memories for me. Aside from those first two months in Leyte, it was on our journey south from Manila at the end of the war that some of my deepest, most troubling personal battles began to catch up with me.

I wasn't sure exactly where we were, but through the broken scattered clouds I could see patches of dark green and light green land as well as glass portions of water. But by sage brush reckoning and country measurements, I figured we should be down over the Batangas area, somewhere where the incident in the little village took place, where the new lieutenant asked me the question about taking a prisoner. I could see several villages below, with a white string-like line, a road snaking its way through the patchy green landscape.

I told Barbara, I didn't know what she might do here, but if I could find a large banana leaf to get under, I could spend the day writing, because this area had some important memories, because it was here that I ended my part in the war.

I wanted to find the little cathedral somewhere down there that I entered 40 years ago and that became the turning point in my war life, while I was on a one-man patrol. So they took us to three different cathedrals in three different villages before we found one that might have been the one or at least fit the right conditions. We rode in a jeepney from village to village, and Sister Clove said, "It's been 40 years and things have changed, but those old cathedrals haven't changed." By the time we got to the third cathedral, we had attracted quite a lot of attention, and we had had the opportunity to talk to quite a few people along the way. The priest in one of the cathedrals remembered the war and the soldiers and had worked with them. In the last cathedral, there were quite a few children and young people, and some were ringing the bell with a long rope on the ground, so I got pictures of me and them and the cathedral. They could have been the grandchildren of the Filipinos I saw 40 years ago from that very bell tower when I rang the bells myself.

Well, with this journey almost over and the curtain about to fall, separating two worlds that in more ways than one really were worlds apart, we would very shortly be heading back into that other world and home. While we had been so caught up in this world, now and in the past, we hadn't had much time to dwell on the world on the other side of the ocean. We thought about it at times, missing the kids and grandkids and wondering how things were going at home. We would liked to have called, but that was pretty difficult from here. And then there had been a number of times that I thought about my own parents and family, as life's reel of memory turned in reverse. But this sentimental, almost unbelievable journey, like a strange, unreal dream, was about to come to a close, but before it did, I still wanted to review and record, so I kept writing.

A Redemption

Sunday, March 3, 1985

It being fast Sunday, we hadn't eaten. We did get ready and go to church. Barbara went to Relief Society and I made priesthood, and we stayed for part of Sunday school before we had to leave to go to the airport. It was good to meet with the saints again. In Manila they had an Anglo branch, and the Filipinos mostly met separately. The temple workers and missionaries met in the Anglo branch as did others who were employed by the Church and several other business firms. There were about 12 or 13 men to priesthood, counting me. The lesson was quite fitting for me, "The Way to Perfection." I told them it had been good for me to be in this city of so many memories, in a church setting, and to be thinking about and discussing the subjects and the spirit that we were this morning. It sort of helped me realize and appreciate the gospel all the more. In a way I was, even if 40 years later, still kind of repenting. I told how we had been to Japan, given back the flag, and kind of apologized and tried to make some amends to that nation, those people, and possibly even to some of the families of those whom I may have helped destroy. It really had helped put all these things in clearer, better perspective. When we discussed that all men are the children of God, I couldn't help but recall my feelings about the Japanese soldiers 40 years ago and my feelings now. So it was indeed a fitting climax to our journey.

Journey's End
March 5, 1985

Over the thin, silver crest of the long wing, silhouetted against the sky, the dawn approached. It was only 1:30 a.m., but it was coming and it was real and so with the onrushing tide of tomorrow ahead, we greeted and entered a new world, leaving yesterday behind, tenderly folded in the bending shades of the falling night that faded into the shadows behind us. And so with the coming dawn, this journey into the bends of the past both closed and opened on a bright new world and note.

Normand and Barbara at dinner at Nagai and Sanae's apartment, with little Shuji.

Nagai and the reporter, Jun Harada.

Normand and the battle flag.

The Laubs and village children at the Catholic cathedral in southern Luzon where Normand had an extraordinary experience in 1945.

Chapter 15

Searching the Arizona Strip

November 12, 1986

It was night, a crisp, clear November night. The last light of day had faded in the west as my wife and I pulled into the lonesome homestead where the Laub family built a cabin and began to clear a little field 52 years and 8 months ago in this little grove of tall pines by the foot of Round Grey Knoll. The country was wild, wide and lonesome. I don't think Mother was very happy there. She longed for her people and a bit of civilization. My two sisters, Ruby, four, and LaRee six, were probably still too young and small to notice or worry too much about where they were. I suppose the responsibility of trying to provide and care for a family in that wilderness location and setting probably weighed pretty heavily on my father, and Mother's sadness and failing health must have robbed him of much of the joy and satisfaction that he could have had as kind of a Robinson Crusoe.

The Past Comes Close

For Merril and myself, what more could life or the entire world ever offer or provide? We had it all. This world was all we needed, ten or fifteen square miles from the full, round, timber-covered dome of Mt. Trumbull on the east with the clear cold water of Nixon Springs gushing out into the big wooden water trough, to the rugged, broken ridge that made our south boundary, where Hell Hole plunged off into the bottom end of the Grand Canyon of the Colorado River. The rim of the Hurricane Fault on the west formed a high 60-mile long plateau, and then the endless stretch of hills, valleys, and timbered flats ran to the north. This may not have been a very big portion of the earth, but to 8- and 10-year-old boys, this was the best of all possible worlds. And so it wasn't with any real sadness or feeling of abandonment that we stayed behind on this Lonesome Pine homestead when Pa and Mother and the girls went back to Utah, 100 miles away for ten days.

Nearly every other day we would take the horses up to Nixon Springs to water and back. And of course, we milked the cows and turned them out to graze and gathered them in at night, fed the chickens and fixed our simple meals of bread and milk for suppers, cracked wheat mush and eggs for breakfast. Just two little boys in a far off wilderness.

Now, as I stand out in this lonesome grove of tall pines a half century later, having come back to commune with my brother and the past, I can't contain the tears and the deep, haunting, yearning, feelings that stir somewhere deep inside. Is it possible to reverse a life and turn back the pages of time? How could we have known, as we shared these sacred, special moments together, that we were building a relationship, a friendship, a unity and oneness that would weld us together like two people are seldom ever bonded, which in less than ten short years would carry us to a part of this land in the U.S. Horse Cavalry, still as the inseparable brothers, and then we would find ourselves on a great troop ship, headed for a place and country so distant that our little minds could not, even in their wildest imagination, comprehend what the future held or what lay ahead.

But certainly, for the moment, that didn't really matter. There we were, just the two of us, going about our routine daily chores and lives. There was the day we went to take the horses to water, and like normal boys, did some playing and exploring along the way. We went a little too far and were late heading home and to make up for lost time, we were hurrying, running our ponies farther than prudent. Mine wasn't used to roughing it like our other horses; he began to falter, stagger, and finally fell to his knees in the dark. A half-panicky cry from me brought my brother, who was in the lead, back. A quick check in the dark showed a jaded, giving-out horse, trembling and sweating. We held an anxious and urgent council as to what to do. It was already dark and late, and we still had miles to go, cows to gather from the hills, and chores to do when we did get home. After a short pause and rest, we decided to try and go on and take the pinto too. So we climbed on the other horse, riding double and leading the pinto. It was kinda like the song of long ago:

> *Two little boys*
> *Had two little toys,*
> *Each had a wooden horse;*
> *Gaily they played*
> *Each summer's day –*
> *Warriors both of course.*
>
> *One little chap*
> *Then had a mishap,*
> *Broke off his horse's head;*
> *Cried for his toy,*
> *Then cried for joy*
> *As his young playmate said:*
> *"Did you think I would leave you crying*
> *When there's room on my horse for two?*
> *Climb up here, Jack. We'll soon be flying;*
> *I can go just as fast with two."*

It was much slower going and well past midnight when we finally got to the shadow of the lonesome pines. And two tired little boys turned their hungry horses loose in the little grain field, which we weren't supposed to do. The cows had finally got lonesome and come home on their own and were standing by the corral gate lowing for their calves. We put them in the corral, and we two exhausted boys went to bed more tired than hungry.

There was a good half moon high in the sky, spreading a silver glow on the great sage and yellow grass, making deep shadows under the towering pines, filtering down through the branches, some of the same branches on which, a half century ago, a gray squirrel and a stripe-backed chipmunk used to play as they watched a little boy who sometimes spent hours watching them. And in the shadows of this strange, haunting silence, with just the two of us, my wife and I, now as close as we two were 50 years ago, there was a strange but familiar beckoning feeling that kept sweeping over me. It was almost as if there was an unseen person or spirit lurking in the shadows or stirring in the motionless pines as they lifted their towering heads heavenward. I felt much like I did when we circled the island of Leyte in the far off Philippines 18 months before. And that moon, untouched a half century ago, was no longer all that far away. In one sense in the world of 1986, the moon didn't seem much farther away than Utah and civilization were 50 years ago from here; the astronauts got to the moon quicker than we had traveled out here then.

As we stood out in that lonesome wilderness, with probably no one within 50 or 60 miles of us two, I experienced a tingling, melancholy feeling and sensation. I was there and not halfway around the world on a jungle island, yet I was trying to bridge the gap between the two. I seemed to tune in on two little boys living and playing and sleeping in the shadow of those same pines and that same moon looked down upon them. Suddenly time seemed to stand still or it vanished away.

Toroweap Valley
November 13, 1986

The next morning was a cool, crisp morning, with a north breeze. It got cool during the night and the wind played in the sheltering pines with soft whispering sounds, and to one whose ear was tuned to hear, there were music and voices in the wind, the deep mournful voices from the past or maybe from eternity. I climbed the little knoll behind the grove of pines to gain a view and perspective of the long ago in the cool, pre-dawn light. It was an interesting experience and with deep feelings as I stood on the hill and watched, as it were, the two little boys a half century ago get up, build a fire, get their breakfast, do the chores, turn the cows out, and go out through the trees in search of their hobbled horses.

I couldn't help but wonder if the people who were here, with the sights and sounds that transpired here, were not somehow and somewhere noted and recorded in the great eternal register and log book. Surely they were—their doings were not unnoticed as part of the great eternal plan and fabric.

As I stood on that little volcanic cinder mound, with the several others scattered around, and looked at the great, broken, lava ridge that makes the Hell Hole summit, or the huge, round dome of Mt. Trumbull, I could only wonder at the great upheaval that once took place to form that high volcanic plateau running for nearly 100 miles north and south from the great chasm of the Colorado River on the south to the Virgin River on the north.

We went down into the lower Toroweap Valley, at what was called the Lower Place to the pond, corral, and small round-topped cabin where we lived for nearly half a year, November 1932 until March 1933. The little 10x12-foot, one-roomed lumber house with a small lean-to on the back was still there, down under a small bench by a big pond, with four or five gnarled old tamarack trees out in front. A half century ago, the tamaracks were young, sprightly bushes. To our west were high three-tiered yellow bluffs jutting out from beneath some higher black volcanic lava cones and flows that evidently came at a later date than the original yellow formations, probably from the great upthrust that formed Mt. Trumbull, Hell Hole, and all the other volcanic cones and hills that are superimposed on top of the old original formations.

It was quite a different winter than we had ever known before. The nearest neighbors were about ten miles up the valley, and my brother and I rode our horses up to their ranch to mail letters or get our mail. After it snowed, it was quite often cold and windy, and I got so cold my little fingers had a hard time opening and closing the gates. But despite its hardships and mature responsibilities, it was a life made to order for two western boys, and we loved it and dreamed dreams and imagined all kinds of occasions which we lived.

I fear it was not a place nor a life for a woman, and I guess Mother became pretty lonesome and homesick at times. My father stuck his head out the window of the little back room, and looking out across the valley, sang parts of an old refrain that went something like this, "Look down, look down that lonesome road, before you journey on." And Mother wiped her eyes with her apron and sobbed some sad and lonesome tears. But much of this lonesomeness, though subconsciously noticed, passed by the two little boys who had a full life and world to occupy their every moment.

Call of the Wild

We were down on the rim of the awesome Colorado, with our pickup parked and our camp less than 50 feet from that breathtaking chasm. We had a cheery fire crackling in a cozy little nook in the ledges under the branches of a piñon tree. As darkness settled over the wild, lonesome canyon wilderness, a three quarter moon began to lighten the broken canyon solitude with a deep, silver shadowed light.

There were just the two of us, Barbara and I, as we continued our journey beyond the bend into the past. As we made that sentimental return, we found some new changes and additions to life's plan, whose purpose was still unfolding and allowing a seeking for further answers and explanations. Again, this became quite a touching, stirring quest, as our journey led us to many places, near, distant, and remote. But I suppose none surpassed or compared with this area, or with this part of our quest, because this, in a way, was where it all began over a half century before.

In that area for the most part the land stands untouched or unchanged in 50 years, maybe even in the last 50 millenniums. It was hauntingly beautiful, different from any other place. As I walked over to the rim of that mighty slice, that deep cut in the crust of the earth, it gave me a strange, haunting, melancholy feeling, the river and the mighty canyon. It's the greatest canyon and fracture in the surface that there is on the earth. This river and this canyon were mystic and unsearchable. I got the feeling as I stood there, particularly as it was bathed in the soft silver light of the clear moon, that I was gazing into the very bosom of eternity and creation. The very beginning, and though it's believed that eons have passed since its creation or formation, I had the strange sensation that it was only hours old, that I was standing there soon after it was finished. Perhaps, this was because this area and scene is not only eternal, it is ageless. And it is quite fitting that this area of eternal beginning was also the area of the beginning of my brother's and my inseparability, that this search and this journey into the past should end up here where it all began over half a century ago.

I sat in the quiet solitude of the canyon wilderness and wrote by the light of a flickering fire. This indeed was an unmatched, unsurpassed place, setting, and experience. If I only had language to capture and describe what my eye beheld and spirit felt as I gazed into the deep blue of the vaulted night sky with its bright moon and glittering stars, a sky that was untouched or tarnished by the smoke, dust, or lights of the modern world.

I couldn't help wonder if the great hand of destiny knew and saw it all, as we played by this mighty canyon that empties into the blue Pacific and listened to the rolling boom of explosions as they blasted the canyon away down the river 100 miles, building Boulder Dam. Could we have known that those rolling booms, like the distant boom of a cannon, was an ominous sign of things to come? Would it have made a difference? No, it wouldn't have made any difference, as two little boys answered the call of the wild and measured out their given time as they were tempered and tested and ever after affected. At that tender age each was seasoned and prepared for what was to come, and they were also forging ties that would bind them as few ever were bound, ties that only death could try to break.

Was it any wonder then that the devastating effect of one brother's death was the end of the world for the one that was left? After I recovered from the initial shock, I had no desire to live or return either, only to get revenge. But in those dark, dreary, and fearful jungle nights, my spirit and soul remembered in a far-off distant sort of way, and tried to reconcile and heal using the bonds that had been developed here, in this land of no beginning or ending.

By 8:00 p.m. the full mantle of night and darkness gathered and closed around the canyon fortress. The silent curtain of night settled over the area, but it was really not all that dark because the glow of the bright moon lit the country with a shadow-like light, and you could hear the low roar floating up from the canyon below, of the mighty river as it churned down the mighty gorge, distinct, mysterious, and haunting. Here one could commune with the wild, with nature, with the eternal, with all that was part of that great scheme of things.

The fire was dying, the glowing embers hot and red, but the flame was gone. I wrote my last lines with Barbara holding the flashlight for me, its light fading away to blend into the night with the rest of this magical creation. Before we retired, we walked out to the rim where we looked down into the canyon where we could hear the river. Much of the canyon was too deep and narrow for the southern-hanging moon to ever reach the bottom with its light, but there was one place where a big side canyon comes in from the south and the rim is broken for a short space, and there the moonbeams reached the river below. And although the river was running muddy and reddish brown by day, the moon gave it a silver shine and literally fulfilled the words of another old refrain I sang for Barbara, "Moonlight on the Silver Colorado."

I believe it was here, in this place and setting, that I may have found or crossed that invisible and mysterious border that separated the present from the past, and entered the world beyond the bend. Even then it was not too far from the present world, with an occasional jet plane flying overhead, but we seemed to have been swallowed or absorbed by the past.

As I tried to put all things in their proper place and perspective and understand the meaning and feelings that prompted, inspired, touched, and haunted me, I was left to wonder if the human soul (heart, mind, and being) was not a world within a world. A world totally contained within itself, neither restricted as to height nor depth, time nor place, but which in a sense, can expand to encompass all things or can contract to limit and exclude everyone and everything except the moment within.

It seemed to me that the call of the wild was buried deep inside many of us, and in some could be awakened by being in this country. And if there was ever a country or place where that call, that message, that invitation is any more evident, that is the canyon country of the Colorado, from up in Utah on down through Arizona and into Nevada. Its message is written in its endless ledges, deep chasms and canyons, carried on and even playing in its whistling winds, or found in its empty wastes of silence.

It was into this world that the Laub family came that November day 54 years ago to make their home, to try and find their place. And maybe the great guiding hand of destiny brought them out to this land of no beginning for the sake of the development of two little boys, who began a companionship and friendship that was to carry them halfway around the world. Even though they were in a remote place and not a part of the world's cares, the distant events that were beginning to take shape were to affect the lives and destinies of those two little boys, who maybe even then, totally unaware, were preparing for that distant time.

Morning broke across the desert, like the muffled roll of drums, as the poet described:

Morning breaks across this canyon like the crescendo of the greatest orchestra ever assembled
And all the world stands struck with awe and unspeakable silence, reverent as the new day comes.

Mystery of My Life
November 1986

At last I finally heard and found it, after nearly half a lifetime of searching, longing, and global travel, and not too strangely nor surprisingly, it turned out to be right back about where it all started a half century ago, in a wild, lonely, isolated area and setting. It was the northwestern rim of the Grand Canyon, the lower end of the Toroweap Valley in Northern Arizona, a wild, isolated, desolate sliver of canyons, ledges, hills and desert, called the Arizona Strip. It had no oiled roads, hotels, or cafes. In fact, it had few if any permanent homes or residents anymore. Its isolation was broken only by the giant jets that flew high above and by the tourist planes that flew up and down the canyon. Except for that, it was an isolated maze and network of canyons, ledges, chasms and bluffs, where the wind and the circling eagles were unhedged and unfettered.

The call of the wild, the mystery of life,
At last I've found you, the answer to my anxious longing, seeking dreams.
And sweet mystery of self and yearning, 'tis the land of my child hood dreams.

After months and years and miles and oceans of travel, searching and longing, of deep inner yearnings and patient, but ofttimes very pressing desire, I had finally arrived at and found that place of beginning, the answer to the call, the fulfillment of desire. If there ever was a place in this vast world of creation where one could find and commune with heaven, with nature and creation, the past, the present or the future, it was in this vast canyon wilderness.

As I sat there beneath the branches of the gnarled old piñon, I was but 20 paces from the rim of the awesome chasm, which literally takes the breath away when one creeps out to its frightening, precipitous edge for a peek into an unbelievable slash in the crust of the earth. Although the experts say this carving and creation has been going on for eons, one's first impression is that this is a view of time at its very beginning, a peek into the very bosom of eternity itself. That here, creation has been frozen in place and time has suddenly stopped. Somehow I couldn't view this wonder of earth as the dredge of eons, but I rather beheld it as a masterpiece of creation, the peak of creative genius. And so, it was not only because we grew up here and is a point and place of our beginnings, it is indeed a place of eternal beginning.

And this was a very natural and desirable place for anyone who was trying to commune with the self, to find a way beyond the bend through the cluttered and violent pages of the past, to find himself, to find peace.

Toroweap Valley where the Laubs lived from November 1932 through the end of summer 1933.

Above, time has decayed the little cabin with the tamarack trees. Below, Normand and his father visit the old cabin..

The grove of lonesome pines where the Laubs lived
On the side of Mt. Trumbull, which rises to the right.

"Here one could commune with the wild, with nature, with the eternal,
with all that was part of that great scheme of things."

"I sat in the quiet solitude of the canyon wilderness nd wrote by the light of a flickering fire."

Epilogue

Redemption in Leyte

February 1995

And once again in the pre-dawn light, we came in over that special island of long ago and far away, Leyte. It was daylight when we landed and the van took us to our hotel just north of Tacloban, on the San Juanico Strait between Leyte and Samar, built in 1984 by Pres. Marcos for the 40th anniversary of the Leyte landing. It was a very beautiful place, but not quite like the little MacArthur beach motel we had ten years before.

Sending a Sacred Book

"This is no small brush fire you've ignited," wrote Elder Lionel Walker from the Philippines in 1987. "You've extended your circle of influence over 7,000 miles and now you need to come back and supervise it."

Writing to us from Tacloban City, Philippine Islands, Elder Walker was referring to a small isolated branch of The Church of Jesus Christ of Latter-day Saints in the jungles of central Leyte, whose amazing and unusual beginning owed much of its existence and success to some special pioneers, especially Ireneo and Engracia Pontejos from the little native barrio of Jaro.

When we took that sentimental journey back to the Philippines in 1985 to retrace those hallowed footsteps where my brother died, besides finding the spot where he was killed, I also had a strong desire to visit the high jungle peaks of central Leyte where I had spent the next two months in days of fighting and nights of personal mourning and silent grief.

"Pack some dried fruit, canned juice, and mosquito repellent," I had told Barbara as we prepared for that odyssey back through time.

"We will be visiting some areas where they may come in handy." In spite of all the modern changes, deep in the heart of the jungle valley, local conditions really hadn't changed all that much. Returning from that jungle mountain rendezvous to Jaro where we had left our waiting driver, we found most of the villagers gathered around his car. Some of them remembered with deep gratitude the American soldiers who had passed through their little barrio 40 years before. With requests to write to them when we got home, some of them gave us their names and addresses written on bits of paper. Engracia Pontejos was one of them.

For the next couple of years, Barbara carried on a long distance letter-writing campaign, especially with Engracia Pontejos, telling her about the Church, the blessing of our son serving a mission, our temples, and eternal families. Then in 1986, as a Christmas present to our special friends in the Philippines, we sent our pictures, our testimonies and enough money for five Books of Mormon to the Philippines Cebu Mission office. We also wrote each of the five families and told them that we were sending them a sacred book which had brought much peace and comfort to our lives and a positive assurance of the love, forgiveness, and saving mission of the Savior. We told them that some missionaries would bring this sacred book to them, and in it would be our pictures and testimony.

To our surprise, the books, pictures and referrals were sent to Elder Lionel and Sister LaRue Lytle Walker, formerly from Pioche, Nevada, whom we personally knew and had worked with as stake missionaries several years before they moved away, and who were now serving a mission in the Philippines. As there were no missionaries or Church members near the Jaro area, the Walkers traveled from Tacloban to Jaro, about 40 kilometers away, and spent the day finding the families, taking some pictures, and delivering the books. "Almost everyone we talked to," wrote the Walkers in their report, "remembered you and were waiting for their sacred book."

EPILOGUE

Three days after receiving their Book of Mormon, the Pontejos family visited the Walkers in Tacloban. They said they had read part of the book, believed it was true and wanted to join the Church. "They were saddened when we told them it wasn't that easy," Elder Walker wrote, "but they took some additional literature and returned home to study and wait for the missionaries to teach them."

The Pontejos family also sent us their own report: "Last Feb. 5th, Elder and Sister Walker handed us the Book of Mormon. It was already four times now the missionaries come to our home. We are really happy and excited to hear their explanation about our Jesus Christ and the Book of Mormon. We attend also the church in Tacloban City."

"That first Sunday they came to church," Elder Walker reported, "they had a slow jeepney and were late. The past three Sundays they have been waiting at the outside gate when the custodian unlocked it, an hour and a half before the meeting starts."

"Five members of the Pontejos family, Ireneo, Engracia, and three daughters were baptized April 12, 1987. Another married daughter is scheduled to be baptized later this month. They are no ordinary family," Elder Walker continued. "They are sincerely converted and very appreciative and don't really understand why the Lord picked them to be the first members from Jaro. They are typically poor people and it cost them more than a day's earnings each time the five of them come to church, just for transportation. We love them very much and need to take the Church to them very soon," Elder Walker explained. "Brother Pontejos will be ordained a priest next Sunday, and because of the seeds you have planted other people are now being taught and baptized."

Missionaries were sent to open up the area for proselyting, and on June 6, 1987 the Jaro Branch was organized with 12 members. Brother Pontejos was called as the branch president and they met in his home. In a few months the membership had grown to 30 and they rented a hall to meet in. When their numbers reached 60 and they had sufficient attendance and priesthood holders, they asked for a chapel. Although it was not possible for them to have a cement chapel, in 1989 they were able to build and dedicate their own little native chapel, with a tin roof and bamboo sides and shutters, which included an office and two small classrooms.

"Brother Normand and Sister Barbara," Engracia Pontejos wrote in one of her letters, "We heartily thank you very much for guiding us to be with the true church. Without you, I and all of my family members would have been ignorant about the Gospel of Jesus Christ and the ordinances of the church. You are a gift from the Lord to us. I can't really forget you all from here to eternity."

The missionaries who followed the Walkers were Elder Elmer and Sister Lila Stubbs Truman from Parowan, Utah. In another happy coincidence, Elder Truman was born and raised in Enterprise, Utah, the same little town where my brother Merril and I grew up. In fact, Elmer and I were the same age, and as boys we played and went to school together, so our direct and personal contact with those from the Philippines continued.

When Elder and Sister Truman returned from their mission, they told us how the Book of Mormon that we had sent to the Pontejos had been wrapped in a blue plastic cover and passed around from one family to another, reportedly being credited with helping in the conversion of 75 others. So our interest and desire to return again to the Philippines and visit those special people we had so briefly met and come to love really began to grow as we continued to correspond with them. Some of the people had hoped we would be back for the 50th commemoration of the Leyte landing, October 1994, and they took our pictures to the beach to look for us in vain among those who did come.

EPILOGUE

Miracle in Leyte

Then in January 1995, the opportunity came our way when we were invited to commemorate the 50th anniversary of the liberation of Manila and of the civilian POWs at Santo Tomas.

"If we are able to go that far," I told Sascha Jansen from Hawaii, one of the POW reunion organizers, "Barbara and I would like to fly on down to Leyte where my brother was killed, for a personal memorial and another special reunion." She was able to arrange the flight for us. So our February 5, 1995 Sunday morning flight from Manila to Tacloban was just about ten years after our first visit, and it was exactly eight years to the day since our Books of Mormon had been delivered to our friends in Jaro. We had tried to contact the Church in Leyte from Manila to find out the time of meetings in Jaro, but we were unsuccessful. So in our hotel room at 8:00 a.m., we were trying to contact the LDS Church or mission in Tacloban, but again without success. We did get the address of the Tacloban chapel, so we hired the hotel van driver to take us there. Sunday school was just getting started, but we met four missionaries, one from Utah was the assistant to the president of the mission. They told our driver how to find the Jaro chapel, and with growing anticipation we headed up that valley road with memories of 50 and 10 years ago mingled together. The real attraction was the group we were hoping to meet.

We arrived at the little chapel about 9:15 a.m. It had a tin roof, cement floor, bamboo sides, and shutters that were open for the breeze to come in. There were no cars or even a parking lot, so we pulled in on the grass. Sunday school was in progress and we could see through the open shutters some people in the chapel. Barbara had written to Engracia Pontejos and told her we were coming back to the Philippines and planned to visit the Jaro Branch if our flight was early enough. So they must have guessed who it was when we drove up, and President and Sister Pontejos came out to meet us. We went in to Sunday school. Although halfway around the world and deep in the heart of the Philippine jungle, the gospel doctrine class, taught by a very sharp native stake missionary on the New Testament, was not only well done with a lot a class participation, but was right on schedule. There were about 25 adults in the class, and there were also children's and youth classes.

Pres. Pontejos conducted the meeting and shared his own humble, powerful testimony. He told them we were special visitors from America, whom his beloved wife, Engracia, with some others had met February 27, 1985 by the Cabayongan River, with a promise we would write. He said that we were the ones who had sent those sacred books eight years ago which had become such a special blessing to them. We too were able to share our own feelings of happiness and gratitude that they had accepted the gospel, had shared it with others, and were continuing to keep a strong and active branch of the Church in Jaro.

For us to be able to meet in this little native chapel, in this particular place, with these humble and grateful people, in the name of the Lord was such a striking contrast to the violent and tragic conditions witnessed here a half century ago, it was really hard to believe. Especially for me, since it wasn't very far from here, in a little clearing quite like this, 50 years, three months and one week before in the midst of war and destruction, that I held my dying brother in my helpless arms, and now I couldn't contain the tears that never fell or were allowed to show back then. And to be able now to rise above the dark despair of those hopeless days of sorrow and silent grief was surely a sign of divine love and a blessing of that peace which passeth all understanding.

It was a cloudy, overcast evening on the Leyte beach as we prepared to depart for Manila, after again being able to visit the place where Merril died. It was raining lightly in the morning when we had our driver take us up to that location. And once again, for a sentimental moment, the past and the present, time and distance, suddenly seemed to melt as that tragic time came back to life and I was able to commune with the past. To spend a few special moments there stirred some very deep memories. But Sister Pontejos probably summed it up best as we prepared to bid them our final farewell, when she said, "Surely, Brother Normand, you can take great comfort in knowing your brother's death in this jungle place was for a very special missionary purpose." And quite literally, it was.

Just two years after they had been given the Book of Mormon, they had a branch and a chapel, and in less than eight years they had 112 members with 20 Melchizedek priesthood holders. They had sent 13 full-time missionaries from their branch; six had returned, seven were then serving, including two of the Pontejos daughters. This is a remarkable record. President Pontejos was serving his second term as branch president, having served some time in the district presidency. He was determined to keep the branch strong. The missionaries serving in the branch told us they had never served in a more spiritual area.

Although President and Sister Pontejos had both been able to go to the Manila Temple, they had not been able to go together or with their family to be sealed. Their great desire to become an eternal family was finally accomplished after much sacrifice in May 1995 when one daughter returned from her mission and another daughter serving a mission in Metro-Manila joined them at the temple for that special occasion.

Now as we witnessed the miracle of that sacred book in the lives of these special people, in this once sad and very special place, our joy was full, we acknowledged that our "cup runneth o'er."

February 1987
Ireneo Pontejos receives his copy of a sacred book sent by the Laubs through the hands of Lionel and LaRue Walker, missionaries in the Philippines, accompanied by Sofia Quiaones and Lila Arbus.

April 12, 1987
The Pontejos family on their baptism day.
Ireneo, Engracia, and three daughters, with the Walkers

EPILOGUE

Normand and Barbara Laub visit the Jaro Branch of
The Church of Jesus Christ of Latter-day Saints in 1995.

Appendix

Maps

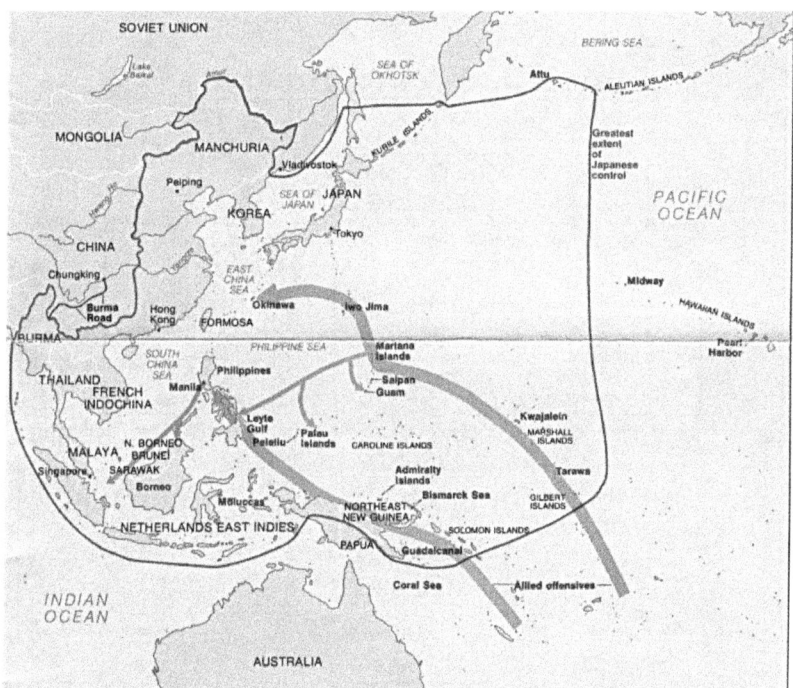

The Pacific Theater operations in World War II.
The somewhat parallel arrows through the series of islands show the strategy used by the Allies in 1943–1945, called "up the ladder" toward the Philippines and Japan.
Normand and Merril fought on the south side of the ladder.

APPENIDX

1ST Cavalry Division
"The 1ST Was First"

Asiatic-Pacific Theater

26 Jun. 1943   8 Sep. 1945

NEW GUINEA
ORO BAY

ADMIRALTY ISLANDS
MOMOTE
LOMBRUM POINT
PAPIT ALAI
HAUWEI
LORENGAU
ROSSUM
PAK-RAMBUTYO

D-Day 29 Feb. 1944

LEYTE-SAMAR
CATAISAN
TACLOBAN
SAN JUANICO STR.
SAN MIGUEL
CARIGARA
ORMOC VALLEY
CATBALOGAN

A-Day 20 Oct. 1944

LUZON

CAGANATUAN
GAPAN
BALIUAG
STA. MARIA
NOVALICHES
BALARA
MARIQUINA
ANTIPOLO
SANTO TOMAS
LIPA

MANILA
"THE 1ST WAS FIRST"

MALEPUNYO
IMOC HILL
ALAMINOS
SAN PABLO
PAGSANJAN
CALAUAG
SINILOAN
PASACAO
KADATALAN
INFANTA

Landed Lingayen Gulf 27 Jan. 1945——First to Enter Manila 3 Feb. 1945

JAPAN
Tokyo Bay-Yokohama-2 Sep. 1945——First Troops in Tokyo-8 Sep. 1945

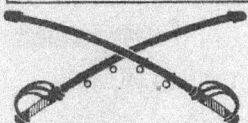  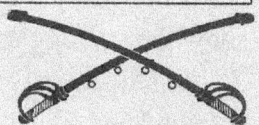

BEYOND THE BEND

This
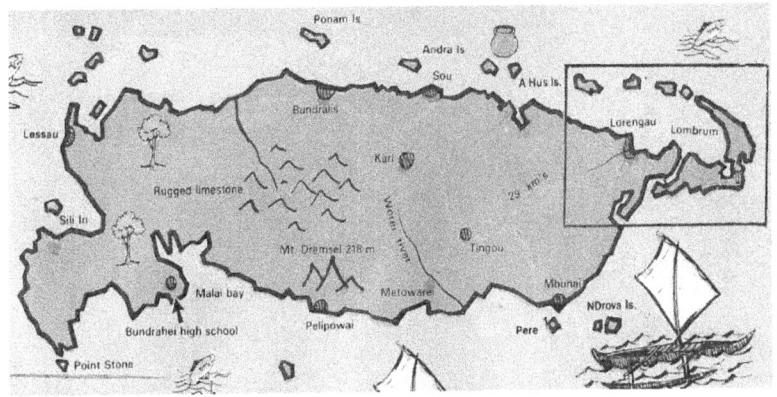
Schedule tells where the 1st Cavalry Division was assigned. The Admiralty Islands.

Above, Manus, the principal island in the Admiralties; the horseshoe-shaped Los Negros, with tiny Koroniat off its northwest tip.

Below, a close-up of Los Negros and Koroniat.

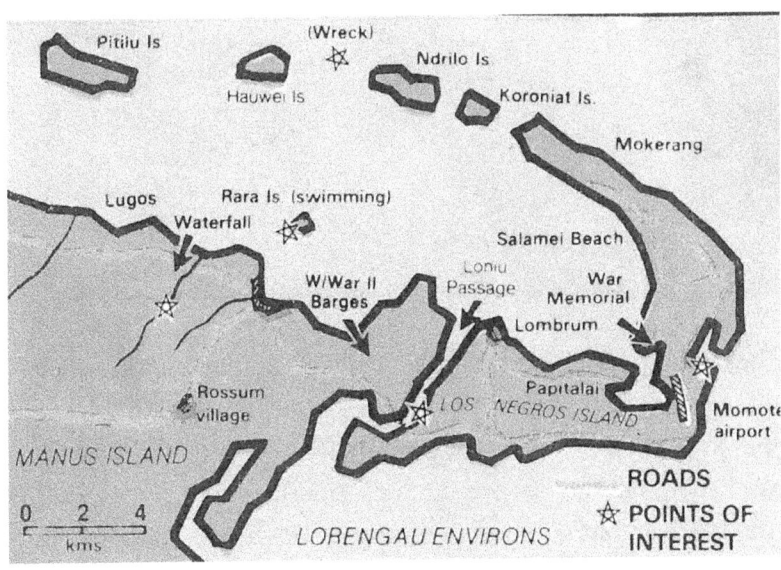

APPENIDX

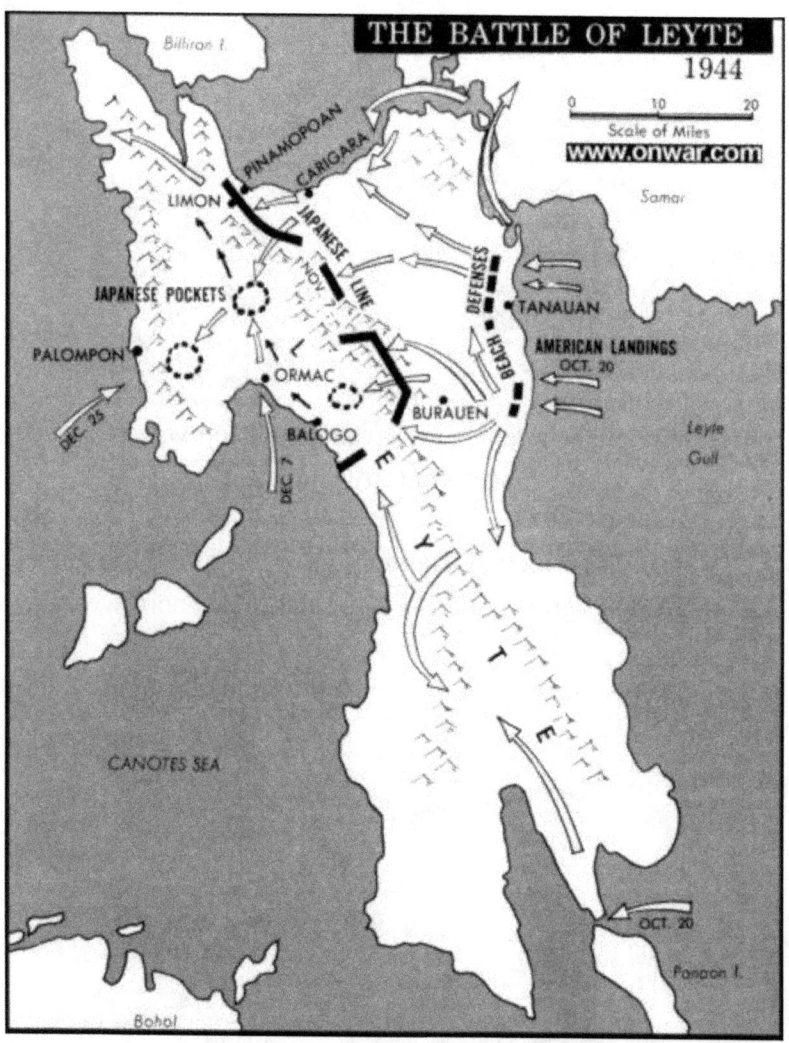

In the Leyte Campaign, Normand and Merril landed on the beach about at the point of the top arrow above "American Landings," and Merril was killed just beyond that point before the mountains, where Normand spent the next two and a half months in jungle combat, often on one-man patrols, before emerging at Ormac on the west.

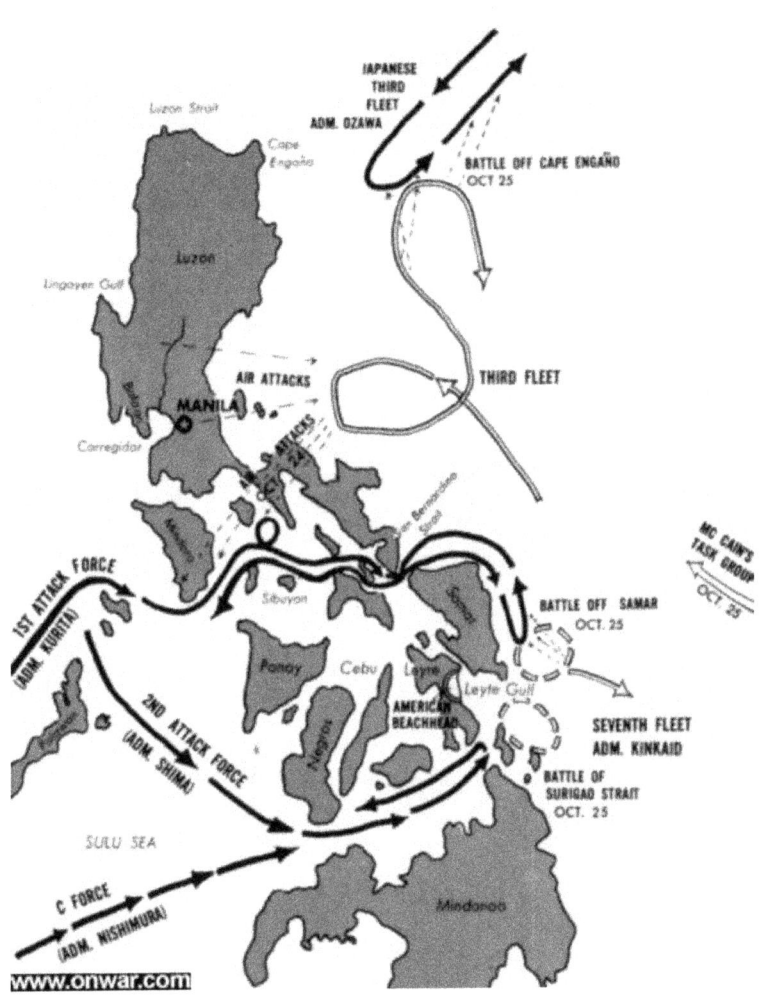

Invading the Philippines.
This map shows the battles in the Allies' initial retaking of the Philippines, including the sea battles that were fought in the few days after the Leyte beachhead.

APPENIDX

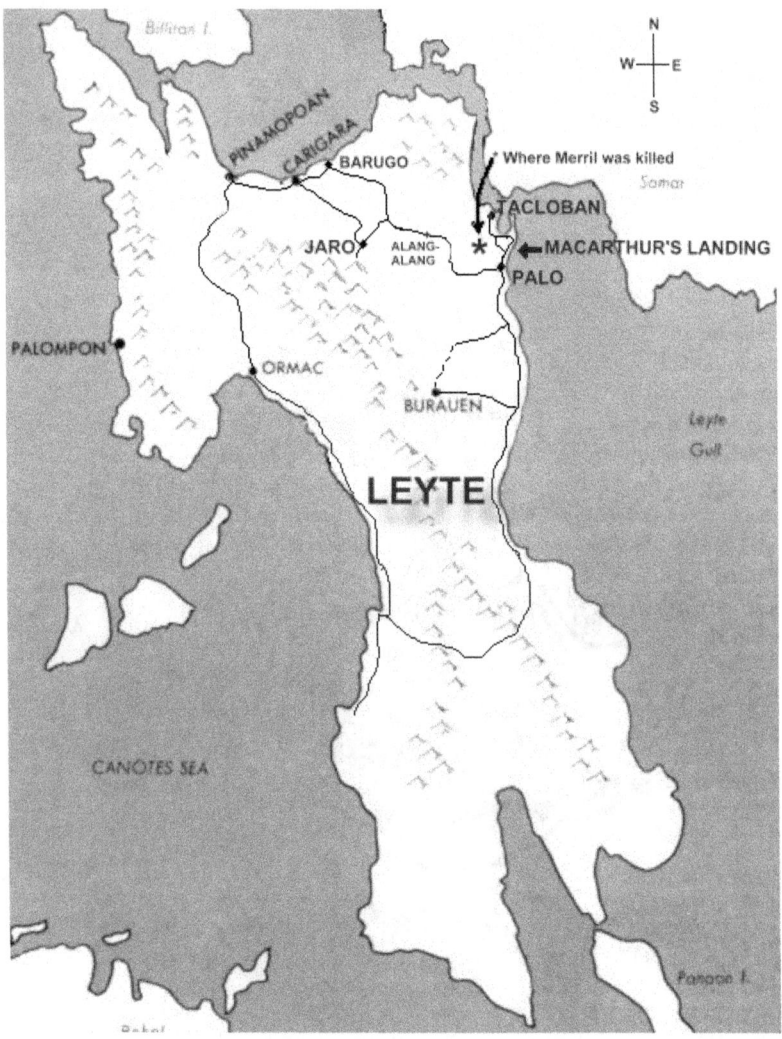

This map of Leyte shows where the MacArthur Landing monument is located, and about where Normand and Barbara found the place Merril was killed. The road they took wound around the coast of the upper part of the island and back, and then they went up through Alangalang to Jaro to get close to the mountain passes.

Southwestern Utah.

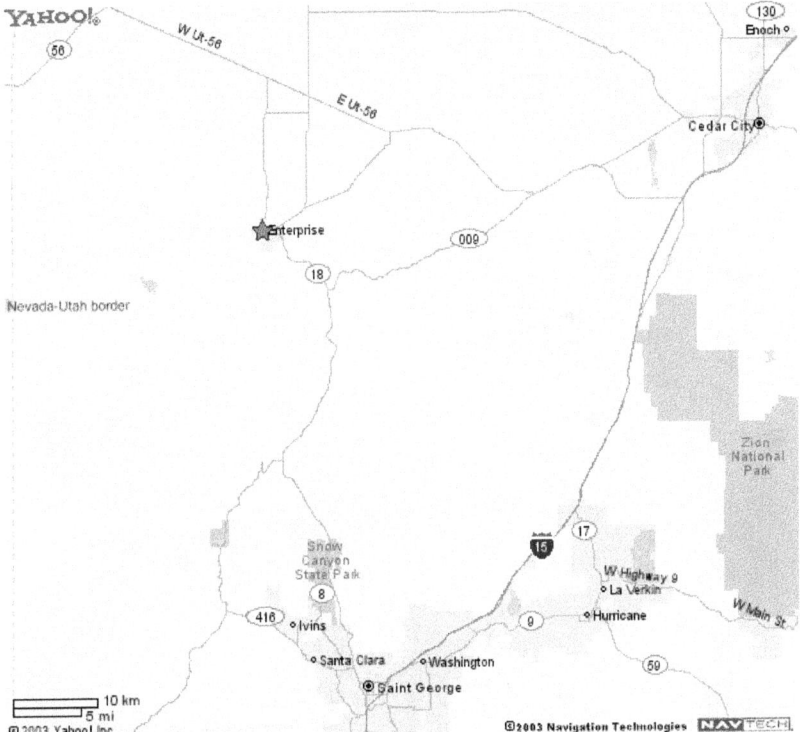

Normand's family lived in Enterprise off and on as he grew up.

APPENIDX

The Arizona Strip.

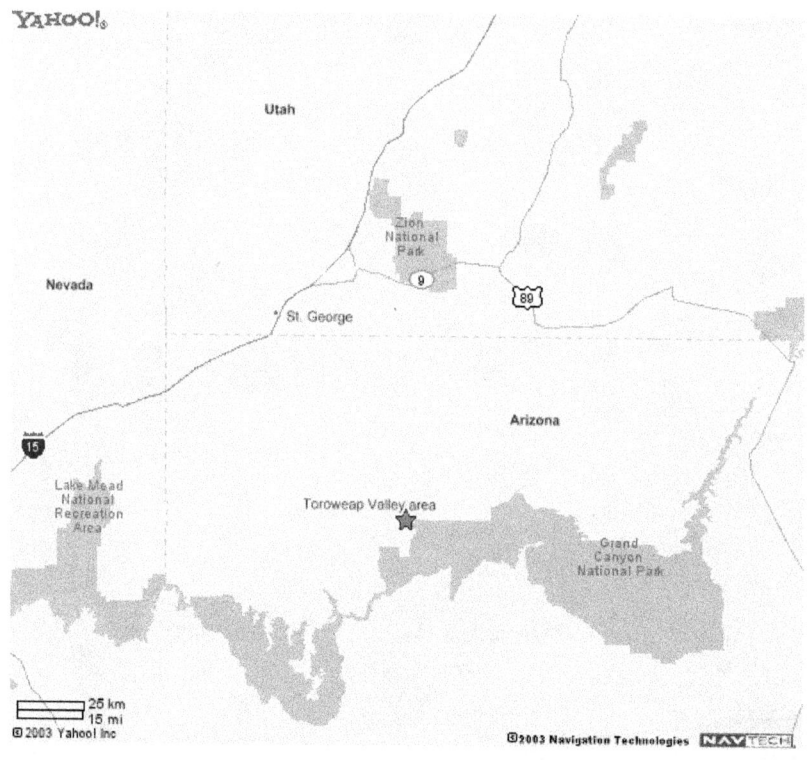

www.ingramcontent.com/pod-product-compliance
Lightning Source LLC
Chambersburg PA
CBHW060820050426
42453CB00008B/521